Cooking
with the
Saints

Cooking with the Saints

Compiled and translated by
Ernst Schuegraf

IGNATIUS PRESS | SAN FRANCISCO

To my mother, who taught me cooking and more

To my wife, who taught me loving and more

To Paul, Monica, Mark and Angela, who made it all worthwhile

Cover art credits:
  Madalena (St. Mary Magdalen)
  Piero della Francesca (ca. 1415/20–1492)
  Duomo, Arezzo, Italy
  Scala / Art Resource, N.Y.

  SS Chiara e Elisabetta (detail of St. Clare)
  Simone Martini (1284–1344)
  Chiesa S. Francesco, Assisi, Italy
  Scala / Art Resource, New York

Photographs of food:
  Ernst Schuegraf

Cover design:
  Riz Boncan Marsella

Text design:
  Riz Boncan Marsella

Composition:
  Shoreline Graphics, Rockland, Maine

© 2001 Ignatius Press
All rights reserved
ISBN 0–89870–779–x
Library of Congress control number: 00–100235
Printed in Hong Kong by C&C offset Printing Co., Ltd. ∞

Contents

Introduction

The idea for this book came on a dark winter evening when there seemed nothing better to do than to look through some cookbooks from the public library to find some exciting and different recipes. Reading two completely different cookbooks, one on cooking in Yorkshire and one on Brittany, I stumbled across two recipes that had names of saints attached to them. Both authors explained in a few sentences the connection of the saint to the recipe. (Saints have a fascination for many people; everybody wants to have someone to turn to and ask for help. Most people have the same attraction to angels.) That is when I wondered whether there might be more such recipes. Reflecting on my childhood in Germany, I could immediately think of several similar recipes. First I thought that it would be entertaining to put together a small collection of such recipes for our own use. After about four weeks of on-and-off-again searching, the collection had grown to about eighty recipes that were linked to about forty saints.

At Christmas 1998 the idea of the book in its present form crystallized, and the suffering for my family began. The joy of each discovery, whether it was a new recipe, a painting of a saint or some other relevant thing, had to be shared with the whole family, who were not quite as excited about the project as I was. Patience began to wear thin.

The family was more enthusiastic about the process of cooking and testing the recipes. The food was well received, but the cook-photographer was not very popular when he announced that dinner would have to wait until photographs of the dishes were taken. Fortunately it appears that saints have a sweet tooth, and many of the desserts and cakes made up for the wait.

In the two thousand years since the arrival of Christianity, cooking has undergone many changes. Cooking utensils have become more sophisticated, more exotic ingredients have become available to the adventurous cooks and the customers' taste buds have in turn become more refined. Christianity itself has contributed in many ways to the advance of cooking. Many popes, bishops and priests have been appreciative of the fine art of cooking and have had good cooks to entertain their guests. The frequent travels of the clergy and their exposure to different foods and cooking methods spread cooking knowledge around most of Europe. The culinary skills of cooks at ecclesiastical houses and noble courts created many exceptional dishes with ingredients considered fancy in their times. The ingredients, such as venison, the king's deer, and cooking methods were generally not available to ordinary folk. In the fifteenth century, use of exotic spices in cooking was considered a sign of wealth in the middle class.

Faced with the long meatless periods of Advent and Lent, or with year-round abstinence from meat, many ingenious monastic cooks succeeded in inventing special dishes with fish that would make such meals more nourishing and enjoyable. Their recipes were often adopted by people outside the monasteries.

In medieval times, as now, the days of the year had saints associated with them. Saints whose feast days were celebrated on the same day over all of Europe

8

were quite important. However, saints of mostly local importance were often celebrated with as much fanfare as the saints on the universal calendar. Celebration of a feast day often included special dishes to be eaten only on that day. The name of the saint was naturally often attached to the dish—for example, St. Joseph's Day Bread, St. Michael's Bannock and Pizza di San Martino. Many dishes do not have the name of the saint in the title but still are associated with a particular feast day. Some of the foods cooked on these special occasions became very popular and were cooked at other times, as well. This happened to many recipes connected with the feast day of St. Nicholas, December 6. Some of the food for that day is now considered standard fare for the entire Christmas season.

In certain parts of Europe, especially in France, it was quite common to give the name of a saint to a village or town, and dishes associated with that region also were linked to the local saint. Lasagna di San Frediano, St. Flour Turnovers and Chicken St. Ménéhould are such recipes. Many more modern recipes were named in a similar fashion; when a cook encountered a special recipe in a certain place, the recipe was named after this location—for example, Mole of Santa Clara.

Many other "saintly" recipes were deliberately created by cooks for dedication to a particular saint for various reasons. The cake Gâteau Saint-Honoré is dedicated to the patron saint of pastry cooks, and Suckling Pig St. Fortunatus is dedicated to the patron saint of cooks. Pork Loin St. Laurent is named after the patron saint of a particular chef.

Often recipes contain ingredients that have a saint's name attached to them, and the recipe title includes the name of the ingredient. The connection to the saint is often lost when the ingredients are translated into English. Coquilles Saint-Jacques translates to scallops, and the fish called San Pietro in Italy or Saint-Pierre in France has the simple English name John Dory; even so, St. Peter's Fish is used occasionally. Wine is often the ingredient that gives the dish its "saintly" connection. Examples are Beef Roast St. Magdalena and Macaroons de Saint Émilion.

Quite a few recipes presented a challenge, since often it was difficult for me to identify with certainty the particular saint associated with a recipe. Local saints were easy, but universal saints more difficult. As an example, there is a recipe connected to St. Felix. A list of saints of the Catholic Church revealed there were fifty-six different saints named Felix. In such cases I have assigned the earliest of those saints to the recipe.

Some readers may notice that there are no recipes here associated with Mary, the Mother of God. There are two reasons for this omission. First, the Mother of God is in a class different from the other saints and deserves special treatment, and, second, there are many, many recipes for her, enough for another volume!

The recipes contained in this book originate in twenty-one different countries, with the majority coming from such Catholic countries as Italy, Spain, France and Germany, but the book also includes many recipes from North America. As my collection has now grown to more than four hundred recipes, it was difficult to choose the recipes to include in this book. The main criterion was variety. The goal was to present a broad spectrum of dishes of every kind, whether soup, dessert or bread, from many different countries, while including as many saints as possible. Some dishes have been left out because they were too similar to a dish included or because I could not discover of the author of the recipe or the connection with the saint. Other recipes and saints have been left out because the link between the two was not well established. However, anybody wanting to bring to my attention the existence of other saint-related recipes is more than welcome to do so.

Some of the recipes presented here are quite old, and the amounts of certain ingredients reflect previous times. The quantity of eggs and butter used in some recipes is staggering: for example, twenty-eight eggs and two pounds of butter in a cake. On some of these recipes, adjustments have been made to present a more modern and healthy version of the dish, but most of them are given unchanged.

This collection of recipes would not have been possible without the help of many friends, who looked through their cookbooks or asked other friends. The encouragement of Hans and Renate Sick at a critical stage was instrumental in getting the book under way. Credit must be given also to Mrs. B. Tauwald, who scoured her collection of antique cookbooks and contributed many recipes. Norbert Igel was tireless in his efforts to find some recipes, and he provided help of any kind when I needed it most. Anne-Marie Gorman helped by providing books with exciting recipes, as well as books with paintings of saints. Gerhard Dueck and Gillian Pink translated some of the recipes and helped me in fine-tuning the cooking instructions. The help of the staff of the St. Francis Xavier University Library is also gratefully acknowledged. Many other friends too numerous to mention assisted in various ways, by providing encouragement, recipes or tips. To them a sincere *Vergelts Gott*, and may they enjoy this collection.

Antigonish, Nova Scotia
February 3, 2000
Feast day of St. Blaise

St. Agnes

AGNES was a young girl living in Rome in the fourth century when it was still illegal to be a Christian. When she was thirteen the son of a prefect fell in love with her, but she refused his offer of marriage because of her commitment to Christianity. The prefect then publicly accused her of being a Christian, and she was to be burned at the stake for her faith. According to legend, the fire refused to burn her, and she was eventually killed by the sword. She died as a virgin at the age of thirteen, firm in her belief in Christ as her spouse. Her death is thought to have occurred about 304, but the exact date is contested.

A church was built at her grave on the Via Nomentana in Rome around 354 by Constance, the daughter of the Emperor Constantine. According to legend, Constance was cured of leprosy by the intercession of St. Agnes. Many other legends about St. Agnes can be found in early Christian writings. Agnes was a famous saint in both the Western and Eastern Church, and she has been venerated by many generations, especially in the Middle Ages, even though her name in recent times has not been very popular. Her feast day is celebrated in the West on January 21.

Because *agnus* means lamb in Latin, Agnes is usually represented in art with a lamb at her side and holding a sword in her hand. She is the patron saint of gardeners.

Mosaic (detail), 6th century, S. Apollinare Nuovo, Ravenna, Italy

AGNESENPLÄTZCHEN

(St. Agnes Cookies)

½ c. (125 g) sugar
3 c. (375 g) flour

1⅓ c. (300 g) butter
apricot jam

Combine the first 3 ingredients and work to a smooth dough. Refrigerate for 10 minutes. Roll out dough to a thickness of about ¼ inch (6 mm). Cut out an even number of circles about 2 inches (5 cm) in diameter. Let dough rest for about 30 to 60 minutes. Bake at moderate heat 350°F (175°C) until golden, about 12 minutes. Spread apricot jam on one circle and cover with second circle.

Makes about 36 cookies.

This recipe is from an old German cookbook first published in 1924.

Mosaic, 5th century,
Sant'Ambrogio, Milan, Italy

AMBROSE was born in 339 in Trier, Germany, and was the son of a Roman prefect. After his father's death he and his brother were raised by his mother and his sister St. Marcellina. He studied Greek and rhetoric and became a successful advocate. He soon attracted the attention of the governing powers and at the age of thirty-one was made the governor of Emilia and Liguria with his seat at Milan.

Shortly thereafter, in 374, the archbishop of Milan died, and Ambrose, as prefect, was responsible for the orderly election of a successor. In the middle of a speech calling for order, it is said that the voice of a small child called out, "Ambrose for bishop." Much to the surprise of Ambrose, who was not even baptized, the crowd took up the slogan, and he was elected. Shortly afterward the emperor confirmed his election. Within the week he was baptized and consecrated bishop. To prepare for his duties he studied Scripture and the writings of St. Basil, Origen and other Church Fathers.

As a bishop he divested himself of all his family wealth in favor of the Church and the poor, and he combined hard work with accessibility to all. He was an eloquent speaker and a prolific writer, spreading monasticism and St. Basil's ideas in the West. He had an important part in the conversion of St. Augustine.

The major problem in his diocese was the fight against the heresy of Arianism, which was supported by some members of the imperial family. Fearlessly, through writings and speeches, Ambrose rebuked attacks by Arian supporters. He had such stature that he was able publicly to reprove the emperor Theodosius for his massacre of thousands of men, women and children in Thessalonica. (After being excommunicated, Theodosius did public penance for the massacre.)

Ambrose died in 397 before he was sixty, and he is buried in Milan in the basilica named in his honor. Ambrose's writings are voluminous and still influential today. He is one of the four great Fathers of the Western Church, and one of the dominant figures of the Church in the fourth century. He wrote and composed several hymns, which he taught his people to sing, but his connection with the Ambrosian Chant or the Ambrosian Rite is uncertain.

His feast day is celebrated on December 7. He is the patron saint of learning and of beekeepers. In art he is usually shown in episcopal vestments.

12

Ambrosius Creme
(St. Ambrose Cream)

2 c. (500 ml) sour cream
½ c. (125 g) sugar
red food coloring
2 egg whites
1 Tbsp. lemon juice
1 Tbsp. rum
½ tsp. vanilla
4 Tbsp. cold water
1c. (250 ml) whipping cream
1½ envelopes gelatin (enough to set 2½ cups [600 ml] liquid)

Beat sour cream and sugar until frothy. Add food coloring. Beat egg whites.

Fold beaten egg whites, lemon juice, rum and vanilla into the sour cream and sugar mixture.

Soften the gelatin in cold water, heat gently, stirring to dissolve, and add to the mixture, while whisking mixture gently to distribute gelatin evenly.

Pour mixture into a bowl and refrigerate until it is set.

Before serving, dip bowl for 20 seconds into hot water. Invert onto plate and remove the bowl.

Decorate by piping the whipped cream around base and the top.

Serves 8.

This recipe is an old one that has been popular in Bavaria for many years and has appeared in many older cookbooks. This more modern version is from Helga Lederer's Gut Essen— Bayrische Küche.

This recipe, from
Anna del Conte's book
GOOD HOUSEKEEPING
ITALIAN COOKERY,
is a dessert that is especially
popular in the summer.

IL MERINGONE DI SANT'AMBROGIO

(Meringue Cake St. Ambrose)

5 egg whites
1¼ c. (300 g) sugar
3 Tbsp. (30 g) pistachios, shelled
½ c. (60 g) chocolate, plain or bitter, grated or finely chopped
2 c. (500 ml) whipping cream
3 Tbsp. candied orange peel
2 Tbsp. powdered sugar
chocolate chips
candied violets

Take 2 sheets of parchment paper and draw a 10-inch (25 cm) circle
on each. Place the paper on 2 baking sheets. Beat the egg whites with
an electric beater until stiff. Fold in ¼ cup (60 g) of the sugar and
continue beating until the mixture is very stiff and glossy. Fold in the
remaining sugar with a metal spoon. Spread the meringue mixture over
the 2 paper circles, gently smoothing the tops with a spreading knife.

Place the meringues in a 300°F (150°C) preheated oven and bake for
20 minutes. Reverse their shelf positions and bake for a further 20
minutes. The meringues should be slightly brown on the top and
just firm to the touch. Allow to cool and then carefully remove the
2 meringue circles from the paper.

Blanch the pistachios, skin and chop finely.

Grate or chop chocolate finely. Beat the cream until soft peaks are
formed. Fold in pistachios, chocolate pieces, candied orange peel
and powdered sugar. Spread ¾ of the cream mixture between the
2 meringue circles and the rest on the top layer.

Cover and put the meringue cake into the freezer for at least 4 hours.
Half an hour before serving remove from the freezer and place in the
refrigerator. To serve, decorate cake with chocolate chips and candied
violets or other candied flowers.

Serves 8 to 10.

St. Andrew

El Greco, 16th century,
Casa y Museo del Greco,
Toledo, Spain

ANDREW was the brother of Peter and a fisherman by trade. He was a disciple of St. John the Baptist before he became an apostle. In all the Gospels he is listed among the first four of the apostles, and he is mentioned specifically by John in the account of the feeding of the five thousand (Jn 6:8).

There is no certainty where Andrew preached, where he died or where he is buried. It is generally agreed that he labored mainly in Greece and the Balkan countries. The Russians claim him as one of their patron saints and assert that he went as far as Poland. Tradition has it that he was crucified on a cross in the shape of the letter X in Patras, Greece, around A.D. 60, during the reign of Emperor Nero. His relics were later transferred to Constantinople.

Ancient legends about Andrew report a trip to Ethiopia. More important is the legend about the transfer of his relics by St. Rule to Scotland in the eighth century. St. Rule stopped at a place in Fife, now called St. Andrews, and built a church there that became a center of evangelization. Because of this, Andrew is considered the patron saint of Scotland.

In art Andrew is usually shown with a cross or a fishing net. The saltire cross, the X, became associated with him first in the tenth century and became his popular sign in the fourteenth. It is now the symbol for Scotland on the Union Jack.

Andrew's feast day is November 30, and it is celebrated by Scots everywhere with special dinners of traditional Scottish fare, normally including haggis. Andrew is the patron saint of fishermen and of Scotland, Russia and Greece.

ANDREASHERZEN

(St. Andrew Hearts)

2 c. (250 g) flour
1 Tbsp. sugar
pinch of salt
4 Tbsp. white wine
1⅓ c. (350ml) cream
2 eggs, small
powdered sugar for dusting

Mix together all the dry ingredients except the powdered sugar. With an electric beater blend the liquid ingredients and eggs. Then add the dry ones and blend thoroughly.

Bake in waffle iron until golden brown. Dust with powdered sugar before serving.

If they are baked in an old-fashioned iron that needs to be dipped in hot oil, the amount of cream should be reduced by half.

Makes about 24 heart-shaped waffles.

An old Bavarian recipe published in the Regensburger Kochbuch in 1890, this is for heart-shaped waffles. If such a form is not available, you can try using the batter in an ordinary waffle iron. White wine is an unusual ingredient for waffles, but these are good.

COUPE SAINT-ANDRÉ

(St. Andrew's Cup)

fruit salad prepared from fresh fruit in season
maraschino liqueur (enough to moisten the fruit)
strawberry ice cream
whipped cream

Moisten the fruit salad with the maraschino liqueur. Top with strawberry ice cream and pipe the whipped cream around the top.

A simple yet delicious fruit salad.

COOKING WITH THE SAINTS

Daube de la Saint-André

(Stew for St. Andrew's Day)

3 lb. (1500 g) topside of beef
1 lb. (500 g) pork back fat (fresh or salted)
3 Tbsp. parsley, chopped
1½ Tbsp. garlic, chopped
3 shallots, chopped
salt
ground pepper
3 c. (750 ml) full-bodied red wine
1 clove
½ onion
1 bay leaf
½ tsp. thyme
½ tsp. sugar

This recipe needs to be started a day ahead for best results. Cooking on the second day is quite effortless. It may be served hot or cold accompanied by a baguette or some crusty French bread.

Trim beef of all fat and cut into ½-inch (1 cm) slices against the grain of the meat. Cut pork fat into chunks and blanch in boiling water for 5 minutes. Rinse, drain and dry the pork fat. Put through a mincer or grind in a food processor. Chop or mince parsley; chop garlic and shallots. Mix this with salt and pepper into the ground pork fat to make a paste. (Omit salt if using salted fat.)

Grease casserole. Layer beef slices and pork paste. Finish with a layer of beef. Simmer wine for 15 minutes to evaporate the alcohol, and pour it still hot over contents of casserole. Stick clove into the onion and put it on top. Add bay leaf, thyme and sugar. Cover with waxed paper and tight-fitting lid.

Put casserole in a preheated very slow oven 250F° (120°C) and cook for 6 hours. Let cool, refrigerate and completely remove the accumulated fat from casserole. An hour before serving, place casserole back in a slow oven (300°F/150°C) and heat. Any fat that might come to the surface during that time should be removed before serving. If there is too much liquid, it should be removed by boiling vigorously. The meat slices may be broken up before serving.

Even though the cooking time is long, no attention by the cook is required during that time.

Serves 8.

This is a recipe for a delicious stew from Paula Wolfert's cookbook THE COOKING OF SOUTH-WEST FRANCE. It is traditionally eaten there in the first cold days of autumn. It may be eaten hot or cold. The amount of pork fat is quite large, but the dish is completely degreased after the first cooking. (The fat is there to keep the meat soft.)

Here is a walnut cake that has been named after St. Andrew. There are many versions of this famous cake. This one was found on the Internet.

Gâteau aux Noix le Saint-André
(St. Andrew's Walnut Cake)

¾ c. (150 g) walnut pieces
⅔ c. (150 g) sugar
½ c. (100 g) butter
3 eggs
6 Tbsp. flour
2 Tbsp. rum
pinch of salt

Optional:
chocolate sauce
whipped cream
liqueur
whole walnuts
chocolate

Some care must be taken that the nuts used for this cake are fresh and not rancid, otherwise the cake will have an off flavor. In an electric blender grind the nuts until they are almost like sand. Put in a bowl and mix with half the sugar. Blend well. Preheat oven to 375°F (190°C). Grease and flour a 10-inch (25 cm) round cake pan and set aside.

Make sure butter is at room temperature and soft. With an electric beater blend together the butter and remaining sugar until light and soft peaks form. Add the nut and sugar mixture, stir until well mixed. Add eggs 1 at a time while beating until mixture is quite smooth. Finally add the sifted flour, rum and the salt. Blend until evenly distributed.

Pour the batter into the prepared cake pan and bake in the middle of the oven for about 30 to 40 minutes. Let cool for 10 minutes and remove from the pan.

This cake may be eaten as is or served with chocolate sauce and decorated with whipped cream that has been flavored with a liqueur. Decorate with walnuts and shaved chocolate or chocolate chips.

Serves 6 to 8.

Saint-Andrés

DOUGH
½ c. (100 g) butter
2 c. (250 g) flour
¾ c. (100 g) powdered sugar
pinch of salt
2 eggs

FILLING
1 c. (250 ml) apple marmalade

ROYAL ICING
2 egg whites
2 c. (250 g) powdered sugar
1 tsp. lemon juice

First, prepare apple marmalade filling (see below) unless you have jars on hand. Second, make the royal icing. Put the 2 egg whites into a bowl and beat slightly. Add 2 tablespoons of the sifted powdered sugar and beat again. Repeat until all the sugar is used up and a thick smooth consistency is obtained. The color should be a solid white. Add the lemon juice and beat again. Cover with a damp cloth until needed.

To make the dough, cut the butter in small pieces and rub them into the flour until the mixture resembles coarse bread crumbs. Add the powdered sugar and salt, mix well together, then add the eggs and work to a smooth dough.

Line small boat-shaped molds (about 3 to 4 inches long [8 to 10 cm]) with the dough, fill with the apple marmalade. Keep some small dough scraps for the top. Spread with royal icing and lay 2 small strips of dough in the shape of an X on top. Bake in a preheated moderate oven 350°F (175°C) for about 10 minutes.

Serves 12 to 16.

This is a recipe for a classic French pastry.

Apple Marmalade

8 c. thinly sliced tart apples, about 3 lbs. (1.2 Kg)
1 orange
1½ c. (375 ml) water
5 c. (625 g) sugar
2 Tbsp. lemon juice

To prepare fruit: wash, pare, quarter and core the apples. Slice thin. Quarter the orange, remove any seeds and slice very thin.

To make marmalade: heat water and sugar until sugar is dissolved. Add the lemon juice and fruit. Boil rapidly, stirring constantly, to 221°F (101°C) or until the mixture thickens. Remove from heat; skim the foam from the surface.

Pour immediately into hot, sterile canning jars to ¼ inch from top. Seal. Process 5 minutes in boiling water bath.

Makes 6 or 7 half-pint jars.

—*from* Mississippi Cooperative Extension

Ludovico Carracci, 16th century, Pinacoteca Nazionale, Bologna, Italy

THE MARTYR ST. ANGELO was born in 1145 in Jerusalem, the son of Jewish converts. At the age of eighteen he became a member of the monastery at Mount Carmel and later retired to the desert as a hermit. John, his brother, became patriarch of Jerusalem. He was sent from Mount Carmel to Rome to obtain the approval of Pope Honorius III for the rules of the Carmelite order.

He then went to Sicily to preach, and he converted many. He publicly reprimanded a local nobleman, Count Beringarius, for his corrupt life-style. In 1120 assassins hired by the count murdered him.

His feast day is May 5, and in art he is usually shown with three crowns at his feet, signifying chastity, eloquence and martyrdom.

Coniglio Sant'Angelo

(Rabbit St. Angelo)

2½ lb. (1kg) rabbit, cleaned
salt
flour for dusting
3 Tbsp. olive oil
1 clove of garlic
2 c. (500 ml) plum tomatoes, canned
1 pinch (sprig) rosemary
1 pinch (sprig) thyme
½ c. (125 ml) dry white wine
fresh basil leaves
salt and pepper for sauce

Clean rabbit and cut into small pieces, trying to take out as many bones as possible. Lightly salt and flour the pieces. Fry them in oil in a heavy saucepan until well browned.

Slice garlic finely. Drain the tomatoes and chop roughly, reserving juice. Next add garlic, tomatoes, rosemary, thyme and white wine to the saucepan and cover.

Cook over moderate heat for about 1 hour. After half an hour add the basil. During cooking, stir occasionally to make sure sauce does not stick. If the sauce is too thick, add some of the drained tomato juice.

Season with salt and pepper to taste and serve hot.

Serves 4 to 6.

Here is a recipe from Antonio Carluccio's book An Invitation to Italian Cooking. He tells us that this recipe is one of the few dishes in his cookbook that have a proper title, rather than a title listing the ingredients. The dish is named in honor of a man living alone on an island facing St. Angelo of Ischia who prepared rabbit in an interesting way.

St. Anne

THE CHURCH has venerated Anne, the mother of the Virgin Mary, since the second century, even though no historical details of her life are known. She and her husband, St. Joachim, are believed to have been both from the tribe of Judah and the royal house of David.

The relics of St. Anne were supposedly transferred from Jerusalem to Constantinople in the eighth century, which gave her a great following in the Eastern Church. In the West her popularity increased significantly in the twelfth century due to a renewed interest in the Virgin Mary. Anne is the patron saint of Brittany and enjoys great affection there. French colonists brought this cult with them to Quebec, and St. Anne de Beaupré is her best-known shrine in North America.

The feast day of St. Anne and her husband, St. Joachim, is July 26. In art St. Anne is often shown teaching her daughter to read. On the continent many paintings and statues show Anne, Mary and the Christ Child.

Anne is not only the patron saint of Brittany, but she is also one of the two patron saints of Canada, as well as the patron saint of housewives, women in labor and cabinetmakers.

CRÈME SAINTE-ANNE

(St. Anne's Cream)

½ c. (125 g) sugar
2 Tbsp. water
1 Tbsp. butter, unsalted
¼ c. (50 g) macaroons, crushed
1¼ c. (300 ml) milk
1 egg
3 egg yolks

Butter 4 ramekins. Put half the sugar in a pan and moisten with 2 tablespoons water. Bring to a boil and cook to amber caramel. Pour the caramel into 4 ramekins, to make a thin layer in each, and allow to set.

Place a thin slice of butter on the caramel in each ramekin and sprinkle each with the chopped macaroons.

Heat the milk to the simmering point. Whisk the egg, egg yolks and remaining sugar until creamy. Beat in the hot milk and pour into the prepared ramekins. The macaroons will float to the top.

Stand the ramekins in a tray of simmering water that comes halfway up their sides. Bake in a moderate oven at 325°F (160°C) for 20 to 25 minutes until set. Allow to cool, loosen edges and turn out onto a plate.

Serves 4.

This is an old French recipe from Brittany, where St. Anne is venerated as a patron saint.

This recipe, an old one from the Alsace region of France, has been reprinted in a German cookbook containing traditional recipes.

ANNA TORTE
(Gâteau Sainte-Anne)

CAKE
4 eggs
1 c. (250 g) sugar
2 Tbsp. dark rum
2 c. (250 g) flour
1½ tsp. baking powder
1 c. (250 g) butter
1 c. (125 g) chocolate, grated
1 c. (100 g) almonds, ground
¼ c. (50 g) mixed peel, chopped finely
1 tsp. vanilla

ICING
1 c. (125 g) powdered sugar
3 Tbsp. water, rum or lemon juice
Optional:
glacé cherries
angelica
chocolate chips

Preheat oven to 350°F (175°C).

With an electric beater blend eggs and sugar until frothy. Add rum and flour mixed with baking powder. Blend in rest of ingredients.

Grease and flour an 8-inch (20 cm) round cake pan and fill with the mixture. Bake for 60 minutes or until done.

Make icing by moistening the powdered sugar with the liquid. Cover cake with icing. You can decorate the cake with glacé cherries, angelica or chocolate chips.

Serves 10 to 12.

St. Anthony (Abbot)

ANTHONY was born in 251 in Coma, Upper Egypt, as the son of well-to-do parents. At the age of twenty, after the death of his parents, he sold all his possessions and retired to live in solitude in the nearby desert. According to legend, he suffered terrible temptations, which he overcame by a strict regimen of prayer and fasting.

Numerous disciples soon wished to join him, and in 305, near Thebes in Egypt, he founded his first monastery, which he governed with kindness and wisdom before returning to his life of solitude. He was strongly opposed to the Arian heresy. His influence and stature contributed to the defeat of the Arians at the Council of Nicaea in 325.

Anthony is generally regarded as the founder of Christian monasticism and had a great impact on the later development of Eastern as well as Western monastic life. Several of his writings survive, including a letter to Emperor Constantine and some letters to his monasteries.

Anthony died in 356, at the age of 105, and was buried, by his own choice, in a place known to none but those who buried him. In 561 his relics were found and transferred to Alexandria. The religious order named Hospitallers of St. Anthony was founded around 1100 and became quite widespread in Western Europe. By special privilege this order's pigs were allowed to roam the streets freely. Later on these pigs provided food for the poor.

Hieronymus Bosch, 16th century, Museo del Prado, Madrid

Anthony was a popular saint in the Middle Ages, regarded as the patriarch of monks and healer of men and animals. He is the patron saint of herdsmen.

St. Anthony's feast day is January 17. The many legends about Anthony inspired some of the more famous medieval artists, who with great imagination depicted his temptations, but a quite common representation was a monk with a pig. His association with a pig has carried over into the culinary domain, where dishes containing pork are often named for St. Anthony, as we find in the following recipe.

OLLA DE SAN ANTON

(St. Anthony's Stew)

½ lb. (225 g) dried white beans, soaked, then drained
½ c. (125 ml) wine, white (optional)
½ lb. (250 g) pork belly, cut into cubes
½ lb. (250 g) pork, lean, cubed
½ lb. (250 g) spareribs
¼ lb. (125 g) chorizo sausage
¼ lb. (125 g) blood sausage (optional)
3 Tbsp. olive oil
1 bay leaf
1 onion
4 peppercorns
1 clove of garlic, finely chapped
½ lb. (250 g) potatoes, peeled and chunked (optional)
1 Tbsp. flour
1 tsp paprika
salt
freshly ground black pepper

This recipe is popular over much of Spain and occurs in many variations. It is from the Guadalajara Province of Spain, where in the villages all the inhabitants collectively fed one pig. On the feast day of St. Anthony there was a draw for the pig, it was slaughtered, and a stew was made for the villagers to share in the winner's luck. This stew attempted to use as much as possible of the fresh pork. This recipe has been updated by eliminating some of the more exotic pork cuts, such as ear or tail.

Soak the beans overnight in cold water. Bring to a boil, strain, rinse and strain again. Put beans in a large pot with a lid. Add enough water to cover; add the wine and bring to a boil. During this time make sure meat and vegetables have been chunked and chopped. Add all the cut-up meat, the sausage, half the oil, the bay leaf and the peeled onion with the peppercorns pushed into it.

Cover and cook over slow heat for about 75 minutes until the beans begin to soften. If potatoes are used, they may be added 10 minutes before the beans are done. Remove the meat, take meat off the sparerib bones, chop and keep warm.

In a small saucepan heat the remaining oil, flour and paprika until the flour bubbles. Remove from heat and stir it into the bean mixture. Bring beans back to the boil, add the meat and let simmer for another 15 minutes. Stir occasionally to prevent the mixture from sticking to the bottom. It may be necessary during this time to add more water to maintain a stewlike consistency. Remove the onion and bay leaf. Adjust the seasoning with salt and pepper.

In some regions of Spain, rice and fennel are added before the final simmering to give the stew more body and flavor.

Serve in bowls, or over rice, with some crusty bread.

Sufficient for 6 to 8 people.

St. Anthony of Padua

ST. ANTHONY, the son of a noble Portuguese family, was born in 1195 in Lisbon, Portugal, and baptized Ferdinand. He joined the Augustinians and studied at Coimbra. Impressed by the Franciscan monks who were martyred in Morocco, he transferred to the Franciscans in 1221 and took the name Anthony. He sailed for Africa to work in the missions, but illness soon forced him to return to Italy.

He was sent to a small hermitage near Forli in Italy, where his exceptional intellectual and oratorical gifts were soon discovered. He then became a lecturer in theology, teaching at various universities in Italy and France. Anthony was a gifted preacher, attracting such large crowds that the churches were too small, and he had to preach in the marketplace. He had a strong devotion to the poor, and an attack on greed and extravagant living was often the main theme of his preaching.

After having served his order as an administrator for a while, he retired to Padua and devoted himself completely to preaching. He died there in 1231 at the age of thirty-six and was pronounced a saint by Pope Gregory IX the following year. He was buried in Padua, and his grave has been the destination for many pilgrims. The many miracles occurring after his death gave him the name of wonder-worker, and he is considered the patron saint of lost articles. This is based on a legend in which a novice who had borrowed a book without permission was asked by an apparition to return it to Anthony.

In the Middle Ages Anthony was a popular saint, his fame being spread by his fellow Franciscans as they traveled all over Europe. In art he is commonly shown with a book and a lily, sometimes with the infant Jesus sitting on the book. His feast day is June 13, which in Portugal, where he is one of the patron saints, is celebrated with great festivities.

This recipe is from Venice, where it is prepared for St. Anthony's feast day.

ZUPPA DI SANT'ANTONIO

(Soup for St. Anthony's Day)

4 eggs
3 Tbsp. flour
½ tsp. salt
½ tsp. baking powder
oil for deep frying
8 c (2 l) chicken broth
1 c (250 ml) spinach, chopped
Parmesan cheese

Whip eggs, flour, salt and baking powder into a very thin dough. With a teaspoon slowly drop little balls of batter into the hot oil. When the drops are golden brown, drain on absorbent paper.

Boil chicken broth, add dough balls and chopped spinach and let them cook for 5 minutes.

Serve soup topped with grated Parmesan cheese.

Serves 8 to 10 persons.

28

Sardinhas Grelhadas

(Grilled Sardines)

2 lb. (1 kg) fresh sardines
½ c. (125 g) coarse salt
3 Tbsp. olive oil

Clean and bone sardines. Head and tail may be left on. Layer the sardines and salt in a baking dish; cover and let stand in the refrigerator for 2 to 3 hours. Rinse the salt from the sardines, then brush each generously with olive oil.

Preheat broiler. Lay sardines on a well-oiled broiler pan, place 4 inches (10 cm) away from heat and broil 2 to 3 minutes on each side, until the fish are quite flaky. Alternatively they may be cooked on a charcoal grill.

Serve very hot with broa or, if none made, with French or Italian bread.

Serves 6 to 8.

In Portugal St. Anthony is the patron saint of lovers, and the boys give their sweethearts presents on his feast day. In Lisbon the feast of St. Anthony is celebrated with great enthusiasm. In the evening before his feast day, sardines are grilled by vendors on the streets and eaten with lots of cornbread.

Broa
(Cornbread)

2 tsp. dry yeast
4 Tbsp. lukewarm water
1¾ c. (250 g) yellow cornmeal
1¼ tsp. salt
1 tsp. sugar
1 c. (250 ml) boiling water
4 Tbsp. olive oil
1¼–2¼ c. (225 g) flour

Sprinkle yeast over the lukewarm water in a small container. Let it stand in a warm location for 2 minutes, stir and let it stand for another 10 minutes.

Meanwhile, process the cornmeal in a blender until finely ground. This is best done in 2 batches. Put about 1 cup of the cornmeal, the salt, sugar and boiling water into a mixing bowl and stir until smooth. Stir in 3 Tbsp. of the olive oil, and then let it cool to lukewarm.

Stir the yeast into the cornmeal mixture. Gradually add the remaining cornmeal and 1¼ cups of the regular flour, stirring constantly. Gather the dough into a ball and put in a warm, draft-free place until it doubles in bulk.

While the dough is rising, grease a 10-inch (25-cm) round pan with the rest of the olive oil. Knead dough for about 5 minutes, adding more flour if it is too sticky. Up to 1 cup (125 g) may be added. The dough should be firm but not stiff. Put dough into the greased pan and let rise for a further 30 minutes until it doubles in bulk again. Preheat the oven to 350°F (175°C).

Bake the bread in the center of the oven for about 40 minutes until the top is golden. Let cool on a rack.

St. Augustine of Hippo

AUGUSTINE was born in 354 in what is now Souk-Ahras in Algeria. His father, a small landowner, was a pagan, and his mother, Monica, was a Christian. Monica raised her son in the Catholic faith, but he was never baptized. With financial support from a friend, Augustine studied at the university in Carthage to become a lawyer but gave this up to study philosophy and teach rhetoric.

During this period he lived quite a loose life and followed the normal ambitions of a young man of his times. For fifteen years he had a mistress with whom he had a son, Adeodatus. During this time he encountered the heresy of Manichaeism and abandoned his Christian faith.

In 383 he went to Rome as a teacher of rhetoric, and, after having been cheated by his students out of his tuition, he went to Milan in 384 to accept a position at the university. There he came under the influence of St. Ambrose, who was bishop of Milan at that time. The sermons of Ambrose showed him how he could integrate the teachings of the Church with his inquisitive intellect. He studied Scripture and theological writings that he discussed with friends and his mother, Monica, who had followed him to Milan.

Benozzo Gozzoli,
15th century, Sant'Agostino,
San Gimignano, Italy

St. Augustine lived a monastic life with his clergy and encouraged greatly the formation of new religious communities. Many of the religious who lived with him founded other monasteries in North Africa. Augustine wrote a simple rule for religious living in communities that formed the basis for the rules of many different orders. He was known to be very hospitable, kind and charitable, and when he died he had no worldly possessions.

In 386 he experienced a great conversion, and on Easter eve 387, he was baptized by Ambrose. Augustine's mother, St. Monica, was very much responsible for the conversion of her son, through her prayers, patience and affection.

Augustine decided to return to North Africa, and on the way Monica died in Ostia. In Hippo he was persuaded by the local bishop to become a priest, and he was ordained in 391. In 395 he was consecrated bishop, and in 396 he became bishop of Hippo. He ruled the diocese there until his death in 430 during the siege of Hippo by the Vandals.

During his time as bishop of Hippo he wrote extensively. Two of his better-known works are his *Confessions* and *The City of God*. Augustine was called upon to defend the Catholic faith against various heresies and thus had to write on many topics, including God's grace, the nature of the Trinity and many other theological problems. Most of Augustine's writings survive, and these have had a great influence on the development of Christian thought and have been translated into many languages.

After his death his relics were transferred to Sardinia and are now buried at Pavia in Italy. His cult started very early, and he was proclaimed a Doctor of the Western Church. In art St. Augustine is normally shown in his episcopal vestments, often in the process of writing or dictating. There is also a remarkable cycle of paintings with scenes of his early life. St. Augustine is the patron saint of brewers because of his early way of life. His feast day is August 28.

CHILES EN NOGADA
(Stuffed Peppers in Walnut Sauce)

SAUCE

50 walnuts, shelled, or 2 c. (200 g) ground walnuts
or ground blanched almonds
milk (if using fresh walnuts)
¼ lb. (100 g) goat cheese, or, if not available, cream cheese
1 hard roll or crust end of a bread soaked in milk
salt and pepper to taste
pinch of cinnamon

To make the sauce:

If starting with fresh walnuts, soak the shelled nuts in milk for about 20 to 30 minutes to loosen the skin and then remove the skins.

Using a blender, grind the nuts, cheese, hard roll in milk together to make a sauce. The sauce should be thin enough to pour; if not, add some more milk. Season the sauce with salt and pepper and a pinch of cinnamon.

STUFFING

3 tomatoes, or 8 oz. (300 g) can of tomatoes, drained
½ c. (100g) almonds, whole, blanched
2 peaches, peeled, chopped
2 pears, peeled, chopped
½ c. (100g) raisins
2 Tbsp. olive oil
½ lb. (250 g) pork, ground
½ lb. (250 g) beef, ground
4 Tbsp. onion, chopped
1 tsp. garlic, minced
¼ tsp. saffron
salt and pepper to taste

To make the stuffing:

Peel tomatoes and chop them. Chop almonds. Peel fruit and chop. Soak raisins in hot water. Set aside.

This recipe is from the Mexican state of Puebla, where the Feast of St. Augustine is celebrated with this dish. An unusual mix of ingredients produces a tasty and filling dish. It requires a bit of effort, shelling and skinning the walnuts. It is important to use fresh walnuts, because it is almost impossible to remove the skin from store-bought shelled walnuts, which tend to be older and may also have an off-flavor. If shelling and skinning the nuts are too cumbersome, shelled or ground walnuts may be used, or even blanched almonds. The flavor will be somewhat different, but the work is considerably less.

Heat the oil in a large frying pan and brown the meat. Add tomatoes, onion and garlic. Cook covered for a few minutes to blend the flavors. Add the almonds, drained raisins, saffron and fruits. Season to taste with salt and pepper and cook till the filling is quite thick and most of the liquid has evaporated.

PEPPERS
7 to 8 bell peppers, medium size, different colors

Put the peppers into boiling water for a couple of minutes, till they have softened somewhat. Remove the top and the seeds.

COATING
¾ c. (100 g) flour
1 tsp. cinnamon
½ tsp. cloves
2 tsp. sugar
2 eggs

GARNISHES
parsley and pomegranate seeds

Prepare the coating mixture by mixing together all the dry ingredients. Beat the 2 eggs slightly.

Stuff the peppers with the meat mixture. Make sure the outside of the peppers is wet before dipping them into the flour spice mixture and then into the egg. Sprinkle again with the flour mixture.

Fry in hot fat at 375°F (190°C) until browned. Drain on absorbent paper. Serve with the cold sauce, garnished with pomegranate seeds and parsley.

Plain or Mexican rice goes nicely with this dish.

Serves 6 to 8 people.

St. Barbara

Jan van Eyck, 15th century, Koninklijk Museum, Antwerp, Belgium

BARBARA has been a popular saint in both the Western and the Eastern Church even though her existence is very doubtful. For this reason Rome removed her from the official list of saints in 1969.

Barbara supposedly lived in the third century and was alleged to have been killed in the persecution of Maximian around 303. The description of her martyrdom was not written until the seventh century, and her first representation in art is not found until the eighth century. Four cities in Italy and the Middle East all claim to have been the place of her death.

Her popularity can be partly attributed to *The Golden Legend*, a thirteenth-century book of legends about various saints. According to legend, her father shut her up in a tower, so that no man could see her.

While her father was away, she had workmen add a third window, in honor of the Trinity, to a bathhouse her father was building. Also, at this time she became a Christian. Infuriated, her father handed her to a judge who condemned her to death. The legend tells us that in return, her father was killed by lightning.

The feast day of Barbara was December 4, and she is usually shown in art with a tower. She is considered the patron saint of dangerous professions, such as artillerymen and firefighters, but she is also the patron of architects, stonemasons and mathematicians.

This is an old traditional German cake recipe that makes a lovely lemon-flavored cake to go with a cup of tea or coffee.

BARBARAKUCHEN

(St. Barbara Cake)

¾ c. (200 g) butter
1 lemon
1 c. (250 g) sugar
4 eggs
1 c. (125 g) flour
1¼ c. (125 g) cornstarch
¾ tsp. baking powder

ICING
1 c. (125 g) powdered sugar
3 Tbsp. lemon juice

Soften butter at room temperature and whisk with electric beater until frothy. Grate lemon peel and add. Alternately add sugar, eggs, and the flour, cornstarch and baking powder to the mixture. Grease and flour a rectangular 12-inch (30 cm) bread pan. Fill with batter and bake at 350°F (175°C).

When cake has cooled somewhat, remove from pan.

Prepare icing by mixing the powdered sugar with the lemon juice. Spread on top of the warm cake.

Serves 8.

Schweinelendchen Barbara

(Pork Tenderloin St. Barbara)

1 lb. (450 g) pork tenderloin
salt and pepper
2 Tbsp. butter
½ lb. (250 g) apples, small
1 c. (250 ml) dry white wine
1 c. (250 ml) whipping cream
4 tsp. cornstarch
4 Tbsp. water
2 tsp. horseradish
pinch of sugar

Cut tenderloin in slices about ½-inch (2 cm) thick and salt and pepper generously. Melt butter in a saucepan, and fry the slices in the butter on both sides until nicely browned. Move from pan to serving plate and keep warm.

Peel apples, cut in half and core. Add the wine to the frying pan, add apple halves, cover and let simmer for 10 minutes. Remove apples and put on top of tenderloin slices.

Add the cream to the wine, stir well and slowly bring to a boil. Mix the cornstarch with 4 tablespoons of water and add to sauce. Boil for 1 minute. Add the horseradish and sugar. Taste and adjust seasoning with salt and pepper. Pour sauce over the tenderloin and apples and serve.

Serves 3 to 4 people.

This is a recipe from a German cookbook entitled Der lachende Feinschmecker *(The laughing gourmet), published in 1979.*

*In Armenia, Syria and Lebanon
the Christmas season begins on
December 4, the feast of St.
Barbara. This is the traditional
dessert for that day, and while
the wheat is cooking, the head of
the household is supposed to tell
the legend of St. Barbara.*

Kamhié

(Dessert for St. Barbara's Day)

3 c. (300 g) wheat, whole grain
8 c. (2l) water, boiling
1 tsp. salt
1 c. (100 g) raisins, golden
½ c. (100 g) pine nuts
½ c. (100 g) walnuts, chopped
½ c. (100 g) almonds, chopped
⅔ c. (100 g) candied mixed peel
½ tsp. rose water
1 c. (250 g) sugar, or a mixture of half sugar and half honey

TOPPING
cinnamon
sugar
walnuts or pistachios, chopped or grated

Wash grain thoroughly under cold running water. Drain well and put
into a heavy saucepan with a tight-fitting lid. A slow cooker may be
used instead. Add the salt and 8 cups of boiling water, cover tightly
and simmer slowly until the wheat is soft but not mushy. This may take
4 to 6 hours.

The consistency should be similar to that of porridge. If there is too
much liquid, it should be drained.

Continuing to cook the grain over low heat, stir in the raisins, pine
nuts, walnuts, almonds, mixed peel, sugar and rose water. Stir until
sugar is dissolved and the mixture thick and moist.

Remove from heat and spoon into individual dessert dishes or one
large bowl. Serve sprinkled with cinnamon, sugar and the chopped
walnuts or pistachios.

Serves 8 to 10.

St. Basil

Mosaic, 14th century,
S. Marco, Venice

THE SON of a very pious family, Basil was born around 330 at Caesarea in Cappadocia (now Turkey). His grandmother, his mother and father, one of his brothers and one of his sisters were all saints. He very early distinguished himself as a student at Constantinople and Athens, and during his studies he struck up a lifelong friendship with St. Gregory Nazianzen. Basil then became a monk, and for a short time he lived in Syria and Egypt until he settled as a hermit near Caesarea. He left his solitude in 364, when the bishop called him to defend the Church against the persecutions of the emperor Valens, who favored the Arian heresy.

In 370 he became bishop of Caesarea, and he put considerable effort into looking after his people. He distributed his inheritance to the poor, and during a famine he organized soup kitchens for the hungry. Basil preached extensively and had a considerable correspondence with the leading people of his time. However, Basil's main contributions to the Church are his extensive theological writings on the Holy Spirit and his rules for monasticism in the Eastern Church. He managed to integrate Christian theology with the best ideas of philosophy and secular culture. For these writings he was named a Doctor of the Church and is venerated in both East and West. His influence in the West was spread by St. Benedict. In the development of the rules for his order, Benedict followed the example set out in the writings of St. Basil.

In art Basil is usually shown with a long pointed beard and a book. His representation in art has been very consistent over the centuries and always includes full hair and a long beard. St. Basil's feast day is New Year's Day in the East, and in the West it is January 2.

This is a very traditional version of a cake made on New Year's Day in Greece in honor of St. Basil. Even though different recipes exist, they all include the hiding of a silver coin in the cake, which is supposed to bring luck to the person who finds it. The head of the family slices the cake and distributes the pieces in a very precise order. The first piece is for St. Basil, the second one for Christ, the third one for the oldest member of the family and on down to the youngest.

VASILOPETA

(St. Basil's Bread)

1 c. (250 g) butter
2 c. (500 g) sugar
3 c. (375 g) flour
6 eggs
2 tsp. baking powder
1 c. (250 ml) milk
½ tsp. baking soda
1½ Tbsp. lemon juice
½ c. (100 g) nuts, chopped
4 Tbsp. sugar

Cream butter and sugar together until light. Add flour and stir until mixture resembles coarse meal. Add eggs, one at a time, beating well after each addition. Stir baking powder into milk and stir into egg mixture. Mix baking soda with lemon juice and add. Preheat oven to 350°F (175°C).

Pour mixture into a greased round cake pan, 10-inches (25 cm) in diameter. Throw in a clean coin. Bake for 20 minutes. Sprinkle top with nuts and sugar and bake 20 to 30 minutes longer until cake is done. When cake is cool remove to serving plate.

Serves 10 to 12.

LAKROR

(St. Basil's Meat Pie)

3 Tbsp. butter
½ c. (125 ml) onion, finely chopped
1½ lb. (750 g) ground meat, preferably a mixture of beef and lamb
2 tsp. garlic, minced
1 tsp. salt
2 tsp. oregano, dried
freshly ground pepper
½ c. (125 ml) parsley, fresh, chopped
½ c. (125 ml) rice, cooked
6 eggs
1 lb. (500 g) phyllo dough
½ c. (125 g) butter, unsalted

Melt the 3 tablespoons of butter in a large frying pan and sauté the onion gently until transparent. Add the meat, garlic, salt, oregano and pepper to taste. Sauté until the meat is nicely browned. Drain off the fat and check the seasoning.

Mix the chopped parsley, rice and eggs, then add them to the meat. Mix thoroughly.

Butter a 9 x 12-inch (23 x 30 cm) pan. Take one sheet of phyllo dough and cut it to the size of the pan. You will need at least 20 sheets, so you may cut them all at once.

Brush the first sheet with melted butter. Repeat this until 10 sheets have been used.

In Albania a special pie with different kinds of fillings is baked in honor of St. Basil on his feast day. As in the previous recipe, a coin is hidden in the pie. This version with a meat filling is made with phyllo pastry.

Place meat filling over the phyllo dough, making sure the filling is spread evenly. Cover with another sheet of phyllo dough, brush with melted butter. Repeat until you have 10 layers. Seal the last sheet especially well, and press down the edges with your fingers.

With a sharp knife, score the surface of the lakror, making a pattern of squares or diamonds. This will make it easier later to cut the pie. Do not cut through all the way, just cut a few of the top layers.

Bake in a moderately hot oven 375°F (190°C) for about 45 minutes or until golden brown.

Makes 6 to 8 servings.

Sano di Pietro, 15th century,
Pinacoteca Nazionale,
Siena, Italy

BLAISE is believed to have been a physician who became the bishop of Sebaste in Armenia early in the fourth century. Even after Emperor Constantine had given peace to the Christians in the West, his colleague Licinius still persecuted the Christians in the East. Blaise, as a Church leader, was accused of being a Christian, tried in court and found guilty. According to legend, he was tortured with iron combs and put to death at Sebaste at around 316.

His feast day is of great importance in the Eastern Church, and the crusaders propagated devotion to him on their return to Europe. The most popular legend about St. Blaise describes him curing a child who was choking to death on a fishbone. Another famous legend tells about a poor widow complaining to St. Blaise that a wolf had stolen her pig. St. Blaise talked to the wolf, and he returned the pig to the widow.

Blessing of the throats on February 3, St. Blaise's feast day, is a custom still today. Blaise is the saint to invoke for help with throat ailments. He is the patron saint of wool combers, patron of Paraguay and one of the patron saints of physicians.

40

BUBENSCHENKEL

(Boys' Thighs)

1 Tbsp. dry yeast
warm water to dissolve the yeast
1 c. (250 ml) milk, scalded and cooled
2 Tbsp. butter, melted
½ tsp. salt
pinch of sugar
3 eggs
6 c. (750 g) flour
oil for deep frying

Dissolve the yeast in a few tablespoons of warm water. Then blend all ingredients into smooth yeast dough. Set aside, let rise for about 1 hour until doubled in size.

Roll out dough to about ½ inch (1 cm). Cut with a pastry wheel into 2 x 4-inch rectangles (5 x 10 cm). Make a cut in the middle of the rectangle almost to the middle. The pieces will look like Bermuda shorts.

Let dough rise another 15 minutes. Fry in hot oil until golden. Serve with a German-style potato salad and a green salad.

This dish contains no meat, but it may be served with a meat dish that has lots of gravy, such as goulash or turkey à la king.

Makes about 18 pieces.

This is an old Swabian recipe to be cooked on the feast day of St. Blaise. There was a pre-Christian, pagan festival on the same day as St. Blaise's feast day, and it is believed that this recipe has its origins in that festival. The dish was later associated with St. Blaise. It is interesting to note that the Pennsylvania Dutch have a similarly named dish called "Boovashenkel", which is translated in the same way. However, the recipe for this dish is quite different as it contains meat. It is essentially boiled beef with potato dumplings. Whether there is a connection between the Pennsylvania Dutch recipe and St. Blaise is not known.

41

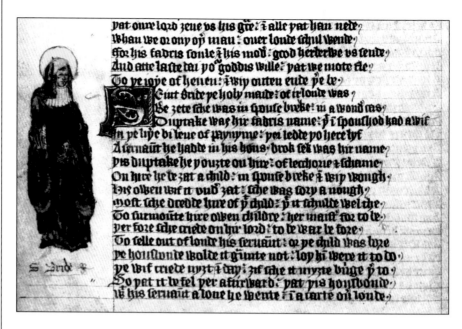

Illustrated Manuscript,
15th century,
Bodleian Library,
Oxford

BRIGID was born of Christian parents, possibly at Uinmeras near Kildare, Ireland, in the fifth century. Her parents, of humble origin, were said to have been baptized by St. Patrick himself, and they brought their children up to be good Christians. Brigid's name can be found as Bridget or Bride in various books.

When she was still relatively young, she became a nun and later founded the monastery of Kildare, the first religious house for women in Ireland. She died there around 525.

Legends say that Brigid as a young nun was asked to look after the cattle, and the cows in her care gave more milk than those looked after by other nuns. Farm duties such as guarding ducks and geese seem also to be associated with the time before she became the abbess of the Kildare monastery. Compassion for friends and strangers was said to have been one of her main characteristics.

Brigid contributed greatly to the spread of Christianity in Ireland and is, with St. Patrick, a patron saint of Ireland. Irish missionaries to Europe spread her fame, and many churches dedicated to her can be found in Wales, Alsace and Flanders. Sometimes it is hard to sort out the three Bridgets, as there is a St. Bridget of Kildare, one of Sweden and one of Northumbria.

In art Brigid of Kildare is usually shown with a cow at her feet or with a goose. She is the patron saint of poets and blacksmiths. Her feast day is February 1, the day when an old pagan festival honoring a goddess was celebrated. Transforming the celebrations to honor a Christian saint was more effective than trying to eliminate the old customs.

Barm Brack

1 c. (100 g) sultanas (if unavailable, seedless raisins may be used)

1 c. (100 g) raisins

1 c. (100 g) currants

1¼ c. (300 ml) cold tea

¼ c. (50 g) candied cherries

¼ c. (50 g) mixed peel

1¼ c. (175 g) soft brown sugar (lightly packed)

1¾ c. (200 g) flour

½ tsp. baking powder

1 tsp. mixed spice (or ½ tsp. each cinnamon and coriander, plus a
   pinch of nutmeg and cloves)

1 egg

Soak sultanas, raisins and currants in cold tea overnight.

Preheat oven to 350°F (175°C).

Add all the remaining ingredients to the fruit and tea and stir well.
Line a 1-lb. (500-g) loaf pan with greased parchment paper and fill with
the mixture. Cook in the oven for about 1½ hours.

Cool on wire rack. Serve buttered.

Serves 6 to 8.

A very well-known Irish recipe for a fruitcake, this Barm Brack proved extremely popular with my family. In Ireland it was customary to bake it in the evening before St. Brigid's Day and serve it the next day, sliced and well buttered.

43

St. Catherine of Alexandria

CATHERINE OF ALEXANDRIA is a saint whose historical existence is cloaked in legends and is even doubtful. She is no longer on the Roman calendar of saints whose feast days are celebrated in the universal Church.

According to legend, Catherine was a noble girl living in Alexandria in Egypt in the fourth century. She was courted by the emperor Maxentius, but she considered herself to be a bride of Christ and refused marriage. The next attempt of the emperor was to convince her to give up her faith by having her argue the merits of Christianity with fifty philosophers. The discussion did not have the hoped-for result, and the emperor condemned Catherine to be tortured on a wheel and put to death. The wheel broke, and ultimately Catherine was beheaded.

The cult of St. Catherine started only in the ninth century, and she became very popular. No first-millennium works of art depicting her have been found, but her story appealed to the imagination of many medieval artists, in whose works she is commonly shown with a wheel.

She was the patron saint of young girls, philosophers and wheelwrights. Her feast day was November 25.

Pasta Santa Caterina

2 lb. (900 g) ripe tomatoes
2 Tbsp. Italian parsley, chopped
2 Tbsp. fresh basil, chopped
2 tsp. garlic, minced
3 Tbsp. freshly grated Parmesan cheese
1 tsp. dried oregano
6 Tbsp. olive oil
½ tsp. salt
½ tsp. black pepper
1 lb. (450 g) spaghetti

Peel tomatoes, remove seeds and cut into small dice.

In a medium bowl combine all the ingredients except the pasta. Marinate at room temperature for about 1 hour.

Cook the pasta in plenty of boiling salted water until tender. Drain thoroughly, and transfer pasta to a heated serving dish. Add the sauce and toss. Adjust seasonings and serve with extra Parmesan cheese.

Serves 8 to 10.

A delightful light summer pasta from V. Laplace's book Pasta Fresca, *it comes from the Hotel Santa Caterina in Amalfi.*

In northern France it is a custom on St. Catherine's day to give heart-shaped cakes to unmarried women who have reached the age of twenty-five. The idea is to encourage them in their search for love (and a husband).

LES COEURS DE SAINTE-CATHERINE

(St. Catherine Hearts)

7 Tbsp. butter, soft
½ c. (125 g) sugar
3 eggs
2 c. (250 g) flour
2 tsp. baking powder
½ tsp. cinnamon
¼ tsp. salt
¼ c. (60 g) candied fruit, mixed
1 Tbsp. orange rind, grated
½ tsp. orange extract
3 Tbsp. water
butter for pan
powdered sugar, for sprinkling

Preheat oven to 300°F (150°C). Chop candied fruit.

Cream the butter. Gradually add the sugar, mixing well; beat in the eggs, one at a time. Sift the flour with the baking powder, cinnamon and salt into the butter mixture. Stir in the chopped candied fruits, orange rind, orange extract and water. Mix thoroughly.

With butter or shortening, grease a heart-shaped pan. Pour the batter into this pan and bake for 20 minutes. Raise the heat to 425°F (220°C) and bake for another 15 or 20 minutes, or until a wooden skewer inserted in the center of the cake comes out clean. Remove from pan when cool. It may be sprinkled with powdered sugar before serving.

Serves 8.

LA TIRE

(St. Catherine's Candy)

1 c. (350 g—250 ml) molasses
1 c. (250 g) sugar
1 c. (150 g) brown sugar
½ c. (125 ml) corn syrup
½ c. (125 ml) water
1 Tbsp. butter
1 Tbsp. vinegar
5 drops vanilla
1 tsp. baking soda

Put all the ingredients except the baking soda into a deep, heavy saucepan. Boil until mixture forms a hard ball in cold water—250°F (120°C) when measured with a candy thermometer. Sift in baking soda and mix well. Pour contents onto a well-buttered platter or cookie tray.

When cool enough to handle, but still warm, pull with both hands until candy becomes a golden brown shade, or whatever degree of light brown you want.

Cut into small pieces. (The candies may then be wrapped in wax paper.)

Makes about 30 pieces.

This recipe comes from Marie Nightingale's cookbook OUT OF OLD NOVA SCOTIA KITCHENS. It is reported there that it has been the custom of the sisters of the Congregation of Notre Dame to observe the feast day of St. Catherine by making this delicious molasses candy in her honor to share with all their pupils. This custom has spread all over French Canada.

This recipe (from P. Estival via the Internet) is a light dessert that can be easily made and may be considered a variation of a classic Pavlova.

ENTREMETS SAINTE-CATHERINE

(Dessert St. Catherine)

MERINGUE
3 egg whites
pinch of salt
5 Tbsp. (75 g) sugar
½ c. (75 g) powdered sugar
cornstarch for dusting

FILLING
1¼ c. (300 ml) whipping cream
1 tsp. sugar
½ tsp. vanilla
3 Tbsp. black currant liqueur (or concentrated juice)
red and black currants, fresh or frozen

Preheat oven to 250°F (120°C).

With an electric beater, beat the egg whites and the salt until stiff peaks form. Slowly add 5 tablespoons granulated sugar and the ½ cup powdered sugar while continuously beating the egg whites.

Cut a sheet of waxed paper, grease one side, put it onto a baking tray and dust the greased side with cornstarch.

Put the meringue into a cake-decorating bag and pipe a circle of meringue onto the paper. The meringue should be about ½ inch (12 mm) thick. (The meringue can also be spread onto the paper with a spatula, but the piping bag creates a fancier base.)

Put the baking tray in the middle shelf of the oven and bake the base for about 1 hour and 15 minutes. Do not let the meringue get brown; it should be a light golden color.

48

While meringue is baking, prepare the filling by whipping the cream and adding the teaspoon of sugar, the vanilla and the black currant liqueur. Continue whipping until everything is well blended. Refrigerate.

Once the base is baked, let it cool. Remove the paper carefully without breaking the base and put the base on the serving dish. Spread the cream onto the base (a piping bag may be used), and decorate it with the currants. If frozen currants are used, add them just before serving to keep their color from bleeding onto the cream.

Serves 8 to 10.

Catherine Wheel Cookies

2 c. (250 g) flour
2 tsp. baking powder
4 Tbsp. currants
½ c. (50 g) almonds, ground
2 tsp. anise seeds
1 c. (240 g) sugar
½ tsp. cinnamon
5 Tbsp. (75 g) butter
1 Tbsp. milk
1 egg

Preheat oven to 400°F (200°C). Grind anise seed with mortar and pestle, if you have one, or chop fine with a knife or process in a blender.

Mix together flour, baking powder, currants, almonds, ground anise seeds, sugar and cinnamon. Melt the butter. Add butter, milk and beaten egg to the flour mixture and mix to a smooth dough. Pinch off walnut-sized pieces of dough, shape into balls and place on an ungreased cookie sheet. Flatten with a fork to make a crisscross pattern and bake in the oven for 10 to 12 minutes until lightly browned.

Makes about 30 cookies.

A well-known recipe that can be found in many books, it makes simple but delicious anise-flavored cookies.

49

This is a French recipe given in
A Good Housekeeping
Compendium, *published in*
London in 1952.

Cécilias

1 c. (100 g) almonds, ground
¼ c. (100 g) sugar
2 tsp. kirsch
1 egg white
2 Tbsp. cocoa
fondant icing
food coloring
2 tsp. melted dark chocolate
slivered almonds for decoration

Mix the almonds and sugar and a teaspoon of kirsch with sufficient egg white to bind it to a smooth paste. Divide paste into two portions. Roll one portion into small balls about ½ inch (1 cm) in diameter. Add cocoa to the other half and make pieces the size and shape of an olive.

Tint some of the fondant icing green and flavor with the remaining kirsch. Dip the plain balls in this.

Add the melted chocolate to some fondant icing and dip the chocolate olives into this. Put a sliver of an almond on each. Allow Cécilias to dry. After they are dry, put them in fancy paper candy cups.

Makes about 24.

St. Charles Borromeo

Orazio Borgianni, 17th century,
S. Carlo, Rome

CHARLES BORROMEO was born in 1538 in Arona, Italy, and as a second son of the family he was early destined for the Church. He took a doctorate in canon law at Pavia in 1559. Soon after his maternal uncle was made pope, Charles was called to Rome, created a cardinal-deacon and made administrator of the vacant see of Milan and papal legate and protector. He was not allowed by his uncle, Pius IV, to take over his diocese until the work connected with the Council of Trent finished in 1565. By that time he had been ordained a priest (in 1563), and two months later he was confirmed a bishop. In 1566 he finally came to Milan.

From that time on Charles Borromeo tried to be the model bishop that the Council of Trent had envisaged. His example became a pattern for the whole Church and contributed greatly to her revitalization after the Council. With boundless energy, needing little food or sleep, he traveled throughout his diocese to exercise a personal ministry through preaching and hearing confessions. He encouraged greatly the efforts of new religious orders, such as the Jesuits, to strengthen religious life. Despite opposition (there was even an assassination attempt made on him), he continued on his path of reforming the Church, setting an example by leading a very austere and ascetic life.

Charles Borromeo died in 1584. He was pronounced a saint in 1610 by Pope Paul V, and his feast day is November 4.

This recipe is likely of Mexican origin, although it was found in a book published in New Mexico. It proved extremely popular with my family.

CHIMICHANGAS SAN CARLOS

3 Tbsp. salad oil (for sautéing meat mixture)
3 onions, chopped
1 garlic clove, crushed
2 lbs. (900 g) beef, ground, lean
4 tomatoes, ripe, peeled and chopped
½ tsp. chili powder, Mexican
½ tsp. cumin, ground
¼ tsp. oregano
1 tsp. salt
12 flour tortillas, warm, preferably large ones
1 c. (125 g) Cheddar cheese, grated
2 avocados, large ripe, peeled and sliced lengthwise
½ c. (125 ml) salad oil (for frying)
sour cream, optional

In a large frying pan heat 3 tablespoons salad oil and cook onions and garlic until transparent. Crumble meat, add and brown well. Add tomatoes and seasonings and mix well.

Cook mixture, stirring often, for 5 minutes, or until it is fairly dry. Drain any excess fat.

On each tortilla arrange some of the meat mixture; sprinkle with cheese and top with slices of avocado. (Reserve 12 slices of avocado for garnish.)

Fold tortillas over the meat like an envelope. This is more easily done with large tortillas than small ones.

54

Add ½ cup oil to a frying pan and fry tortillas until golden, taking care not to open the envelope. A small weight, like a glass, on top of the envelope may prevent it from opening. Drain on absorbent paper.

Serve the chimichangas garnished with an avocado slice and the sour cream.

Serve with a salad or some fresh vegetable, such as tomatoes or cucumber slices.

Serves 6 for dinner, 12 for lunch.

EGGS ST. CHARLES

1 egg
4 Tbsp. milk
4 fillets of fish, about 4 oz. (100 g) each (sole, tilapia, snapper)
½ c. (60 g) flour
½ c. (50 g) cornstarch
4 Tbsp oil or butter
4 poached eggs
1 c. (250 ml) Hollandaise sauce
salt, pepper

In a shallow bowl beat the egg with the milk. Season the fillets with salt and pepper, then dredge the fish in flour. Dip the fish in the egg-milk mixture and then coat with cornstarch.

Heat the oil or butter in a pan, then fry the fish on moderately high heat until crisp, about 3 to 4 minutes a side. Drain on absorbent paper.

Put fish on 4 serving plates and top each fillet with a poached egg. Spoon Hollandaise sauce over each egg and serve. Can be served as a light lunch.

Serves 4.

Here is a recipe from the Internet that is a more substantial variation of the popular Eggs Benedict.

St. Clare of Assisi

Simone Martini, 14th century, S. Francesco, St. Martin's Chapel, Assisi (detail)

CLARE was born in 1194 in Florence, the daughter of a knight, but we know nothing else about her early life. When she was eighteen she was so impressed by the preaching of Francis of Assisi that she became the first woman to embrace the same life of poverty and austerity as Francis. She remained a trusted adviser to Francis until the time of his death.

Clare started her religious life at a Benedictine convent until Francis was able to offer her and her companions a small house next to San Damiano in Assisi. In 1215 she became the abbess of a community of women who wished to live according to the rule and spirit of St. Francis. Soon other members of her family joined her, as well as some members of wealthy families of Florence. The way of life, unusual for its time, was one of extreme poverty, the nuns living entirely from alms collected from the people. Similar to the Franciscans, Clare's nuns, or, as they were called, "Poor Clares", spread all over Europe, especially Spain.

Clare never left her convent at Assisi. She was devoted to serving her community and the town of Assisi. She continued following the ideals of St. Francis even after his death in 1226. For the last twenty-seven years of her life she suffered from various illnesses until she died in 1253. One of the great medieval contemplatives who firmly believed that poverty is essential for religious life, she was pronounced a saint by Pope Alexander IV two years after her death.

The feast day of St. Clare is August 11, and she is the patron saint of embroiderers and of television. In art she is often shown with a monstrance, referring to the time she prevented Assisi from being sacked by foreign troops by holding up a monstrance for protection.

56

Pasteis de Santa Clara
(St. Clare Turnovers)

PASTRY
½ c. (100 g) butter, chilled
1¾ c. (200 g) flour
1 egg, slightly beaten

FILLING
½ c. (125 g) sugar
½ c. (50 g) almonds, ground
4 egg yolks

Rub butter into the flour and add a little bit of very cold water until a pliable dough is obtained. Cover and refrigerate until filling is finished.

Melt the sugar in a little water and boil until thick. Add the ground almonds and yolks. Mix and simmer while stirring until very thick.

Roll out dough to ⅛-inch (3 mm) thickness, cut into 3-inch (8 cm) diameter circles. Divide the filling among them, placing it in the middle of each circle. Wet the edges and fold over, forming a half-moon shape. Seal and brush with the beaten egg and bake on a greased cookie sheet at 400°F (200°C) until golden, about 20 minutes. When baked, dredge in sugar.

Makes about 24 turnovers.

A recipe from a monastery in Coimbra, Portugal, this has been preserved for generations.

57

A recipe from a Spanish monastery of Poor Clare nuns.

ENSALADA FESTIVA DE SANTA CLARA
(Festive Salad Santa Clara)

6 eggs, hard-boiled
3 tomatoes, medium, sliced
12 sardines in oil
2 avocados, medium, sliced
1c. (150 g) carrot, grated
½ lb. (250 g) cheese (sharp, such as aged Cheddar), grated
8 oz. (250 g) tuna, canned
8 oz. (250 g) asparagus, canned or fresh
4 Tbsp. wine vinegar
4 Tbsp. olive oil
Optional: lettuce leaves, washed

Cut eggs into slices. Slice tomatoes and halve the slices. Leave sardines and asparagus whole. If fresh asparagus is used, it should be cooked for 5 minutes in hot salted water or steamed until just tender. Slice avocado and grate carrots and cheese.

This salad is supposed not only to taste good but also to be pleasing to the eye. Careful arrangement on a serving platter, making the different colors stand out, is essential. The salad may be put on one large platter or on individual plates. Lettuce leaves may be used as a base, if desired.

Spread the grated carrot in the center of the plate and put the tuna and sardines on top. Surround this with grated cheese, slices of egg, tomato and avocado and the asparagus. Keep in mind the more colorful the arrangement, the better. Season the salad with vinegar and oil; the oil from the sardines may be used.

The ingredients in this salad may be varied; you could add or substitute slices of beet, cucumber, kiwi fruit, sweet bell peppers, ham, shrimp, pickles, etc.

Serves 8 to 12 hungry persons.

Rosquillas de Santa Clara

(Santa Clara Fritters)

1 Tbsp. dry yeast
1 Tbsp. water
1 egg
3 Tbsp. sugar
½ c. (125 ml) olive oil
4 tsp. anise seed
1½ c. (200 g) flour (approximately)
oil for deep frying
powdered sugar for dusting

Soften the yeast in a tablespoon of water. Beat the egg with the sugar until creamy. Add the oil, anise and yeast. Stir in the flour. Keep adding flour until the dough does not stick to your fingers anymore.

Knead for 5 minutes and then form balls the size of a nut.

Fry these balls in plenty of hot oil and drain on a paper towel. They may be dusted with powdered sugar before serving.

This makes about 24 fritters. The recipe can easily be doubled or tripled.

This is another Spanish monastery recipe that has been handed down through generations of nuns and whose origin cannot be traced.

*An unusual dish from Mexico,
it can be made quite spicy,
though the heat is moderated by
the chocolate. It is worth a try
for all lovers of hot and spicy
foods, especially those who like
chili pepper.*

MOLE OF SANTA CLARA

MEAT

6 lb. (3 kg) chicken breasts without skin and bones

4 c. cold water

SAUCE

12 mulato chiles

3 pasilla chiles

2 ancho chiles

2 chipotle peppers

4–8 Tbsp. peanut oil

½ c. (100 g) almonds, whole, unblanched

½ c. (50 g) seedless dark raisins

1½ tsp. sesame seeds

1 c. (200 g) tomato, coarsely chopped

1 tsp. garlic, minced

stock from the chicken

2 tsp. salt

¾ tsp. anise seed, ground

1 Tbsp. fresh cilantro, minced

¼ tsp. cinnamon, ground

¼ tsp. fresh ground black pepper, scant

⅛ tsp. cloves, ground

2 oz. (60 g) bittersweet chocolate, chopped fine

2 Tbsp. packed brown sugar

GARNISH

toasted sesame kernels

onion, sliced paper-thin in rings, halved

Put poultry in a stockpot with 4 cups of cold water. Bring to a boil. Skim foam off top, reduce heat and simmer until tender (about 1½ hours). When poultry is done, remove it and refrigerate (or freeze if preparing for later use). Strain stock into a bowl, cover and refrigerate. After stock has chilled, skim off top. Reserve stock for later use in the recipe.

Sauce
Pull off the tops of the dried chiles by the stems. Tear chiles into strips. Remove all seeds and veins. Reserve 1 to 3 tablespoons of the seeds (depending on how hot you want the mole to be). If the chiles are too dry to tear apart, cover them with boiling water and soak a few minutes until softened.

(Chiles can burn sensitive skin. You may want to wear gloves. In any case, be careful not to touch your eyes while preparing chiles.)

Put 1 or 2 tablespoons of peanut oil into a large skillet or pot over high heat. Fry the chile strips, reserved chile seeds, almonds, raisins, sesame seeds, tomato and garlic in batches until the chiles have changed color and stiffened. Be sure to fry the chipotle thoroughly, or it will be too hot. (This is a very hot pepper and you might want to omit it, depending on your tolerance.)

After each batch is fried, transfer to a food processor and add a ladle of stock. Process mixture to a coarse paste. Continue until all batches have been processed.

Add 2 to 3 tablespoons of peanut oil to the pan, and place over medium heat. Add all of the chile paste. As the paste cooks, stir in the salt, anise, cilantro, cinnamon, black pepper and cloves. Be careful, because the mixture could spatter. Add stock, a ladleful at a time, mixing after each addition, until sauce is smooth and thick enough to coat the back of a metal spoon.

Add chocolate and brown sugar. Stir until chocolate is melted and sugar is dissolved in the sauce. Simmer at least 40 minutes over very low heat, stirring occasionally.

Serving: Cut chicken into medium-sized slices. Add to mole in skillet or stewpot and cook over medium heat, stirring frequently, until poultry is heated throughout. Serve hot, garnished with toasted sesame seeds and fresh onion slices.

If making mole in advance, refrigerate or freeze the sauce (separately from the meat), then reheat and serve sauce and meat together as above.

Serves 10.

St. Clement

CLEMENT was a Roman by birth who was converted to Christianity by either St. Peter or St. Paul. He accompanied Paul on some of his travels and in the letter to the Philippians was called his "fellow laborer". In 88 he succeeded Peter as bishop of Rome and fourth pope.

In 96 a bitter dispute broke out among members of the Church in Corinth, a faction revolting against the leaders of their church. Clement wrote a letter to the church emphasizing the necessity for people to follow Christian teaching, the need of a hierarchy and the preeminence of the bishop of Rome. The letter also provides evidence for the residence and martyrdom of Peter and Paul in Rome. Clement died around 100 during the reign of the emperor Trajan.

Tradition has it that for his missionary activities in Rome, Clement was sent into exile in the Crimea to labor in the quarries. According to legend, he was killed by having an anchor hung around his neck and being thrown into the sea. Miracles attributed to Clement abound in *The Golden Legend*.

Clement's relics are supposedly buried in San Clemente in Rome, where there is a series of frescoes showing legends about his life. St. Clement's feast day is November 23, and he is the patron saint of marble workers.

Many churches in Europe were dedicated to Clement, and one of these churches, in the city of London, found its way into the old English nursery rhyme: "Oranges and lemons say the bells of St. Clement's." This rhyme is the reason English chefs associate dishes containing orange and lemon juice with St. Clement, a connection not found anywhere else in Europe.

St. Clement's Chicken

This dish, with a nice spicy sauce, can be prepared easily and quickly.

6 chicken breasts, boneless
2 garlic cloves, minced
½ tsp. ground ginger
½ tsp. cinnamon
2 Tbsp. olive oil
2 oranges
1 lemon
1 Tbsp. ginger root, grated
1 Tbsp. honey
¾ c. (175 ml) chicken stock
½ tsp. salt
½ tsp. fresh ground black pepper
fresh coriander, parsley or chopped chives for garnish

Mix together the garlic, ground ginger and cinnamon and rub it over the chicken.

Heat the oil in a large, heavy saucepan that can be covered. Add the chicken and brown on both sides. While it is browning, grate the peel of one orange and one lemon and set aside. Squeeze the juice of the two oranges and the lemon and mix the juice with the grated rind, grated ginger root, honey and chicken stock.

Add this mixture to the chicken in the pan and bring to a boil. Add salt and pepper. Cover tightly and cook so that the liquid is barely bubbling for about 20 minutes. Turn the chicken several times during cooking.

Serve garnished with chopped chives, coriander or parsley.

Serves 4 to 6 persons.

St. Clement's Sweet Potatoes

Here is an unusual way of preparing sweet and regular potatoes. The subtle flavors of the potatoes require a fairly bland main dish to be really appreciated.

¾ lb. (350 g) sweet potatoes
¾ lb. (350 g) white potatoes
1 orange
4 Tbsp. butter
2 Tbsp. sugar
salt and pepper
1 lemon

Peel and cube potatoes. Put sweet and white potatoes into two separate pans of boiling salt water. Cook until tender. Drain and return to pan.

Grate the rind of half the orange and squeeze out 2 tablespoons of orange juice. Add juice and rind to the sweet potatoes with half the butter and sugar. Blend the ingredients together until smooth.

Mash the white potatoes and stir well over low heat. Season to taste with salt and pepper. Grate the rind of the lemon and squeeze out 2 tablespoons of lemon juice and mix with the remaining butter and sugar. Add to the mashed potatoes. Stir well to make the mixture smooth.

Put the 2 vegetables side by side in a hot serving dish and garnish.

Serves 6.

63

St. Clement's Mousse with Caramel Oranges

MOUSSE
2 lemons
1 orange
1 tsp. gelatin
1 c. (250 ml) whipping cream
3 egg yolks
½ c. (125 g) sugar
3 egg whites

CARAMEL ORANGES
2 large oranges
1½ c. (200 g) sugar
½ c. water
2 Tbsp. Grand Marnier
6 Tbsp. cold water

CANDIED PEEL
finely pared rind of 1 lemon and 2 oranges
boiling water
1 Tbsp. sugar
2 Tbsp. water

A brilliant dessert by Judi Geisler from The Masterchef competition for young chefs held annually in Britain, it is somewhat time-consuming to make but well worth the effort.

Grate rind of 1 lemon and of 1 orange and set aside. Finely pare the rind from the other lemon and set aside for candied peel. Extract juice of 2 lemons and 1 orange. In a small bowl sprinkle gelatin over the juices and let soften. Lightly whip cream in another bowl.

In a large bowl whisk egg yolks, ½ cup sugar and grated lemon and orange rind together until thick and pale. Gently heat the bowl with the gelatin in a pan of hot water until the gelatin dissolves. Add to egg yolk mixture and stir until it begins to set, then fold in the whipped cream.

Beat egg whites until stiff, then fold into the mousse. Divide into 4 molds and put into the refrigerator for at least 1 hour to set.

To make the caramel oranges, finely pare the rind of 2 oranges and save for the candied peel. Peel oranges, removing all the white pith. Cut crossways into slices and then halve each slice. Put 1½ cups (200 g) sugar and ½ cup (125 ml) water in a heavy pan and dissolve over low heat. Boil until the syrup caramelizes to a golden brown color.

Mix the Grand Marnier with 6 tablespoons of cold water. Remove the syrup from the heat and add the diluted Grand Marnier while protecting your hands carefully. Stir carefully over low heat until caramel dissolves. After caramel mixture has cooled, pour it over the orange slices and chill in the refrigerator for at least 1 hour.

Cut reserved lemon peel and orange peel into thin strips. Blanch in boiling water for two minutes, drain. Dissolve 1 tablespoon sugar in 2 tablespoons of water in a small saucepan over low heat. Add citrus rind. Let simmer until all water has evaporated. Put on a plate and let cool.

To serve, dip the molds into hot water for a few seconds and then turn them out onto a serving plate. Surround with the caramel orange slices and decorate with candied peel strips.

This dessert sounds somewhat complicated but is not difficult to make, and it is certainly worth the effort.

Serves 8 to 10.

Note: *This is an excellent, traditional recipe. The eggs should be fresh. This recipe contains uncooked eggs and therefore may present a health problem for some people.*

St. Clement's Tartlets

SWEET SHORTCRUST PASTRY
2 c. (250 g) flour
1 Tbsp. sugar
pinch of salt
4 Tbsp. butter
4 Tbsp. shortening
5 Tbsp. ice water
1 tsp. lemon juice

FILLING
1 orange
2 lemons
½ c. (125 g) sugar
2 eggs, separated
5 Tbsp. orange juice, fresh
3 Tbsp. lemon juice, fresh
7 Tbsp. butter, melted
1 tsp. orange flower water
¼ tsp. vanilla

CANDIED LEMON SLICES
1 lemon
½ c. (125 g) sugar
4 Tbsp. water
whipped cream for garnish

This is a recipe from the restaurant attached to a California winery named St. Clement.

Sweey Shortcrust Pastry
First make the pastry. In a medium bowl combine flour, sugar and salt. Cut in butter and shortening until mixture resembles coarse bread crumbs. In a measuring cup whisk together ice water and lemon juice. Sprinkle over flour mixture until moistened all over. Gather dough into a ball, divide in half, wrap and refrigerate for at least 1 hour.

On a lightly floured surface roll out dough about ⅛ inch (3 mm) thick. Cut out circles large enough to line 3-inch (8 cm) tart pans. Press dough into corners. Leave pans on baking tray; cover and refrigerate while preparing filling.

Filling
To make the filling, grate the rind of 1 orange and 2 lemons. In a food processor mix the sugar and the rind until well blended. Add 2 egg yolks and process until thick and pale yellow.

Squeeze orange to make 5 tablespoons of fresh orange juice, and lemons to make 3 tablespoons of lemon juice. Gradually beat the juices, orange flower water and vanilla into the egg-yolk mixture. Beat in the melted butter until well blended. Set aside. In a medium bowl beat the 2 egg whites until stiff. Fold slowly into juice mixture.

66

Ladle filling into prepared tartlet shells. Bake in preheated oven at 350°F (175°C) for about 20 minutes until filling is set in center. Cool in molds on wire rack. Carefully remove tartlets from molds.

Candied Lemon Slices
To prepare the candied lemon slices, halve lemon lengthways, seed and cut into slices. Heat sugar and water over medium heat, stirring constantly until syrup boils. Stop stirring and cook for 3 more minutes. Add lemon slices and cook 5 minutes, until translucent. Using a fork, arrange slices in a single layer on waxed paper. Reserve syrup.

To serve, arrange lemon slices on top of tartlets and brush with a little of the reserved syrup. Garnish with a small amount of whipped cream.

Makes 10 to 12 tartlets.

St. Cloud

S CLOV.

CLODOALD, or Cloud, was born as the third son of King Clovis of the Franks around 524. After his father was killed in battle, his grandmother St. Clothilde brought him up. His uncles plotted to take over the kingdom and murdered his two older brothers, but the eight-year-old prince Cloud was taken safely to Provence. When he was of age he became a hermit, going to Paris and living as a disciple of St. Severinus. He was ordained and gathered many followers. This group later took up residence at Nogent near Versailles at a location that became later Saint-Cloud and still retains the name today. Cloud died in 560 and is buried there.

His feast day is September 7, the day of his death. Because of a pun on *clou* (nail), he is the patron saint of French nail makers. He also is the patron saint of the diocese of Saint Cloud in Minnesota.

St. Cloud Tartlets

SWEET SHORTCRUST PASTRY

2 c. (250 g) flour

1 Tbsp. sugar

pinch of salt

4 Tbsp. butter

4 Tbsp. shortening

6 Tbsp. ice water

FILLING

1 c. (250 g) green plum jam

DECORATION

5 oz. (125 g) puff pastry

½ c. (125 ml) whipping cream

1 tsp. sugar

¼ tsp. vanilla

12 glacé cherries

angelica strips, optional

A recipe from one of the many editions of Mrs. Beeton's cookbook. Written in the late nineteenth century, the book has been reissued many times and is still available today. It is considered a classic in England. This recipe contains an unusual jam made from green plums, which may not be easy to obtain.

In a medium bowl combine flour, sugar and salt. Cut in butter and shortening until mixture resembles coarse bread crumbs. Sprinkle ice water over flour mixture until moistened. Gather dough into a ball. Refrigerate for at least 1 hour.

On a lightly floured surface roll out dough about ⅛ inch (3 mm) thick. Cut out circles large enough to line 3-inch (8 cm) tartlet pans. Press dough into corners. Put tartlet pans on baking tray and fill with jam and bake in a preheated oven of 375°F (190°C) for about 10 to 15 minutes.

Roll out puff pastry to about ⅛-inch (3 mm) thickness and cut out rings about ½ inch (1 cm) less than the diameter of the tartlet molds. Bake in a hot oven 400°F (200°C) until golden; when cool, place the rings on the tartlets. Whip the cream; when firm, add sugar and vanilla. Fill the center with the whipped cream, top with a glacé cherry. Angelica strips may be added for further decoration.

Makes about 10 to 12 tartlets.

Pouding Froid à la Saint-Cloud

(St. Cloud Pudding)

SPONGE CAKE

1 tsp. sugar

1 tsp. flour

1 c. (125 g) flour

⅛ tsp. salt

3 eggs

½ c. (125 g) sugar

1 tsp. grated lemon rind

PUDDING

1 Tbsp. butter

4 Tbsp. (50 g) almonds, blanched

3 eggs

4 Tbsp. (50 g) sugar

2 c. (500 ml) strong coffee

2 Tbsp. whipping cream

3 Tbsp. apricot jam

DECORATION

glacé cherries

angelica

candied pineapple

This is another of Mrs. Beeton's recipes, this one for a dessert with an unusual texture that is popular with coffee lovers and best served with cream or a fancy sauce.

The cake may be made the day before. Grease and dust a 6-inch (15 cm) pan with a teaspoon of flour and sugar mixed together. Sift 1 cup flour and ⅛ teaspoon salt. Beat the eggs and sugar over a pan of hot water until thick and creamy. Fold the flour mixture and lemon rind lightly into the egg and turn the mixture into the pan. Bake in a warm oven at 350°F (175°C) for 30 minutes.

Thickly butter a 3-cup (750 ml) soufflé dish. Chop the almonds coarsely, and bake them in a moderate oven until golden brown. Sprinkle liberally over the buttered surface of the soufflé dish.

Crumble the sponge cake and fill the soufflé dish with the crumbled cake and any remaining almonds that did not adhere to sides of the dish. Beat the eggs and sugar to a liquid. Warm the coffee and pour over the egg liquid. Stir, add the cream and pour into the prepared soufflé dish. Cover with buttered paper and steam very gently for 1½ to 2 hours.

Cool slightly, then turn out and cool completely.

Heat the apricot jam with the same amount of water and when cool pour over the pudding. Decorate with rings of cherries, angelica and pineapple.

Serves 6 to 8.

KALBSCOTELETTEN À LA SAINT CLOUD
(Veal cutlets St. Cloud)

4 veal cutlets, 5 oz. (125 g) each
salt and pepper
1 truffle (optional)
2 Tbsp. butter
4 bacon strips
SAUCE
3 Tbsp. butter
3 Tbsp. flour
1 c. (250 ml) veal or chicken stock
salt and pepper
2 Tbsp. sherry, sweet

Tenderize the veal cutlets with the back of a heavy knife, so that they become quite thin. Season with salt and pepper. If you have a truffle or a flavorful mushroom, insert small pieces of it into the cutlets. Melt butter in a frying pan and slowly braise the cutlets in the butter until browned. Cool.

Cut each bacon rasher in half. Put 4 of the pieces into the bottom of a casserole, put a cutlet on top of each. Top each cutlet with another bacon piece.

To make the sauce, melt the butter in the same frying pan, add the flour and cook for 1 minute. Over low heat add the stock, stirring constantly and scraping off all the brown bits from cooking the cutlets. Season the sauce with salt and pepper. Add the sherry after the sauce has thickened, stirring it well.

Pour sauce over the cutlets in the casserole and cook in a moderate oven 350°F (175°C) for about 30 minutes or until the meat is tender. This dish goes well with plain rice or mashed potatoes.

Serves 4.

This recipe is from the German UNIVERSAL LEXIKON DER KOCHKUNST (*Encyclopedia of Cooking) published in 1909.*

St. Constantine

THIS particular Constantine was the first bishop of Perugia, in central Italy. During the persecution of the Christians in the reign of the Roman emperor Marcus Aurelius, he and numerous Christians from his flock were put to death for their belief.

According to legend, he escaped from a fiery furnace, was caught several times and was eventually beheaded in Foligno. He died in 178.

His feast day is celebrated on January 29, and he is the patron saint of Perugia. He was buried in the cathedral of Perugia, but his relics were transferred in 1205 to San Costanzo. His cult is concentrated in Umbria. In art he is often shown as a bishop.

Torcolo di San Costanzo

(Cake of St. Constantine)

4 Tbsp. sugar
1 Tbsp. dry yeast
1 c. (250 ml) lukewarm water
1 Tbsp. olive oil
2 Tbsp. clarified butter
pinch of salt
1 Tbsp. anise seed
4 c. (500 g) flour
4 Tbsp. pine nuts
½ c. (100 g) mixed peel
powdered sugar

Mix the sugar and yeast with 1 cup (250 ml) of lukewarm water and let it stand for 10 minutes. Add olive oil, melted clarified butter and salt to the mixture.

Chop anise finely or grind it with mortar and pestle.

Measure flour into a large bowl, add anise and pour yeast mixture over it. Stir, and work to a dough, adding lukewarm water as necessary. The dough should not be sticky. Add pine nuts and mixed peel and knead for 2 to 3 minutes until everything is well blended. Cover with a towel, and let dough stand in a warm room until it has doubled in bulk.

Punch down and fill into a well-greased ring-shaped pan. Bake in the middle of a preheated oven 350°F (175°C) for about 40 minutes or until golden brown. To serve, dust with powdered sugar.

Sufficient for 8 to 12 people.

This cake is quite light and goes well with coffee or tea. The recipe is from Perugia, where the cake is baked for the feast day of St. Constantine.

73

Michael Wohlgemuth,
15th century, Parish Church,
Langenzenn, Germany

CUNEGUND was raised piously by her parents, Siegfried of Luxembourg and his saintly wife, Hedwig. She married Henry, Duke of Bavaria, who later was elected emperor of the Holy Roman Empire as Henry II. In 1013 they went together to Rome to receive the imperial crown from Pope Benedict VIII.

It was partly due to the encouragement of Cunegund that the emperor established the diocese of Bamberg in 1006, despite the opposition of the neighboring bishops. Henry and Cunegund built a cathedral there, and Pope Benedict came to consecrate the cathedral in 1020. Cunegund secured many privileges for the city to ensure its survival.

Her husband, Henry, died in 1023 and was buried in the cathedral that he and Cunegund had built. On the anniversary of his death, Cunegund became a nun and retired to a monastery at Kaufungen in Hesse that she had founded in previous years. She lived there as a simple nun, praying and looking after the sick until her death in 1033. She was buried in the cathedral in Bamberg next to her husband. She and her husband were both pronounced saints, one of the few couples who have been canonized.

Many legends exist about Cunegund, her generosity and faith. Many of these legends are shown on the tomb in the Bamberg cathedral. The rings of the following recipe are also associated with a legend. One day when the emperor was hunting, he had not had a good day and was therefore in a bad mood as he sat down with Cunegund for dinner. As it was late in the afternoon, the bells of the newly built cathedral rang at their normal time. Henry and Cunegund had both donated money for the bells. The emperor's bell was heard with a very somber sound, like that of a funeral bell, while the bell of Cunegund had a very cheerful ring. This seemed to upset the emperor considerably, and when Cunigund noticed this, she threw her ring toward her bell. When the ring hit the bell, it changed the sound to a much lower tone and made it more like that of her husband. This pleased the emperor greatly. According to the legend, the throw covered a distance of around six miles.

The feast day of Cunegund is March 3. In art she is often shown together with her husband, St. Henry, holding the cathedral they founded. St. Cunegund is one of the patron saints of Luxembourg.

KUNIGUNDENRINGE
(Rings of St. Cunegund)

3 Tbsp. (45 g) sugar
¾ c. (200 ml) milk, lukewarm
2 Tbsp. dry yeast
4 c. (500 g) flour
1½ tsp. salt
1 egg, at room temperature
1 c. (250 g) butter, unsalted

Dissolve 1 tablespoon of sugar in the lukewarm milk. Add the yeast and stir. Let stand for 10 minutes or until it is quite frothy.

Pour the flour, the remaining sugar and the salt into a bowl and mix well. Beat the egg slightly and blend into the frothy yeast. Add yeast and egg mixture to the flour and stir until well blended. The dough should be soft but not sticky. It may be necessary at this stage to add more milk or flour to make a soft dough.

Knead for 5 minutes until smooth and elastic. Cover with a towel and let rise in a warm place for about 30 minutes. The dough should double in size. After this put the dough in the refrigerator and leave it there until it is quite cool, approximately 1 hour.

For the following step it is essential that the dough and butter are cold and at the same temperature. The butter should not be very hard. Remove the dough from the refrigerator and roll it out on a lightly floured table into a rectangle. It should be about ¼ inch (6 mm) thick. Cut the cup of butter into thin slices and put them on ⅓ of the rectangle. Fold the buttered part over onto the dough so that the butter is covered. The remaining ⅓ of the dough should be folded over the already folded part. With a rolling pin gently press down on the dough. The trick is not to let any butter escape from the sides. Roll until you have another rectangle. Fold it over twice as before and put in the refrigerator to let it cool for another half-hour.

Repeat the procedure of rolling and folding the dough 4 times.

To make the rings, roll out the dough to about ¼ inch (6 mm) thick. You may cut out rings of about 6 inches (15 cm) with a 3-inch (8 cm) hole in the middle. The cutout may be baked as is. If you want more rings, cut strips about 18 inches (45 cm) long and about 3 inches (8 cm) wide. Join the ends and shape the dough into a ring. You can brush the rings with an equal mixture of egg yolk and milk.

Place the rings on a baking sheet sprinkled with water and let rise for about 20 minutes until they have doubled in size. Preheat oven to 450°F (230°C). Bake the rings in the middle of the oven for 10 to 15 minutes until golden. Transfer immediately to a wire rack and let them cool.

This will make 12 to 16 rings.

This recipe is from Bamberg, a city in northern Bavaria, where the feast day of St. Cunegund on March 3 is celebrated by baking these special pastry rings that are normally not available during other times of the year. Cunegund is a very common name for girls in that area. This recipe comes from an old bakery in Bamberg that was established in the 1800s.

75

School of Giotto di Bondone,
14th century, S. Francesco,
Maddalena Chapel, Assisi

DAVID, or Dewi, was born around 460 near Cardigan, Wales. His father was Sant, a king of South Wales, and his mother was St. Non. David studied with St. Paulinus before being ordained and becoming a monk. At Mynyw he founded a monastery that followed closely the traditions of the monasteries in Egypt founded by St. Anthony. David had great influence on the further development of Welsh monasticism. Later he was appointed bishop and transferred the principal Welsh See to Mynyw.

David participated at the important synod of Brevi and gave a speech there. According to legend, a white dove settled on his shoulder during that address.

David died around 500, and he was buried at Mynyw, which is now called St. David's, the westernmost town in Wales. In the twelfth century a large cathedral was built at his shrine, which became the destination for many pilgrims.

Several hundred years later many legends were attached to St. David, mainly for reasons of ecclesiastical politics, and, as with St. Patrick, his stature and influence were overstated.

In art David is usually shown as a bishop standing on a hill with a dove on his shoulder. He is the patron saint of Wales, the only patron saint of Britain who is actually buried in the country in which he was born. His feast day is March 1, and Welshmen everywhere celebrate it by wearing leeks.

76

St. David's Leek Pie

SHORTCRUST PASTRY
2 c. (250 g) flour
pinch of salt
3 Tbsp. (50 g) butter
3 Tbsp. (50 g) shortening
ice cold water

FILLING
3 c. (400 g) leeks (about 6), sliced
2 Tbsp. (30 g) butter
1¼ c. (300 ml) milk
2 eggs
4 Tbsp. (30 g) Cheddar cheese, grated
pepper, salt

Put flour and salt in a bowl. Rub or cut the butter and shortening into the flour until the mixture resembles coarse bread crumbs. Sprinkle with enough cold water so the dough can be gathered into a smooth ball. Refrigerate for 20 minutes.

Line a 9-inch (23 cm) pie dish with half the pastry. Trim roots and green tops from the leeks and wash thoroughly. Cut into thin slices. Melt the butter in a sauce pan and cook the leeks until soft. Cool to lukewarm and put into pastry shell. Beat milk and egg together and season well. Pour mixture over leeks and sprinkle with the grated cheese. Cover with the remaining pastry and seal edges firmly. Bake in a preheated oven at 400°F (200°C) for 40 minutes until golden and serve right away.

Sufficient for 6 as a side dish or for 4 as a light lunch.

This recipe is from Mary Novak's book COOKING MONTH BY MONTH.

St. Denis

DENIS, or Dionysius, was born in Italy, and in 250 he was sent with six other missionary bishops to France to convert the Gauls. Denis became the first bishop of Paris and settled on an island in the Seine. He was very successful in converting the people living in the surrounding area. During the persecution of the emperor Decius, around the year 258, he and his companions where beheaded and their bodies thrown in the Seine. Their remains were retrieved and buried by a Christian lady named Catulla. A chapel was built over their tomb, which later became the great abbey of Saint-Denis and the burial place for the kings of France.

Legends about St. Denis are abundant because in the eighth century he was deliberately confused with two other saints of the same name. Denis became a popular saint because of all "his" miracles and deeds—which really were those of three different persons. This confusion was propagated by the medieval book *The Golden Legend*.

Denis is the patron saint of Paris and of France, and his feast day is October 9. In art he is usually shown as a bishop, often while being beheaded. A common image, based on a legend, shows him carrying his head under his arm.

Talmouses de Saint-Denis
(St. Denis Turnovers)

½ c. (175 g) cream cheese
2 eggs
1 Tbsp. flour
salt and pepper
1 lb. (500 g) puff pastry

Mix cream cheese, 1 egg and flour, and season generously with salt and pepper.

Roll out puff pastry to about ¼-inch (6 mm) thickness. Cut out rectangles or circles of about 3 inches (8 cm). Put a teaspoon of the cheese mixture in the middle. Moisten edges with water, fold over and seal.

Brush with the slightly beaten egg and bake in hot oven 400°F (200°C) until golden brown.

Makes about 20 talmouses.

This is a recipe from an old cookbook published in Amsterdam in 1747 and quoted in Larousse Gastronomique.

79

Here is another of
Mrs. Beeton's recipes.

Saint Denis Tartlets

SWEET SHORTCRUST PASTRY
2 c. (250g) flour
1 Tbsp. sugar
pinch of salt
4 Tbsp. (60 g) butter
4 Tbsp. (60 g) shortening
6 Tbsp. ice water

TARTLETS
¼ c. (50 g) butter
¼ c. (50 g) sugar
2 egg yolks
¼ c. (50g) almonds, ground
1 Tbsp. cornstarch
½ tsp. vanilla
1 egg white
raspberry jam
powdered sugar for dusting

In a medium bowl combine flour, sugar and salt. Cut in butter and shortening until mixture resembles coarse bread crumbs. Sprinkle ice water over flour mixture until moistened. Gather dough into a ball, refrigerate for at least 1 hour.

On a lightly floured surface, roll out dough about ⅛ inch (3 mm) thick. Cut out circles large enough to line 3-inch (8 cm) tartlet pans with the dough circles.

Cream the butter and sugar together until thick; beat in the 2 egg yolks, 1 at a time. Add the ground almonds, cornstarch and vanilla. Lastly fold in the stiffly whisked egg white.

Place a teaspoon of jam in the bottom of each tartlet pan and fill with the mixture. Place two narrow strips of pastry across the top. Bake in a fairly hot oven 400°F (200°C) for 15 to 20 minutes.

When cool, dust with powdered sugar.

Makes 12 to 15 tartlets.

Brioche Saint-Denis

(Praline Cake)

PRALINE

⅓ c. (100 g) sugar
½ lemon, juice of
½ c. (100 g) almonds, blanched

CAKE

1 Tbsp. dry yeast
pinch of sugar
1 Tbsp. warm water
4 c. (500 g) flour
pinch of salt
6 eggs
2 Tbsp. sugar
1½ c. (350 g) butter

This is a recipe from Keith Floyd's Floyd on France.

To make the praline, put sugar and lemon juice in a heavy saucepan over moderate heat until sugar is melted. Turn the heat up and, stirring frequently, cook sugar to a golden brown. Add almonds and remove the mixture from heat. Pour mixture onto a baking tray covered with lightly greased aluminium foil and let cool. Remove from foil and crush with rolling pin to a coarse sandlike powder.

Mix yeast with a pinch of sugar and the warm water and leave for 10 minutes. Put flour and salt in a bowl. Beat the eggs with the sugar, pour into the bowl, followed by the yeast. Stir, and work into a smooth dough by kneading. Add the butter little by little until the dough is smooth again. Cover and allow to rest in a warm place until well risen. Beat down and let rise again. Preheat oven to 375°F (190°C).

Knead half of the praline into the dough and press it into a buttered 8-inch (20 cm) round cake pan. Cover with remaining praline. Bake in the oven for 40 minutes.

Serves 6 to 8.

St. Dominic

DOMINIC GUZMAN was born in 1170 in Calaruega, Spain, the youngest of four children. He was educated by his priest uncle and studied at the University of Palencia, was ordained and became an Augustinian. Sent to Rome on a task, he

passed through France and encountered the Albigensians, a heretical group. In Rome his request for permission to go to preach in Russia was denied by the pope, but he was asked to oppose the Albigensian heresy at home. Dominic was very successful and with the support of the local bishop established a house for women converts. Out of this work grew the second order of St. Dominic.

Dominic continued preaching and attracted several followers, and in 1215, at an ecumenical council in Rome, he requested again that a new order be established that would be entirely devoted to sound learning, preaching and teaching. Only a guarded approval was granted, but Dominic was allowed to select a rule. He decided to adopt the Rule of St. Augustine. An excellent organizer, he added a constitution that provided rules for day-to-day living. Honorius III confirmed the order and its constitutions in 1216.

The Dominicans were the first order to abandon manual labour and devote themselves to preaching and poverty.

The last seven years of Dominic's life were spent in organizing the order, which had become quite successful, with monks spreading all over Europe. The Dominican order also became a force in the missions in Asia and later on in the Americas.

Dominic died in 1221 in Bologna, where he is buried. Pope Gregory IX declared him a saint in 1234. His feast day is now August 8.

In art he is usually shown in the habit of the Dominicans, holding a lily, sometimes with a black and white dog. The dog is a pun (*Domini canis*) on the name of Dominic and the Dominicans.

Fra Angelico, 15th century,
Galleria Nazionale dell'Umbria,
Perugia, Italy (detail)

Coniglio San Domenico

(Rabbit St. Dominic)

2¼ lb. (1 kg) rabbit
3 artichokes, medium
1 lemon
6 Tbsp. olive oil
½ c. (125 ml) onion,chopped
½ c. (100 g) black olives
1 sprig marjoram
6 leaves of sage
salt and pepper
½ c. (125 ml) white wine
chicken stock
1 Tbsp. tomato paste
2 tsp. parsley, fresh

Disjoint the rabbit and cut into medium-sized pieces.

Trim artichokes down to the tender heart, removing the choke, and cut into quarters. Squeeze lemon juice into a bowl, add water and then the artichokes, to prevent discoloration. (Canned artichokes may be used instead.)

Heat oil in a large pan and fry the chopped onion. Add rabbit pieces, olives, marjoram, sage, salt and pepper, wine and some stock. Stir well, cover the pan with a lid, let simmer for 45 minutes to an hour, adding stock if necessary. Add artichokes, tomato paste and parsley and simmer for a further 10 to 15 minutes.

Serves 4.

This is a recipe whose origin is recorded, so we know the association with the saint for whom it is named. Antonio Carluccio in his cookbook Italian Feast *reports that he met four Dominican monks, and he cooked a meal for them from their own garden produce and the rabbits they raised.*

83

St. Elisabeth of Hungary

Hastings Book of Hours,
15th century,
British Library, London

ELISABETH was born in 1207, the daughter of King Andrew II of Hungary. When four years old, she was promised in marriage to Louis, son of the Landgrave of Thuringia. After Louis had become Landgrave and she was fourteen, they were married. The marriage was a very happy one, with three children. With Louis' permission, through many acts of mercy Elisabeth indulged in helping the poor. She spent enormous amounts of money on almsgiving, founding hospitals and providing for helpless children, especially orphans.

In 1227 Louis joined the emperor Fredrick II on his crusade; he died three months later because of the plague. Elisabeth was driven from the court by her brother-in-law and settled at Marburg, where she became a member of the Third Order of St. Francis, following a life of poverty and providing relief for the sick and the poor. Her life was one of austerity and suffering caused by an insensitive spiritual director. St. Elisabeth died at the early age of twenty-four in 1231 and was buried in Marburg. She was canonized by Pope Gregory IX in 1235, and her grave became the object of many pilgrimages, until in the sixteenth century her relics were moved to an unknown place by the Lutheran Philip of Hesse.

In art she is usually shown wearing a crown and giving food to the poor, or with a cloak full of roses (an image based on a legend). Her feast day is November 17, and she is the patron saint of the Third Order of St. Francis.

ELISEN LEBKUCHEN
(St. Elisabeth's Lebkuchen)

2 c. (500 g) sugar
5 eggs
2 tsp. cinnamon
½ tsp. cloves, ground
1 pinch of cardamom
1 pinch of mace
2 tsp. grated rind of lemon
1 c. (200 g) mixed peel
2½ c. (500g) almonds, not blanched
1 c. powdered sugar
4 Tbsp. lemon juice

With an electric beater, blend sugar and eggs until the mixture is pale yellow and creamy. Add spices, lemon rind and finely chopped mixed peel. Grind almonds finely, and add to mixture. The result should be spreadable, like soft margarine. Extra ground almonds may have to be added if the eggs were large.

Drop tablespoonsful of the mixture onto a well-greased cookie sheet and let them stand for a few hours.

Bake in a slow oven 325°F (160°C) until golden.

Mix some powdered sugar with lemon juice, and glaze the cookies with this after they have cooled.

Yields about 40.

This recipe is quite old and is a favorite in Germany around Christmas time. This version comes from the BAYERISCHES KOCHBUCH, a cookbook popular in Bavaria since the 1920s. This book contains many more recipes for traditional German Christmas cookies.

ELISABETHEN-BROTTORTE

(St. Elisabeth's Bread Cake)

2 c. (100 g) rye bread crumbs, fresh
5 eggs
⅔ c. (150 g) sugar
4 Tbsp. raspberry juice or white wine
½ c. (100 g) mixed peel
½ c. (100 g) almonds, ground
1 Tbsp. cinnamon
1 tsp. cloves, ground
1 Tbsp. lemon rind, grated
powdered sugar or icing

Prepare the bread crumbs. They can be made from slices of rye bread chopped finely in an electric blender.

With an electric beater, beat the eggs and sugar until creamy. Moisten bread crumbs with the raspberry juice or white wine. Chop the mixed peel finely. Add all the ingredients to the egg-sugar mixture and stir until smooth.

Butter and flour a 10-inch (25 cm) round cake pan and pour in the batter.

Bake in a preheated oven on a low rack at 325°F (160°C) for about 45 minutes. If the cake browns too quickly on the top, cover it with buttered aluminum foil.

The cake can be iced with a mixture of rum, water and powdered sugar or served sprinkled with powdered sugar.

Serves 6 to 8.

This unusual German cake recipe does not use flour but crumbs from a loaf of rye bread instead, though the other ingredients are not unusual for a coffee cake. It is certainly not a recipe that would have been cooked by many poor people, because of the expensive ingredients. This recipe proved to be very popular with my family.

86

St. Émilion

Engraving, 15th century,
Bibliothèque Nationale de
France, Paris

ÉMILION, or Emilian, was born in Vannes, France, and became a Benedictine monk at the abbey of Saujon. Later he became a hermit in the forest of Combes near Bordeaux. He died in 767. His feast day is celebrated on January 7. Otherwise very little is known of his life. His name, however, is familiar to many because of a famous wine bearing his name.

COOKING WITH THE SAINTS

This is a typical French recipe for almond macaroons.

MACARONS DE SAINT-ÉMILION

(St. Émilion Macaroons)

2 c. (200 g) almonds, ground
1½ c. (200 g) powdered sugar (for use in the dough)
6 Tbsp. sweet white wine
1 drop vanilla
3 egg whites
1 Tbsp. powdered sugar (for sprinkling cookies)

Preheat oven to 350°F (175°C).

Mix the almonds with the powdered sugar, white wine and vanilla.

Beat the egg whites until stiff and whisk in the almond mixture. Transfer to a saucepan and whisk over very low heat to dry out the mixture a little, then allow to cool.

When cool, drop the dough by rounded teaspoonfuls on a well-buttered baking sheet and sprinkle with additional powdered sugar. Bake on a low rack in the oven until crisp or until the edges turn slightly brown, about 15 minutes. Do not allow to brown completely.

Makes about 40 macaroons.

St. Émilion au Chocolat

(Chocolate Pudding à la St. Emilion)

¼ lb. (100 g) ratafia biscuits
2 Tbsp. rum
½ lb. (200 g) plain chocolate
½ c. (100 g) butter
½ c. (100 g) sugar
1 c. (250 ml) milk
2 eggs, beaten
2 Tbsp. whipped cream

Soak the ratafia biscuits in rum. Melt the chocolate in a bowl over a pan of hot water. Cream butter and sugar together, then add the chocolate.

Put milk and eggs into a saucepan and heat the mixture gently so it thickens enough to coat the back of a wooden spoon. Do not boil. Pour this mixture into the chocolate, stirring continuously.

Cool until the mixture begins to thicken. Spoon half the mixture into a dish, cover with a layer of the ratafias, leaving some for the top. Cover biscuits with remaining chocolate. Swirl whipped cream through the center and put remaining ratafias around the edge. Refrigerate pudding for several hours until serving time.

Serves 6.

Here is a fancy version of chocolate pudding.

89

St. Encratis

Bartolomé Bermejo,
15th century,
Museo de Bellas Artes,
Bilbao, Spain

St. Encratis, known in Spain as Santa Engracia, was a Christian woman living in Saragossa in the third century. At that time Saragossa was a Roman town. When the Roman emperor Diocletian ordered all Christians to be persecuted, Encratis was thrown into prison. She defended her faith vigorously, and this goaded her persecutors to inflict on her the most extreme tortures, including flagellation. According to legend, she withstood all the cruelties and eventually died in prison around 303. Several other Christians died with her at the same time, and they were buried in adjacent graves. In 592 a monastery and church were erected near the gravesite.

The king of Aragon Juan II enlarged the monastery, which was later destroyed during the Napeolonic wars but then rebuilt. The relics of St. Encratis and her companions can be found in Saragossa in the crypt of the Basilica Santa Engracia.

Encratis is the patron saint of Saragossa, and her feast day and that of her companions is April 16.

90

Pastelitos Santa Engracia

(Potato Fritters St. Encratis)

2 lb. (1 kg) potatoes
2 eggs, small
3 Tbsp. cream
1 tsp. salt
½ tsp. pepper
2 c. (300 g) meat, cooked and finely chopped (chicken, turkey, beef, pork)
2 eggs
flour
oil for frying

Cook the potatoes in their skin until done. When cool enough to handle, peel them and push them through a sieve. A potato press may be used instead, but do not use a blender. Add the 2 small eggs, cream, salt and pepper. Mix well.

Form about 8 small balls. Flatten each ball with the palm of your hand. Season the meat with some extra salt and pepper. Distribute the meat over the 8 balls, placing it in the middle of each. Fold the edges over and cover the meat completely. This makes 8 rather large fritters, or they can be made smaller by dividing the potato mixture into 12 balls.

Roll the fritters in flour and then in the 2 slightly beaten eggs. Fry in plenty of oil. If used for a light lunch, serve them with a simple green salad.

Serves 6 to 8 persons.

This recipe is from the Monasterio del Sagrario in Spain.

St. Felix

THE LIST of saints of the Catholic Church contains sixty-six saints with the name Felix, ranging in time from the first to the sixteenth century, including several popes. Geographically they can be found all over Europe and North Africa. The St. Felix in the picture is usually shown with a fellow saint named St. Adauctus.

This particular Felix was a priest in Rome in the third century, and during the persecution of the emperor Diocletian he was asked to renounce his beliefs. Felix refused and was tortured and condemned to death by the sword. As Felix travelled to his execution, a stranger was heard to confess his belief in Christianity. He was seized and beheaded with St. Felix. Since the name of the stranger was not known, he was called Adauctus, which means "the one added". The execution occurred around 304, and they were buried on the Ostian Way in Rome.

St. Felix and St. Adauctus are found in the earliest lists of saints of the Church. A church was built over their grave, forgotten until rediscovered in 1905.

In art Felix is usually shown in priestly garments together with St. Adauctus. The feast day for the two is August 30.

Buñuelos de San Felíu

(Fritters St. Felix)

1c. (250 ml) milk or water
5 Tbsp. butter
2 Tbsp. sugar
pinch of salt
1c. (125 g) flour
4 eggs
1 Tbsp. anise liqueur or brandy
olive oil for deep frying
powdered sugar

Place the milk, butter, sugar and salt in a heavy pan and heat until it just boils. Lower the heat and add the flour all at once, beating it with a wooden spoon until it forms a smooth ball of dough.

Remove from heat and beat in the eggs, 1 at a time. Beat until cool and very smooth.

Add anise liqueur. If brandy is used, add ¼ teaspoon of anise seed and the brandy.

Heat oil for deep frying in a heavy saucepan to about 350°F (175°C). Drop teaspoons of batter into the hot oil. Fry until golden and puffed up. Remove, drain on absorbent paper and sprinkle the puffs liberally with powdered sugar.

Serve warm.

Makes about 24 fritters.

This is a recipe from Spain for very light and fluffy anise-flavored fritters. These kinds of fritters can be found in many countries bordering the Mediterreanean Sea.

St. Florentin of Samur

SCS FLO RENTIVS

Mural, 11th century,
Hôtel Musée Gouin,
Tours, France

THERE are many saints named Florentin, Florent, Florentius or Florence, and sometimes it is not easy to find the connection between a specific saint and the recipes named for him.

One of these saints, Florentius, was born in Bavaria and, attracted by the fame of St. Martin of Tours, became one of his disciples. He was ordained by Martin and was sent out to evangelize Poitou. After he retired, he became a hermit at Mt. Glonne, where he was followed by numerous disciples. He built for them a monastery that was later known as St. Florent-le-Vieux. He died there in extreme old age around the year 440. Many miracles were attributed to him.

Not many artists have represented this particular Florentius. Normally he is shown as a monk, as on this mural originally from the church of St. Martin in Tours. His feast day is September 29.

94

Pommes de Terre Saint-Florentin

(Potatoes St. Florentin)

1½ lb. (750 g) peeled potatoes
2 Tbsp. butter
½ tsp. salt
¼ tsp. pepper
1 pinch nutmeg
2 egg yolks
½ c. (100 g) lean ham, chopped
1 egg
1 Tbsp. milk
½ c. (60 g) crushed vermicelli
oil for deep frying

Boil potatoes in lightly salted water until cooked. Drain and dry well. Mash potatoes, add butter, salt, pepper and nutmeg. Beat in egg yolks. Chop ham and add to potato mixture and on a floured board roll into a cylinder about 3 inches (7 cm) diameter. Press into oblong shape. Cut into slices about ¾ inch (2 cm) thick.

Prepare an egg dip by beating one egg with the milk. Dip the slices in the egg mixture and then into vermicelli crushed with a rolling pin. Some white bread crumbs may be added. Deep fry the slices in hot oil.

Makes about 24 slices.

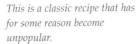

This is a classic recipe that has for some reason become unpopular.

95

GÂTEAU SAINT-FLORENTIN
(St. Florentin Cake)

GENOESE SPONGE CAKE
4 eggs
½ c. (125 g) sugar
⅔ c. (90 g) flour
4 Tbsp. melted butter

FILLING
3 Tbsp. water
½ c. (125 g) sugar
2 egg whites
1 Tbsp. butter
4 Tbsp. kirsch
¾ c. (125 g) glacé cherries or fresh strawberries

ICING
½ c. (125 g) sugar
1 tsp. glycerin
5 Tbsp. water
red food coloring

Sponge Cake

Grease a square 8-inch (20 cm) pan, line the base with greased waxed paper. Preheat oven to 350°F (175°C).

Combine eggs and sugar in a large bowl, place over a saucepan of simmering water but do not allow bowl to touch water. Using an electric beater, beat until mixture is thick and creamy, about 10 minutes.

Remove the bowl from the hot water, and beat the mixture until it returns to room temperature. Sift half the flour over the egg mixture and carefully fold in the flour. Repeat with remaining flour.

Quickly fold in the cooled melted butter.

Pour mixture into the pan and bake for about 20 minutes until sponge feels elastic to the touch. Turn cake onto wire rack to cool. When cool, remove paper at the bottom and split cake in half horizontally.

Filling

To make the filling, put water and sugar into a heavy pan. Cook rapidly until the sugar reaches 230°F (110°C). Remove the pan from the heat. Beat the egg whites until stiff peaks form. Slowly trickle the sugar syrup into the egg whites while continuing to whisk the mixture. (Try not to pour the sugar syrup directly on the whisk itself.) When the sugar has been blended in completely, add the melted butter and ¼ of the kirsch.

Icing

Use the rest of the kirsch to soak the top and bottom half of the cake. Spread egg-white mixture over bottom half. Cover with the glacé cherries or strawberries. Put top half of cake on the filling.

To make the fondant icing, heat sugar, glycerin and water in a heavy saucepan over high heat until the sugar has reached soft ball stage 240°F (115°C). Add a few drops of food coloring and mix in. Pour mixture on a heat-proof surface, and while it cools keep folding the edges to the center with a spatula until it becomes opaque.

When the icing is cool but still pliable, put it on top of the cake. Leave the sides without icing, so that the fruit and filling will show.

Serve the cake within 1 hour of making it, or the meringue will get soft.

Serves 8 persons.

QUENELLES OF VEAL ST. FLORENTINE

QUENELLES
1 lb. (500 g) veal
2 Tbsp. butter
½ c. (60 g) flour
½ c. (125 ml) stock
1 egg
salt and pepper
2 eggs
1 c. (100 g) breadcrumbs, fine, dry

SPINACH PURÉE
1 lb. (500 g) spinach
3 Tbsp. water
2 Tbsp. butter

TOMATO SAUCE
1 small onion
2 Tbsp. bacon, chopped
1 Tbsp. butter
1½ c. (375 ml) canned tomatoes
½ c. (125 ml) dry red wine
salt and pepper

This is a recipe that appeared in only one of the many editions of Mrs. Beeton's Cookery.

Normally dishes that contain spinach are called simply "Florentine", so maybe this recipe's name was a mistake by Mrs. Beeton. For a mistake, it tastes very good.

Quenelles

First make the quenelles by processing the chopped meat in a food processor until smooth. It is best to do this in 2 or 3 batches so as not to overload the machine.

In a saucepan melt the butter, add the flour and cook slightly. Add the stock and stir and cook until the mixture becomes very thick and smooth, then allow to cool. Blend in the processed veal and the egg, stirring constantly and continuing until well blended. Season to taste with salt and pepper.

Shape the mixture into oval quenelles with two spoons previously dipped in hot water. Brush with beaten eggs and coat with bread crumbs. Make the tomato sauce next.

Sauce

To make the sauce, sauté the finely chopped onion and the bacon in the butter until the onion is transparent. Chop the tomatoes roughly and add to onion and bacon mixture. Add wine and simmer covered for about 10 minutes. Add salt and pepper. If a smooth sauce is preferred, process it in a blender or purée it through a sieve.

98

Spinach Purée

In a saucepan put the spinach with the water and butter and cook until spinach is tender. Drain spinach liquid. Chop the spinach and return to the pan and keep warm.

Fry the quenelles until golden brown.

To serve, put a mound of spinach on a plate and place the quenelles on top. Pour tomato sauce around the spinach. It may be decorated with little puff pastry cutouts if available.

Serves 4 persons.

St. Flour

FLOUR, or Florus, of Lodève, is a saint about whom we know very little. He was a missionary of Gallo-Roman origin working in the south of France. He became the first bishop of Lodève, in the Languedoc region of France. He evangelized the area, and when he died in 389 a small Christian community was established where he was buried, at what is today Saint-Flour. The cathedral named St. Peter contains his relics.

In the twelfth century a priory was founded in Saint-Flour, and in the thirteenth century Saint-Flour became the see of a new diocese.

St. Flour's feast day is celebrated on November 3. Recipes bearing the name St. Flour come from the Auvergne area of France.

Pommes de Terre Saint-Flour

(Potatoes St. Flour)

½ c. (100 g) bacon, lean, diced
½ lb. (250 g) cabbage
1 lb. (500 g) potatoes
salt, pepper
1 tsp. garlic, crushed
2 Tbsp. chicken stock
2 Tbsp. grated cheese

Dice bacon and fry till crisp. Drain bacon and discard all but 2 tablespoons fat.

Shred the cabbage and sauté it in the 2 tablespoons of bacon fat until crisp. Put cabbage and bacon on the bottom of a greased casserole dish.

Peel potatoes and cut into round slices about ¼ inch (12 mm) thick and arrange on top of the cabbage, mixing in the bacon. Season with pepper and salt. Mix the crushed garlic with the stock. Sprinkle the potatoes with the garlic-flavoured stock and then top them with the grated cheese. Cook in a slow oven 300°F (150°C) for about 30 minutes or until potatoes are done.

Serves 4 as a side dish and 2 to 3 as a light lunch.

This is an interesting combination of bacon, cabbage and potatoes.

101

Omelette à la Saint-Flour

TOMATO SAUCE
1 small onion
2 Tbsp. bacon, chopped
1 Tbsp. butter
1 c. (250 ml) canned tomatoes
salt and pepper

FILLING
1 Tbsp. butter
½ c. (125 ml) cabbage, chopped
pinch of salt

OMELETTE
1 small onion
bacon strips, thick sliced
pork fat
4 eggs

To make the sauce, sauté the finely chopped onion and the bacon in the butter until the onion is transparent. Chop the tomatoes roughly and add to onion and bacon mixture. Simmer covered for about 10 minutes. Add salt and pepper to taste.

To make the filling, melt butter in a small saucepan, add chopped cabbage and sauté for 2 minutes. Add a generous pinch of salt and cover. Braise over low heat for 4 minutes.

Slice onion thinly. Cut bacon into small pieces and blanch in boiling water for 1 minute. Brown onion and bacon in some pork fat.

Beat the eggs, adding onion and bacon. Make 2 omelettes out of this mixture. Put 1 omelette on a plate, cover with the braised cabbage, top with the other omelette and surround with the tomato sauce.

Makes enough for 2 persons.

Here is a combination of bacon and cabbage in a double-decker omelette surrounded by tomato sauce.

RISSOLES DE SAINT-FLOUR
(St. Flour Turnovers)

This is another recipe from the region around Saint-Flour, France.

PASTRY
½ c. (125 g) butter
2 c. (250 g) flour
1 tsp. salt
2 egg yolks
3 Tbsp. cold water

FILLING
1 c. (125 g) Cantal or Gruyère cheese, diced or grated
2 egg yolks
2 tsp. chives, chopped
1 tsp. chervil, chopped
salt and pepper
oil for deep frying

To make the pastry, rub or cut the butter into the flour until the mixture resembles coarse bread crumbs. Add salt, egg yolks and enough water to make a ball of smooth dough. Chill for 30 minutes.

To make the filling, mix all the ingredients together and add salt and pepper to taste.

Roll out the dough to about ¼ inch (6 mm) thickness and cut out 3-inch (8 cm) circles. Put a teaspoon of filling in the centre of each circle, brush the edges with water, fold over and seal tightly. Chill for 30 minutes.

Heat oil in deep fryer to 350°F (175°C). Fry a few turnovers at a time for 5 to 6 minutes or until golden brown. Drain on paper towels and keep them warm while frying the others. Serve immediately.

Makes about 24 turnovers.

St. Fortunatus

Venantius Honorius Clementianus Fortunatus was born near Treviso in Italy about 535 and was educated at Ravenna. He was a very good poet, and he used this skill while traveling around Europe as a wandering minstrel and visiting various courts. First in 565 he went to Germany, and he spent some time in that country. After two years he went to Poitiers in France. There he spent some time at the court of King Clotaire. Liking the environment, Fortunatus decided to stay, remaining there for twenty years. Eventually he was ordained a priest and became adviser and secretary to the king's wife, Radegund, who later became a saint. About 600 he was appointed bishop of Poitiers, and he died in Poitiers around 605.

Fortunatus was a fluent writer who liked to write in verse, not only on religious topics but on secular matters as well, including customs at court and cooking and eating. His poems provide great insight into the life-style of his time. Fortunatus wrote several outstanding hymns in Latin; the best known is "Pange Lingua Gloriosi". He also authored several lives of saints, written in fluent Latin verse. He is usually referred to as Venantius Fortunatus to distinguish him from a contemporary bishop who is called Fortunatus the Philosopher. It is likely that Venantius Fortunatus was made the patron saint of cooks because he reported so much about the life at court, including the meals. This is probably why the famous chef Auguste Escoffier named this special recipe after him— the patron saint of cooks.

His feast day is celebrated on December 14. In art there are not many representations of him, but the most famous one is that in the town hall of Poitiers.

Cochon de Lait Saint-Fortunat

(Suckling Pig St. Fortunatus)

1½ c. (375 ml) stock, veal or chicken
¾ c. (150 g) barley
suckling pig, including the liver
4 Tbsp. butter
36 chestnuts
½ lb. (250 g) chipolata sausages
2 Tbsp. fresh herbs, chopped
salt
4 Tbsp. brandy
4 Tbsp. olive oil
2 c. (½ l) chicken or veal stock

First simmer the barley in the stock until soft but not mushy, about 45 minutes. Drain. Then clean the suckling pig. Retain the liver. Cut liver into ¾-inch (2 cm) cubes and sauté in half the butter. In a pan with a tight-fitting lid, braise chestnuts in remaining butter over low heat. Cook the sausages and chop them.

Mix liver, chestnuts, sausages and fresh herbs with the cooked barley and blend well.

Rub the inside of the suckling pig with salt and moisten with the brandy. Put in the stuffing and sew up the cavity.

Put the pig into a roasting pan, brush with oil and cook at 350°F (175°C). Brush with oil during cooking to make skin crisp and golden. The piglet may be turned over carefully at about half of the expected cooking time. The cooking time will depend on the weight of the pig, but approximately 12 minutes per pound should be sufficient. The internal temperature of the thickest part should be 170°F (75°C), and the outside will be nicely browned and crisp.

When cooked, remove to a serving dish. Add 2 cups of stock to the juice in the pan and simmer for a few minutes. Serve gravy separately.

Depending on the size of the piglet, this may serve from 16 to 30 hungry people. A great dish for special occasions.

A tart applesauce or a red currant sauce mixed with horseradish goes well with this dish. Horseradish and red currant jelly should be mixed at about 2 parts of horseradish to 1 part of red currant jelly. The latter proved extremely popular when this recipe was tested with a large crowd of friends.

This recipe comes from the greatest chef of the last two hundred years, Auguste Escoffier. Born in 1847 in the French town of Villeneuve-Loubet, Escoffier started as a cook at the age of twelve and retired from cooking duties in 1921. He cooked at the most famous hotels of his time, the Savoy in London, the Ritz in Paris and the Carlton in London, where he retired. He was called the "King of Chefs and the Chef of Kings".

This recipe from his book Ma Cuisine *honors the patron saint of cooks with an unusual combination of meats and stuffing ingredients. To cook this for a large crowd is not a small effort but is worth the time. The result is spectacular and generally appreciated by those who eat it.*

Born in Assisi, Italy, in 1181, Francis was the son of a wealthy merchant. The child, baptized John, was called Francis because his father was in France at the time of his birth. He was an extravagant and pleasure-seeking youth who participated in 1201 in an attack on Perugia, where he was captured and held as a prisoner for a year. During this time he became very ill.

Fresco, Giotto di Bondone, 14th century, S. Francesco, Assisi

After his recovery, Francis participated in another military adventure, but at Spoleto he had a vision that changed his life. He devoted himself to the care of the sick and the poor. While praying at the church of San Damiano, he heard a voice that said, "Go and repair my house, which you see is falling down." He interpreted this as a command to repair the church he was in. Francis helped the priest there and renounced all his worldly possessions. In 1209 he heard in the Gospel at Mass the call to poverty and preaching. He then gave away his shoes and other clothes and wore only a simple garment tied with a cord. Others soon joined him, and when they numbered eleven Francis led them to Rome to seek approval from the pope for their new religious order. After some hesitation Innocent III granted approval in 1210, and the spread of the Franciscan order began. Francis insisted that all brethren should live in simplicity and poverty and entirely from alms. After hearing Francis preach, St. Clare became one of his followers and established an order (later called the Poor Clares) for women who wanted to follow the rule of Francis.

Francis preached all over Italy and soon set out on a mission to North Africa to evangelize the Muslims. Through ill health he was forced to return to Italy, but in 1219 he went to Egypt to talk to the Sultan. This was during one of the crusades. How he managed to get through the enemy lines is still a mystery. Unsuccessful in this endeavor, he made a pilgrimage through the Holy Land before returning to Italy. His order spread beyond Italy, but Francis relinquished the leadership and retired to a monastery in 1221. Ill health and blindness plagued the last few years of his life, and he died in 1226. He was made a saint in 1228, and his relics are today in the great basilica dedicated to him in Assisi. The influence of St. Francis and his order has been remarkable. Even today children still look at a crib in church at Christmas time, a custom started by St. Francis. His popularity has persisted; he has been the subject of several films, and his actions have inspired many.

For artists St. Francis was a great subject, for his habit of talking to animals and the various adventures in his life were easy to paint. The most famous paintings of the life of St. Francis, painted by Giotto, are in his church in Assisi. Francis is one of the patron saints of Italy as well as the patron saint of merchants, ecologists and animals. His feast day is October 4.

106

Paletta di Mandorla

(Almond Slices)

1 c. (225 g) butter
1½ c. (350 g) sugar
4 eggs
4 c. (500 g) flour
2 c. (400 g) almonds, whole, finely chopped, or 4 c. (400 g) almonds, ground
1 tsp. baking powder
1 tsp. vanilla

Cream butter, sugar and eggs. Add the other ingredients and knead until smooth. Form 2 rolls about 1 inch (3 cm) diameter.

Bake in a preheated moderately hot oven 375°F (190°C) for 10 to 12 minutes until golden brown.

When cool, cut into slices ¾ inch (2 cm) thick, and toast in the oven for 3 minutes.

Makes about 50 slices.

This recipe from the Umbria region of Italy is served on the feast day of St. Francis. It is supposedly one of the few foods that St. Francis let himself really enjoy.

The recipe, according to tradition, originated with St. Clare.

Puños de San Francisco

(Cuffs of St. Francis)

DOUGH
¾ c. (150 g) sugar
4 eggs
1 c. (125 g) flour

FILLING
2 c. (½ l) milk
1 cinnamon stick
1 lemon
7 Tbsp. flour
½ c. (125 g) sugar
1 egg
3 egg yolks
powdered sugar

This recipe, from Monasterio de San Antonio de Padua, a Spanish monastery of Poor Clare nuns, is prepared only on very special occasions when the nuns want to thank their donors and friends.

First make the batter by beating sugar and the 4 eggs together until they are light and fluffy. Stir in the flour and mix until smooth. Line a large cookie sheet 12 x 16 inches (30 x 40 cm) with parchment paper and butter it well. Turn up the edges of the paper and push them into the corners. Pour batter onto cookie sheet and distribute evenly over the sheet by tilting it. Bake on the middle rack of a hot oven 375°F (190°C) for 5 minutes or until golden. Cool for 45 minutes.

In the meantime make the filling: Put the milk into a saucepan, add the cinnamon stick and the peel of the lemon. Bring to a boil carefully so that the milk does not scorch on the bottom. In a bowl mix flour and sugar, then add the whole egg and 3 egg yolks. Blend well. An electric beater comes in handy for this. Slowly add the hot milk.

Put the mixture back in the saucepan. Return saucepan to the stove and over low heat bring it to a boil while stirring constantly. This process requires close attention so as not to burn the custard-like filling. After it has thickened, remove it from the heat and set the saucepan in cold water, stirring constantly so a skin does not form.

Cut the thin baked layer of cake in half horizontally. Remove from parchment paper. When the filling is lukewarm, pour it on the bottom half of the cake and distribute it evenly. Top with the other half of the cake. Let filling cool completely. When cool, cut the puños with a very sharp knife into rectangles 2 x 4 inches (5 x 10 cm) or squares 2 x 2 inches (5 x 5 cm).

Dust with powdered sugar before serving.

Makes about 16 large puños.

COOKING WITH THE SAINTS

St. Francis Xavier

Anthony van Dyck,
17th century, Pinacoteca,
Vatican Museum, Vatican City

FRANCIS XAVIER was born on April 7, 1506, in Spain. Like Ignatius of Loyola, Francis was a Basque. He was educated at the University of Paris, where at the age of nineteen he met Ignatius. After much soul-searching he eventually joined Ignatius and his group, which later became the Company of Jesus, known as the Jesuits. The Jesuits had offered themselves to be at the service of the pope. When the king of Portugal asked the pope to send priests for the new missions in India, Ignatius selected Francis Xavier. He was appointed the pope's representative for missions in the Far East, and in April 1541 he sailed from Lisbon.

It took Francis thirteen months to reach Goa, where he immediately began his missionary work, first with the small Portuguese colony, but later extending it to the native population. On his journeys, which lasted more than ten years, he took little besides his prayer book and a book of meditations.

After leaving Goa, Francis worked with fishermen on the coast of South India; then he went to Malacca and the Moluccas, and eventually in 1549 he went to Japan. He died in 1552 on a lonely island, in the presence of just one companion, while trying to get permission to enter China. He is buried at Goa. In 1622 Pope Gregory XV canonized Francis Xavier and Ignatius.

In art, St. Francis Xavier is usually shown as a missionary, as he is the patron saint of all Catholic missions. His feast day is December 3.

110

Xaver Suppe

(Soup for St. Francis Xavier's Day)

1½ c. (200 g) flour
½ c. (125 ml) cream
½ c. (125 g) butter
½ c. (70 g) Parmesan cheese, grated
½ tsp. salt
½ tsp. pepper, white
pinch of nutmeg
2 eggs
2 egg yolks
1 Tbsp. parsley, chopped (for dough)
12 c. (3 l) chicken stock
2 Tbsp. chervil, chopped
2 Tbsp. parsley, chopped (for soup)

Over low heat work the flour, cream, butter and Parmesan cheese to a solid dough. Work in the salt, pepper, nutmeg, the eggs and egg yolks and the 1 tablespoon of parsley. Put the mixture into a piping bag with a big nozzle and pipe pea-sized balls onto a buttered tray. Let stand for about 30 minutes.

In the meantime heat some salted water until it boils, then drop in all the "dough peas". Cook for 5 minutes, then remove them with a slotted spoon and add to the warm chicken stock. Season soup to taste and add the chervil and 2 tablespoons parsley.

Serves 10 to 12 people.

This is a delicious soup that is easy to make and can serve a crowd.

111

St. Frediano

Filippo Lippi, 15th century,
Louvre, Paris.
St. Frediano (left) and
St. Augustine kneel before
Madonna and Child.

In ITALY he is known as Frediano; in Ireland, where he was born in the first half of the sixth century, he is known as Frigidian. Reputedly the son of a king, Frediano was ordained a priest in Ireland. On a pilgrimage to Italy he became a hermit on Mount Pisano near Lucca. In time he was made bishop of Lucca against his will. He accepted only when pressured to do so by Pope John II.

Frediano fled the Lombard invasion of Lucca and on his return rebuilt the destroyed cathedral and helped the needy and the sick. He was known for his holiness and desire for solitude. He formed a community of clergy and lived with them.

Frediano died around 588 and is buried at Lucca. In 1507 the group that he founded was merged with another order.

Frediano's feast day is March 18, and in art he is usually shown in the garments of a bishop with his crozier. According to legend, he diverted a swollen river that threatened Lucca by drawing a path for the river in the sand with his crozier, thus leading it away from the city walls.

Lasagne di San Frediano

(Lasagna St. Frediano)

½ lb. (250 g) lasagna noodles
½ lb. (250 g) ground pork or veal
2 Tbsp. unsalted butter
½ c. (100 g) lean ham
½ lb. (250 g) mushrooms
1 small onion, finely chopped
1 clove of garlic, chopped
2 Tbsp. olive oil
salt and pepper
1 c. (250 ml) dry white wine
½ c. (125 ml) stock
½ c. (70 g) grated Parmesan cheese

WHITE SAUCE
3 Tbsp. butter
3 Tbsp. flour
1½ c. (375 ml) milk
salt, pepper
grated nutmeg

This recipe comes from the district of San Frediano in Milan. It is unusual in that it does not contain any tomatoes.

Cook the lasagna noodles in lots of salted, boiling water until done. Set aside. Meanwhile, prepare the white sauce by melting the butter in a saucepan, adding the flour and then adding the milk, stirring constantly. Season with salt, pepper and nutmeg.

Brown the meat in half the butter, add the chopped ham and cook briefly. Set aside.

Clean mushrooms and slice finely. Sauté the finely chopped onion and garlic in the oil and remaining butter till they barely change color. Add mushrooms and cook briskly until just cooked. Season with salt and pepper. Pour in the wine and cook until most of it has evaporated before adding half the chicken stock. Cover and cook for about 10 minutes. Combine meat and mushroom mixture and cook gently for another 15 minutes, stirring occasionally and adding more broth when it thickens.

Oil a casserole lightly and make 3 layers of noodles, mushroom and meat sauce and Parmesan cheese, finishing with a layer of noodles. Cover with the white sauce and sprinkle with more Parmesan cheese. Put in an oven preheated to 400°F (200°F) and cook for 20 to 25 minutes until the top is golden. Serve accompanied by a green salad.

Sufficient for 6.

GEORGE is an immensely popular saint, though little of his life is known. A few things can be said with certainty. An officer in the army of Emperor Diocletian, he was asked to give sacrifice to the gods but refused because he was a Christian. He was tortured and beheaded at Nicomedia, now in Turkey, around 303. The veneration of St. George is very ancient, and he is found in many early descriptions of martyrs.

Russian Icon, School of Novgorod, 14th century, Tretyakov Gallery, Moscow

Everything else we know about St. George is legend. The fictional story about him slaying the dragon and rescuing the king's daughter, so familiar to all of us and shown in many paintings, was popularized by *The Golden Legend*. In the Church the dragon is a symbol of the devil, so St. George's victory over it is a symbol of his martyrdom.

The association of St. George with England began with the crusades. At the siege of Antioch, an English writer, William of Malmesbury, reported a vision of St. George and St. Demetrius assisting the crusaders. Richard I placed himself and his army under the special protection of St. George. This made George a patron saint of soldiers, and his fame spread to England with the returning crusaders. Edward III made him the patron saint of the Order of the Garter, and at Windsor a chapel in his name was built by Edward IV and Henry VII. At the battle of Agincourt Henry V made a famous speech that invoked St. George as the patron of England.

From that time on, St. George's Day, April 23, became a major feast day in England. The characteristics that are personified in St. George were popular all over Europe and represent the ideals of Christian chivalry and knighthood. This explains his broad appeal in the Middle Ages.

Devotion to St. George has declined in many areas, and in the modern calendar of the universal Church his Mass is celebrated as a memorial, rather than as a feast. Despite that, his feast day is still celebrated by Englishmen all over the world, especially by those outside of England. Wearing red roses and having special dinners on that day is common for expatriate English.

In art St. George is usually shown as a soldier or knight on horseback slaying the dragon. Many famous artists have produced well-known paintings. St. George is not only the patron saint of England and of soldiers but is also considered to be one of the patrons of Venice, Genoa and Portugal.

Melachrino Cake

CAKE

1 c. (200 g) butter

1½ c. (350 g) sugar

5 eggs

2 c. (400 g) semolina

1½ c. (200 g) flour

2 tsp. baking powder

2 tsp. baking soda

2 tsp. cinnamon

2 tsp. ground cloves

1¼ c. (250 g) nuts, chopped

SYRUP

1 orange

1 lemon

2 c. (500 g) sugar

4 c. (1 l) water

2 Tbsp. brandy

1 cinnamon stick

This is an old Greek recipe traditionally associated with St. George, given to me by an employee of the Greek Embassy in London.

Soften the butter at room temperature and beat it until quite light. Add the sugar and continue beating until the mixture is light and fluffy.

Separate the eggs, and beat the egg whites in a separate bowl until stiff peaks form.

Add the egg yolks, 1 at a time, to the butter and sugar, beating thoroughly after each egg yolk.

Add semolina and flour mixed with the baking powder and soda. Add cinnamon, cloves and nuts. Blend in well. Carefully fold in the beaten egg whites. Butter and flour a 10-inch (25 cm) round cake pan and put the mixture into it. Bake in a moderately hot oven 375°F (190°C) for about 50 minutes until the cake is firm to the touch but not hard. Let cool for 10 minutes, then remove from pan and put on a plate with a high rim.

In the meantime prepare the syrup. Grate half the orange rind, and squeeze out 2 teaspoons of lemon juice. In a saucepan bring the sugar and water to a boil, add the lemon juice, orange rind, brandy and cinnamon. Simmer over low heat for about 15 to 25 minutes until the syrup lightly coats the back of a spoon and is reduced to about ⅔.

Before serving, pour the hot syrup over the cake and let it soak for a couple of minutes.

Serves 10 to 12.

Creamed St. George's Day Mushrooms

2 lb. (1 kg) St. George's Day mushrooms
4 Tbsp. butter
1 Tbsp. lemon juice
½ c. (125 ml) whipping cream
1 tsp. cornstarch
3 Tbsp. dry cider
salt and pepper

Here is an English recipe for St. George's Day mushrooms. These mushrooms can be found in markets in England around Saint George's feast day.

Wash and clean mushrooms, pat dry and slice in half if mushrooms are large. If St. George's Day mushrooms are not available, other mushrooms can be substituted.

Melt butter and sauté mushrooms for about 5 minutes. Stir in lemon juice and half the cream. Simmer for 5 to 7 minutes. Remove mushrooms from pan. Mix cornstarch with cider and remaining cream. On full heat add this mixture to the pan and heat thoroughly. Season with salt and pepper. Pour sauce over mushrooms and serve. Suitable as a side dish or a light lunch.

Serves 8.

St. George's Toast

2 Tbsp. ham, cooked, lean
4 sardines, skinned, boned
½ tsp. cayenne pepper
salt
4 slices of toast

This recipe is from an English cookbook published in the 1930s. Though the combination of flavors is unusual, it makes a nice accompaniment for a glass of wine.

Chop ham finely. Skin and debone sardines carefully. Mix the first three ingredients together by pounding them and season with salt if necessary. The mixture should look like a paste. Alternately you can use a food processor.

Cut toast into fingers. Spread paste over the toast fingers and put under the grill. Grill until they are hot and steaming.

Goes well with a glass of wine or makes a light lunch.

Serves 2 to 4 persons.

116

St. Germain of Auxerre

Antoine Coypel, 17th century,
Musée des Beaux-Arts,
Dijon, France.
In this painting St. Germain
is portrayed giving a medal
to St. Genevieve when she
was a child.

GERMAIN was born around 378 in Auxerre in France, and he was trained there and in Rome as an advocate in Roman law. He married a noble Roman lady and was named governor of his home province.

Later, in 418, he was named bishop of Auxerre. Germain was ordained and, taking on a life of poverty and austerity, he built monasteries and churches in his diocese.

At the request of the British bishops, Germain went to Britain in 429 to combat some heretics, an endeavor that he completed successfully. It was on this trip that the famous "Alleluia victory" occurred, where a force of Britons was saved by Germain's intervention from destruction by a much larger force of marauding Picts and Saxons.

On his return to Auxerre he convinced Auxiliaris, the prefect, to reduce taxes, reputedly by healing Auxiliaris' sick wife. In 440 he returned to Britain again to argue with the heretics and founded numerous schools to teach the proper faith. After his return to France he tried to mediate between the natives and a Roman general charged with putting down their revolt. Germain went to Ravenna to convince the emperor Valentinian III to call off the attack. However, this proved unsuccessful, as news of yet another uprising had reached the emperor. Germain died in Ravenna on July 31, 448. According to his last wish, he was buried at Auxerre, where his remains were destroyed during the French Revolution.

In art Germain is often represented in his robes as a bishop. His feast day is July 31 according to *The Oxford Dictionary of Saints* and the 1946 Roman Martyrology.

117

FILETS DE SOLE SAINT-GERMAIN

(Fillets of Sole with Béarnaise Sauce)

FISH
½ lb. (250 g) fresh white bread
4 fillets of sole, 6 oz. (150 g) each
salt and pepper
8 Tbsp. melted butter

SAUCE
4 Tbsp. white vinegar
1 spring onion
4 black peppercorns
¼ tsp. dried tarragon
2 egg yolks
½ c. (125 g) butter

An easy-to-prepare dish with a classic French sauce, this recipe transforms a simple meal of fish into a gourmet adventure.

Tear the bread into chunks and process in a blender to make fresh bread crumbs. Season the fillets with salt and pepper, then dip in melted butter and finally dip in the bread crumbs. Place fish on a buttered tray, sprinkle with remaining butter and grill gently until golden brown.

To make the sauce, combine the first 4 ingredients in a saucepan, bring to a boil, reduce the heat and simmer uncovered until mixture is reduced by half. Strain.

Place egg yolks in top half of a double boiler, and stir in the strained liquid. Cut butter into small cubes.

Put top half of double boiler over barely simmering water in the bottom half. The water should not touch the base. Gradually whisk in the butter, a cube at a time, watching carefully that it does not get too hot and cause the sauce to curdle. After all the butter has been added, the sauce should have a fairly thick consistency.

Pour sauce over the individual fillets and serve with noisette potatoes. These are prepared by making small balls from a potato with a melon scoop and frying them in butter.

Serves 4.

Purée Saint-Germain

(Pea and Lettuce Purée)

½ lb. (250 g) lettuce
12 small green onions (scallions)
2 lbs. (1 kg) fresh shelled peas
3 sprigs of parsley
8 Tbsp. butter
1 tsp. sugar
½ tsp. salt
4 Tbsp. chicken stock
boiled potato (optional)

Shred lettuce and chop green onions. Put peas in a saucepan with the lettuce, onions, parsley, half the butter, the sugar, salt and the chicken stock. Bring to a boil and cook slowly until peas are tender. Remove parsley and drain peas, reserving the juice.

Put mixture in a blender and process to a fine purée. Reheat in the top of a double boiler, adding the rest of the butter and, if too thick, some of the reserved juice. Do not overheat or the glorious green color will be lost. If the purée is too thin, some puréed boiled potatoes may be added to thicken it. Serve as a vegetable side dish with grilled meat such as tournedos or noisettes.

Sufficient for 8 to 10 people.

A classic French dish, this makes a good accompaniment for many main courses. It is popular with children because of the sweetness of the peas.

HEDWIGSOHLEN

(Shoe Soles of St. Hedwig)

DOUGH

½ c. (125 ml) milk, lukewarm

4 Tbsp. sugar

1 tsp. dry yeast

1 lemon

2 c. (250 g) flour

4 Tbsp. butter

½ tsp. salt

1 egg

TOPPING

2 Tbsp. sour cream

1 egg yolk

sugar

Mix half the milk with a teaspoon of the sugar and the yeast. Let stand until frothy. Grate the peel of half of the lemon. Mix this and all the other dough ingredients with the yeast mixture to make a smooth dough. It may be necessary to add flour or liquid so the dough is pliable.

Let dough rest for about 45 minutes. Cut dough into 10 small balls and form each ball into the shape of the sole of a shoe.

The dough should then be about ¼ inch (6 mm) thick. Put the "soles" onto a greased baking sheet, let rest and rise for about 20 minutes.

Bake the breads in a preheated oven at 400°F (200°C) for about 20 minutes until golden brown. Five minutes before the end of baking time, brush the top of each "sole" with the mixture of the sour cream and egg yolk. Sprinkle with sugar and return to the oven for the last 5 minutes.

Makes about 16.

St. Helen

HELEN was born around 250 and may have been the daughter of an innkeeper. Two places claim to be her birthplace: Colchester in England and Drepanum, a vanished seaside resort in Turkey. In 270 she married the Roman general Constantius Chlorus, who encountered her on one of his travels. When he became emperor in 292, he divorced her for a match more appropriate for his rank. Helen retired to Treves (Trier) in Germany, the place where she probably became a Christian.

Helen's son Constantine, who was born either at York in England or at Nish in Serbia, eventually became emperor of the Roman Empire after his father's death. Constantine greatly respected and honored his mother, even minting a coin in her honor. Under him the persecutions of the Church stopped, and the Church lived in peace.

In 312, at about the age of sixty, Helen became a Christian. With Constantine's acquiescence she generously gave to the Church, supported the poor and looked after prisoners. She made a pilgrimage to the Holy Land to supervise the construction of a church on Mount Calvary. She died in Jerusalem around 330.

Fresco, Piero della Francesca, 15th century,
S. Francesco, Assisi.
St. Helen (dark blue cape) has her right hand on the cross.

Helen's fame is based on a legend that during the construction of a church on Mount Calvary she found the True Cross. The legends surrounding the discovery and identification make fascinating reading. This event had a great impact on the theological discussions of the time, as the new religion and its beliefs were being questioned in many Mediterreanean schools and universities. Subsequently the True Cross became an important relic, especially in the battles of the crusades, where a major part of it was eventually lost in the fourteenth century. Many churches all over Europe still claim to be in possession of a piece of the True Cross.

The imaginations of many artists have been inspired by the legends surrounding the finding of the True Cross and the miracles that occurred. Piero della Francesca's series of frescoes in Assisi is quite comprehensive in its coverage of these legends.

Helen is usually depicted as an elderly Roman lady venerating a cross. Her feast day in the West is August 18, and in the East she is celebrated together with her son Constantine on May 21.

Lienzer Helenenbrot

(St. Helen's Bread from Lienz)

SOURDOUGH
½ c. (60 g) flour
5 Tbsp. water
1 Tbsp. dry yeast
pinch of sugar

BREAD
8 c. (1 kg) rye flour, or a mixture of rye and wheat flour
1 Tbsp. dry yeast
3 c. (750 ml) water
1 Tbsp. salt
3 Tbsp. mixture of spices—caraway, fennel, anise, coriander, fenugreek (only a bit of this, as it is very strong)

This is an old Tyrolian recipe for a very tasty rye bread. The more rye flour used, the more spices the dough can take. The crunchiness of a bread's crust is in Germany and Austria the sign of a good bread. Thus, the harder and crunchier the better.

The sourdough starter must be prepared 3 days in advance by mixing the ingredients together and leaving the mixture in a loosely covered glass jar in a warm room. It will bubble vigorously the first day, then it will subside and should be stirred once every day. If it is not used after 3 days it may be stored in the refrigerator for 3 more days.

To make the bread, measure the flour into a big bowl. Make a well in the middle and add the yeast dissolved in some of the water. Let stand for 10 minutes. In the meantime, add the salt to the water.

Chop spices, or grind them coarsely with mortar and pestle. Add sourdough starter, water and spices to the flour, stir with a wooden spoon until it can be kneaded by hand without being sticky. Some flour may have to be added at this point.

Knead dough for 3 minutes, cover and let rest in a warm place until nearly doubled. Knead again for 2 minutes and form 2 loaves. Cover and let the loaves rest until doubled in size.

The bread may be baked in a loaf pan, but it is better to put it on a baking sheet. This gives a better crust. The top may be brushed with slightly salted water and sprinkled with more spices.

Put a shallow pan of water in the bottom of the oven, and preheat oven to very hot 425°F (220°C). Bake the bread for about 1 to 1½ hours on the middle rack of the oven. After 60 minutes reduce heat to 350°F (175°C).

When baked, remove from the oven. Cool.

Makes two 2-pound loaves.

124

St. Hildegard of Bingen

HILDEGARD was born in Bökelheim, Germany, in 1098, and, because she was a sickly child, she was given at the age of eight to the care of a recluse called Jutta. When Hildegard was old enough to become a nun, a small community had grown up around Jutta. When Jutta died in 1136, Hildegard became abbess of the community. About 1147 her group of Benedictine nuns, having outgrown their premises, moved to Rupertsberg, near Bingen. Hildegard reformed several monasteries and founded another one. She died after a full life at the age of over eighty in 1179.

From the age of seventeen on, Hildegard had visions that were recorded by her confessor. Twenty-six of these visions were published in a book. These mystical writings gave her immense popularity among the ordinary people. She also made very important contributions in many other areas, such as natural science, music, medicine, theology and cooking. Her correspondents included Henry II of England, Emperor Fredrick Barbarossa, Pope Eugenius III and many other clergy, and she had no hesitation in reproving them if she thought they done something inappropriate.

Hildegard was never formally canonized, but she was added to the list of saints in the fifteenth century. In art she is usually shown as a nun reading or writing. Her feast day is September 17, and she is one of the patron saints of the sick.

Hildegard's studies in natural science and cooking led her to the writing of a cookbook, which is still quite popular in Germany. It emphasizes the use of spelt, an ancient form of wheat, as a remedy for many ailments. For one of Hildegard's own recipes, see the section for St. Margaret of Antioch.

Miniature by St. Hildegard, 12th century, from "Scivias", Codex Rupertsberg (facsimile)

HILDEGARDPLÄTZCHEN
(St. Hildegard Cookies)

½ c. (110 g) butter
¾ c. (200 g) sugar
2 eggs
3½ c. (450 g) flour
1 tsp. baking powder
2 tsp. cinnamon
2 tsp. nutmeg
½ tsp. cloves

Whisk butter and sugar together, then add eggs. Sift in flour, baking powder and spices. Work dough to a smooth ball. If it is too dry, 1 or 2 tablespoons of milk or water may be added. Roll dough out to about ¼ inch (6 mm) thickness and cut out circles about 3 inches (8 cm) in diameter. Preheat oven to moderate 350°F (175°C).

Put cookies on a cookie sheet on the middle rack and bake for 10 to 12 minutes until golden.

Makes about 40 cookies.

The recipe for these rather spicy cookies comes from Germany; they go well with coffee or tea.

125

St. Honorat of Arles

HONORAT, or Honoratus, was born in the latter half of the third century; his father was a Roman consul. He eventually settled in Gaul (France) and was well educated. Early in his youth he renounced the worship of the gods, and converted with his brother Venantius to Christianity. Their father did not like their decision, and so with their spiritual director they fled to Greece to live. There Venantius died, and Honorat became sick and was forced to return to France. He first lived as a hermit in the mountains, near Marseille, and then, when others of a similar mind joined him, he founded the famous monastery at Lerins. This monastery was well known for the holiness and charity of its monks.

In 426 Honorat was consecrated archbishop of Arles, despite his strong opposition. He died there in 429 and was buried in Arles. In 1391 his relics were transferred to Lerins and later to Grasse. Honorat was a well-known writer of great elegance.

St. Honorat's feast day is January 16. In art he is shown either as bishop or as abbot.

126

RÂBLE DE LIÈVRE SAINT-HONORAT

(Saddle of Hare à la St. Honorat)

1 saddle of hare

MARINADE
1 stick of celery, chopped
1 onion, chopped
1 sprig of thyme
½ c. (125 ml) dry white wine

SAUCE
1 Tbsp. red currant jelly
½ tsp. crushed peppercorns
1 c. (250 ml) beef or chicken stock
4 Tbsp. butter
1 c. (250 ml) whipping cream
¼ lb. (100 g) mushrooms, sliced
3 Tbsp. wine vinegar

First prepare the meat by removing the skin. The bone may also be removed at this point; it makes the marinade more effective, and cooking and eating easier.

Put the meat in a dish with the chopped celery, onion, thyme and white wine. Marinate for at least 24 hours. Take meat out of marinade, put it with a spot of butter in a hot saucepan and cook for 5 minutes on each side till nicely browned. Remove from the saucepan and keep warm.

Add marinade to the saucepan with the red currant jelly, the peppercorns and the stock. Let it reduce by ⅔, strain and mix in the butter, the cream, the sliced mushrooms and the vinegar. Stir until thick.

Place the saddle of rabbit on serving dish and pour sauce over it. Serve immediately.

Serves 2 persons.

This is a French dish for rabbit in which the meat is marinated, quickly cooked, and served with the delicious sauce expected of a French cook.

This is a very sophisticated recipe for lobster that will make a good meal for special occasions. The original recipe has been slightly modified so that it can more easily be made in a domestic kitchen.

Homard Saint-Honorat

(Lobster St. Honorat)

2 lobsters, cooked

SAUCE

2 Tbsp. butter

2 Tbsp. ham, lean, uncooked, diced

4 Tbsp. carrot, finely diced

4 Tbsp. onion, finely diced

4 Tbsp. celery, finely diced

1 bay leaf

2 Tbsp. brandy

1¼ c. (300 g) tomatoes, fresh, chopped

sprig of thyme

salt and pepper

2 Tbsp. butter (for cooking lobster tail and oysters)

2 Tbsp. butter (for flour to thicken sauce)

2 Tbsp. flour

½ c. (125 ml) cream

¼ tsp. garlic, minced

1 Tbsp. parsley, chopped

1 Tbsp. tarragon, chopped

1 Tbsp. chervil, chopped

RICE PILAF

2 Tbsp. butter (for onions and rice)

2 Tbsp. onion, finely chopped

½ c. (100 g) rice

1 c. (250 ml) chicken stock

8 oysters, shells removed

Break off the tails of the lobsters, and split them length-wise down the middle. Remove the meat, and cut it into thick slices. Set aside. Remove meat from the claws and knuckles, and reserve the tomalley (the green stuff inside the lobster).

Sauce (step 1)

To make the sauce, melt 2 tablespoons butter and cook the ham in it for one minute. Add carrots, onion, celery and bay leaf and cook until vegetables are soft. Chop the meat from the claws and knuckles and add to the vegetables along with the reserved coral. Cook for a couple of minutes. Add the brandy and light it.

After the flame has died down, add the chopped tomatoes, thyme, salt and pepper. Cook covered for about 20 minutes. In the meantime prepare the rice pilaf.

Pilaf

In a saucepan melt the butter, and cook the onion in it until it is soft but not browned. Add the rice and cook it for several minutes. Add the chicken stock, cover the sauce pan, turn the heat to low and cook for about 18 minutes without disturbing it.

In a small frying pan melt 2 tablespoons butter and sauté the lobster tail slices. Take them out and keep warm. Fry the oysters in the same saucepan, take them out and keep them warm.

Sauce (step 2)

To finish the sauce, mix 2 tablespoons butter and flour together, add it to the sauce that is still simmering, and stir until the sauce has slightly thickened. Add the cream and keep the sauce warm, but do not let it boil. Taste for seasoning and adjust with salt and pepper if necessary. Add the herbs just before serving the sauce.

To serve, fill the empty lobster tails with the rice pilaf. Top with the slices of the lobster tail and cover with the sauce. Put 2 fried oysters on top of the sauce. Any leftover sauce and rice may be served separately.

Serve with a dry white wine.

Serves 2 to 4 people.

St. Honoré of Amiens

Honoré was born at Port-le-Grand near Amiens in the sixth century. He was ordained and later became bishop of Amiens and governed the see until his death there at around 600. During his time as bishop, a priest found the relics of three saints who had been forgotten for three hundred years, and Honoré provided an appropriate surrounding for them by building a new church.

In 1060 Honoré was declared a saint, and his popularity in France increased tremendously as a consequence of some remarkable miracles.

His feast day is May 16. He is the patron saint of millers, bakers, pastry chefs and confectioners, but how he became connected with these professions is not clear. One of the most famous French cakes, the Gâteau Saint-Honoré, is named in his honor.

130

St. Honoré Trifle

GENOESE SPONGE

4 eggs

½ c. (125 g) sugar

7 Tbsp. flour

4 Tbsp. butter, melted

DECORATION

3 egg whites

2 Tbsp. sugar

12 macaroons

½ c. (125 ml) sherry

1 c. (250 ml) whipping cream

8–10 glacé cherries

8–10 angelica strips

Grease a square 8-inch (20 cm) baking pan, line the base with greased waxed paper. Preheat oven to 350°F (175°C). Combine eggs and sugar in a large bowl, place over a saucepan of simmering water, but do not allow bowl to touch water. Using an electric beater, beat until mixture is thick and creamy, about 10 minutes.

Remove the bowl from the hot water, beat the mixture until it returns to room temperature. Sift half the flour over the egg mixture and carefully fold in the flour. Repeat with remaining flour.

Quickly fold in the cooled melted butter. Pour mixture into the pan and bake for about 20 minutes until sponge feels elastic to the touch. Turn cake onto wire rack to cool.

Beat the egg whites until stiff, add sugar and continue until all the sugar is blended in. Pipe meringue around the outside of sponge and put in a cool oven 250°F (120°C) until the meringue hardens.

Remove, cover bottom with macaroons, soaking them with sherry without touching the border. Let soak for at least 1 hour. Whip cream, add the sugar, put on top, and garnish with the cherries and angelica before serving.

Serves 8 to 10.

This recipe, from Mrs. Beeton's cookbook, somewhat resembles the famous French cake but is much simpler to cook.

GÂTEAU ST. HONORÉ

BASE
½ lb. (220 g) puff pastry

CROWN AND PUFFS (CHOUX PASTRY)
5 Tbsp. butter
½ c. (125 ml) water
½ c. (125 ml) milk
½ tsp. salt
1 tsp. sugar
1 c. (125 g) flour
4 eggs

EGG WASH
1 egg yolk
1 Tbsp. milk

PASTRY CREAM (FILLINGS)
3 eggs
4 Tbsp. sugar
6 Tbsp. flour
4 Tbsp. cornstarch
1¼ c. (300 ml) milk
¼ tsp. vanilla
½ c. (125 ml) whipping cream, for filling puffs

CARAMEL
½ c. (100 g) sugar
2 Tbsp. butter
3 Tbsp. water

Here is the classic French cake in honor of the patron saint of pastry chefs. This one uses puff pastry instead of the normal shortcrust pastry.

To make the base, roll out the puff pastry on a lightly floured surface and make a circle 10 inches (25 cm) in diameter. Brush a baking sheet with a bit of water and transfer pastry circle to it.

To make the choux pastry, dice the butter and put butter, water, milk, salt and sugar in a saucepan, set on high heat and boil for 1 minute while stirring. Take the pan off the heat and quickly add the sifted flour and stir. When the mixture is very smooth, return the pan to the heat and stir for one minute to dry out the dough a bit. Transfer paste into a bowl. Immediately beat in the eggs, 1 at a time, until the mixture is very smooth. Spoon the choux pastry into a piping bag with a wide nozzle, ½ in (12 mm) wide.

Next prepare the egg wash by mixing the egg yolk with the milk. With the egg wash, brush a ring on the outside of the pastry circle about 1 inch (2.5 cm) wide. On top of the egg wash, pipe a border around the outside of the pastry ring.

Whip the cream. To make the caramel, cook the sugar in a saucepan with the butter and water until it turns golden amber.

On another lightly buttered baking tray, pipe 18 small puffs about ¾ inch (2 cm) in diameter. Brush with egg wash and press lightly with the back of a fork. Preheat oven to 425°F (220°C). Bake the puffs and base for 10 minutes, then lower the temperature to 400°F (200°C) and cook the puffs for a further 10 minutes and the base for a further 15 minutes. When the puffs come out of the oven, cut a hole in the bottom of each puff to let the steam escape. Dip the top of each puffball into the caramel and set aside to cool. When cool, fill each puff through the hole in the bottom with whipped cream. Attach each puff onto the outside of the base with a little bit of the caramel.

To make the pastry cream, beat together 2 egg yolks, 1 whole egg and the sugar. Reserve egg whites. Stir in the flour, cornstarch and the vanilla. Heat the milk gently and gradually beat in the egg mixture. Return the mixture to the pan, bring to a boil, stirring all the time, and boil for two minutes. Cover with buttered paper and cool.

Whip the 2 egg whites until stiff and fold together egg whites, any remaining whipped cream and the pastry cream. Fill the center of the cake with this mixture. Drizzle remaining caramel over the cream and decorate with candied flowers, strawberries, or even candied fruit. If possible, decorate just before serving.

Serves 6 to 8.

St. Hubert

Master of the Life of the Virgin, 15th century, National Gallery, London

FEW FACTS about Hubert's early life and conversion are known. He was ordained a priest by St. Lambert, lived first as a hermit, and later worked as a pioneering priest in the Ardennes region of Belgium. When Lambert was murdered at Liège about the year 705, Hubert was made bishop in his place.

Some years later he transferred St. Lambert's remains from Maastricht to Liège, built a cathedral and eventually moved the seat of the diocese there, thus becoming the first bishop of Liège. He died in 727 on a trip to Brabant and was buried in Liège. In the ninth century his remains were transferred to the abbey of St. Hubert in the Ardennes, close to the border with Luxembourg.

Hubert's fame is based on a legend that his conversion occurred while he was hunting on Good Friday. Earlier connected with St. Eustace, this legend was attached to Hubert around the fourteenth century, and it is probably why he became the patron saint of hunters. As some of Hubert's life was spent in the woods as a hermit, he is the patron also of woodcutters and foresters, as well as of the city of Liège, and his intercession is sought against rabies. His feast day is November 3.

Hubert's conversion while hunting is a popular theme for artists, but he can also be found portrayed in bishop's robes. In cooking, there are many recipes with Hubert's name in them, all involving game of one kind or another.

Salpicon Saint-Hubert

(Ragout à la St. Hubert)

½ c. (120 g) butter
½ c. (125 ml) carrot, chopped finely
½ c. (125 ml) celery, chopped finely
4 Tbsp. onion, chopped finely
4 Tbsp. flour
1 bay leaf
4 Tbsp. mushroom essence (optional)
4 Tbsp. truffle essence (optional)
3 c. (750 ml) strong meat stock
½ c. (125 ml) dry sherry
salt and pepper
½ lb. (250 g) mushrooms
1 lb. (500 g) game meat, diced

Any game meat (venison, boar, hare, pheasant, partridge or quail) is fine for this recipe. The flavor is greatly improved if the meat stock is prepared with game meat.

Melt half the butter in a pan and fry the finely chopped carrot, celery and onion till golden brown. Add flour and cook for 1 more minute. Add the bay leaf, the optional mushroom essence and truffle essence and the stock. Reduce stock by boiling until you have only 2 cups (500 ml). Add the sherry and adjust the seasoning with the salt and pepper. Remove bay leaf and purée in a blender or put through a fine sieve.

In another saucepan sauté the sliced mushrooms with the remaining butter until soft, then add the diced game meat. When warm, add this to the sieved liquid.

This salpicon is very good for filling vol-au-vent cases, or it may be served with plain rice.

Serves about 4 as an entree and is enough filling for about 20 vol-au-vent cases.

This is a very versatile French recipe for leftover cooked game meat of any kind. It makes a good hors d'oeuvre or main course.

135

Côtes de Chevreuil Saint-Hubert

(Venison Cutlets in the Style of St. Hubert)

CHOPS
8 venison chops
¾ lb. (350 g) sausage meat
½ lb. (200 g) mushrooms
4 juniper berries
4 Tbsp. butter, clarified (or 2 Tbsp. oil and 2 Tbsp. butter)

MARINADE
½ c. (125 ml) red wine
1 onion, chopped
3 Tbsp. brandy
3 Tbsp. olive oil
salt and pepper

POIVRADE (PEPPER SAUCE)
1 onion, chopped
1 carrot, diced
2 Tbsp. oil
2 Tbsp. flour
2c. (500ml) beef stock
1 Tbsp. tomato paste
bouquet garni
6 Tbsp. red wine vinegar
6 peppercorns
4 Tbsp. red wine
salt and pepper

An excellent recipe from Janet Grigson's book The Mushroom Feast, *this dish can easily be adapted to veal or beef if venison is not available.*

Mix together all the ingredients for the marinade, seasoning well. Marinade chops for several hours, or overnight.

Pepper Sauce

The sauce can be made earlier. Brown the onion and carrot in the oil, stir in the flour, then the beef stock and tomato paste, and finally add the bouquet garni. Simmer covered for 2 hours. Strain and skim off the fat.

Put the vinegar in a small pan, add peppercorns and the marinade from which the chops have been removed. Reduce over medium heat by half. Add to the brown sauce and simmer for another 30 to 45 minutes. Pour in the 4 tablespoons wine. Season with salt and pepper. Reheat gently before serving.

Let chops drain well and pat dry. Mix the sausage meat with the chopped mushrooms and the juniper berries. Use the clarified butter (or butter and oil mixed) to brown the chops on one side only. When cool enough to handle, spread the sausage mixture on the browned side of the chops.

Place chops in an ovenproof dish, fairly close together, and bake them for 20 minutes in a moderately hot oven 375°F (190°C). Baste with the remaining butter.

Serve with mashed potatoes and the sauce.

Serves 6 to 8 persons.

POTAGE SAINT-HUBERT

(Soup St. Hubert)

1 lb. (500 g) lentils
4 Tbsp. onion, finely chopped
1 c. (125 g) leek, finely sliced
1 bay leaf
½ tsp. thyme
1 pheasant
salt and pepper
½ c. (125 ml) cream

Soak the lentils in cold water for 2 to 3 hours. Drain.

Chop onion, cut the white of the leek into small rings. Cook the lentils, leek, onion, bay leaf and thyme in plenty of salt water. Even though brown lentils are the normal variety to use, red lentils taste just as good and make a more attractive soup.

Roast the pheasant; even an older bird will do. When it is cooked, cut the meat off the bone. Dice the meat from the breast and set aside.

Chop the other meat , strain the lentils, put them into a food processor and purée with a little bit of the lentil stock.

Pour into a saucepan and heat gently, adding more lentil stock until the consistency is right for a soup. Adjust seasoning. When the soup is quite hot, add the cream and the diced meat.

Serves 10 to 12 people.

Note: If you want to try this recipe and cannot find a pheasant, use a chicken of about 3 pounds.

HASENRÜCKEN ST. HUBERTUS

(Saddle of Hare St. Hubert)

2 saddles of hare
salt and pepper
4 juniper berries
2 strips of fatty bacon, smoked
4 Tbsp. butter
½ c. (125 ml) dry red wine
¾ c. (200 ml) sour cream
2 Tbsp. cranberry sauce

Skin the saddles, season them with salt and pepper. Crush juniper berries with a rolling pin and rub over the meat. Cut bacon into thin strips and, using a larding needle, put the strips into the meat.

Put the butter in a casserole dish, add the two saddles, add the red wine and roast in a hot oven 400°F (200°C) for 30 minutes. During roasting, baste a couple of times with the juices. Turn off heat after 30 minutes and let meat rest for another 10 minutes.

Prepare sauce by checking the roasting juice for seasoning; add salt and pepper if necessary. Mix with the sour cream and the cranberry sauce. Put saddles on a serving plate and serve the sauce separately. Serve with spätzle or rice and braised red cabbage. Apple or cranberry sauce may be served with it.

Serves 2.

This recipe, which is a rustic yet simple way to cook the best part of a hare, originates in Germany, where game meat of any kind is extremely popular.

*This recipe is a classic
French dish for hare,
for which one can use joints,
such as the front legs, that are
not very popular for roasting.*

PETITES TERRINES DE LIÈVRE SAINT-HUBERT

(Terrine of Hare St. Hubert)

1 lb. (500 g) meat of hare, minced or chopped finely
½ lb. (250 g) sausage meat
½ c. (100 g) fatty bacon, chopped
½ lb. (200 g) mushrooms, chopped
1 truffle, chopped (optional)
salt and pepper
½ tsp. thyme
6 Tbsp. brandy
6 Tbsp. sherry, dry
2 eggs
18 small round circles of fatty bacon
6 Tbsp. melted butter or lard

Mix together hare meat, sausage meat, chopped bacon, mushrooms and truffle. Add salt, pepper and thyme. Stir in brandy, sherry and eggs until well distributed. Fill 18 ramekins with the mixture and top with a circle of bacon.

Preheat oven to 340°F (170°C). Put ramekins into a bain-de-marie and cook in the oven until the mixture is set, about 1 hour.

Tilt each ramekin slightly, press down gently and pour off the juices. Cover thinly with lard or melted butter. Serve with wedges of toast, Melba toast or crusty bread.

Makes 18 servings.

140

Wildschweingulasch Sankt Hubertus

(Goulash of Wild Boar St. Hubert)

¾ lb. (300 g) wild boar meat
salt and pepper
1 tsp. caraway seeds
1 tsp. marjoram
2 tsp. grated lemon rind
2 Tbsp. olive oil
½ c. (125 ml) onion, chopped
½ c. (125 ml) carrot, diced
5 Tbsp. leek, sliced fine
¾ c. (200 ml) beer
4 Tbsp. cornstarch
4 Tbsp. red wine vinegar
1 c. (250 ml) meat stock
2 Tbsp. maple syrup
2 Tbsp. tomato paste
4 Tbsp. plain yogurt or crème fraîche
2 tsp. mixed herbs, rosemary, thyme, savory

If you do not have access to wild boar meat, you can substitute lean pork.

Wash meat, drain and pat dry and cut into small cubes. Season meat with salt, pepper, chopped caraway, marjoram and lemon rind. In a frying pan fry the meat in the olive oil until nicely browned. Transfer meat to a casserole dish.

Add vegetables and beer to the frying pan and cook for a minute while scraping off all the browned bits. Put this mixture into the casserole dish, cover it and put it into a moderate oven at 350°F (180°C). Cook for 1 hour or until meat is tender.

Mix cornstarch with the vinegar, add the stock, maple syrup, tomato paste, yogurt or crème fraîche and the mixed spices. Add this mixture to the casserole and cook for another 15 minutes until it has thickened. Serve the goulash with noodles, spätzle or some crusty bread.

Serves 4.

This is a recipe from Germany, where wild boar is considered a delicacy and is widely available.

This is a modern German recipe with a nice combination of spices.

FRISCHLINGSKEULEN ST. HUBERTUS

(Legs of Young Boar St. Hubert)

2 hind legs of a young boar (marcassin)
1½ Tbsp. salt
2 tsp. paprika
¼ tsp. coarse black pepper
¼ tsp. sage
½ tsp. thyme
½ tsp. oregano
5 Tbsp. olive oil
1 c. (250 ml) meat stock
4 Tbsp. dry red wine
4 Tbsp. cream

If no wild boar legs are available, the dish can be tried with a shank end of pork.

Carefully remove skin from the legs and rub all sides with the salt. Preheat oven to 425°F (220°C).

Mix all the other spices together and rub the mixture over the legs. Brush legs with the oil. Put the remaining oil in a roasting pan, add the legs and put in the oven.

After 15 minutes pour the stock in the roasting pan and cook for another hour. Add the red wine in the last 15 minutes. After cooking is finished, move legs from pan to a serving dish. Add the cream and adjust the seasoning. Serve sauce separately.

Sufficient for 8 persons.

Rehkeule St. Hubertus mit Ingwer

(Leg of Venison with Ginger à la St. Hubert)

MARINADE

6 c. (1½ l) water

½ c. (125 ml) red wine vinegar

1 bay leaf

5 peppercorns

5 juniper berries

1 Tbsp. freshly grated ginger root

1 large onion, quartered

MEAT

1 leg of venison, deboned, about 1½ lb. (750 g)

4 strips of lean bacon

salt and pepper

4 Tbsp. olive oil

2 Tbsp. carrot, chopped

2 Tbsp. celery, chopped

2 Tbsp. leek, sliced fine

2 Tbsp. tomato paste

1 c. (250 ml) meat stock

3 Tbsp. flour

2 Tbsp. sour cream

This modern German recipe for venison contains an unusual ingredient for such a dish, fresh ginger root. The result is very tasty.

Wash leg carefully; remove as much skin as possible. Next make a marinade with 6 cups (1½ l) of water, the vinegar, the spices and the quartered onion. Place in a glass dish or bowl. Cover and let the meat stand in the refrigerator in this marinade for 3 days. Turn meat over once a day.

Remove meat and pat dry. Cut bacon in thin strips. Using a larding needle, thread the strips through the meat. Salt and pepper the meat.

Preheat oven to 425°F (220°C). In a large pan with the olive oil brown the meat on all sides.

Transfer to a roasting pan and add the chopped vegetables. Put in the oven, and after 15 minutes add the tomato paste and meat stock. Cover pan and roast for about 90 minutes. Check occasionally that there is sufficient liquid left; if not, add some more stock or water.

Remove meat and keep warm. Mix the flour with some cold water and add to thicken the sauce. When thickened, add sour cream and adjust seasoning.

Cut meat into thick slices, put on a serving plate and pour the sauce over it. Serve with spätzle or boiled potatoes and braised red cabbage.

Serves 6.

Lepre alla Sant'Uberto

(Hare Casserole with Red Wine)

3½ lb. (1.5 kg) hare
½ c. (125 ml) onion, chopped
½ c. (125 ml) carrot, chopped
½ c. (125 ml) celery, chopped
6 Tbsp. olive oil
1 clove of garlic, sliced
2 bay leaves
3 cloves
2 sprig of rosemary
1 sprig fresh sage
1 c. (250 ml) dry red wine
salt and pepper
1 Tbsp. flour
2 tsp. grated orange rind
2 tsp. red currant jelly

This recipe is a delightful casserole for a cool fall evening. It comes from Valentina Harris' book Complete Italian Cookery Course. *It is a good example of the popularity of hare or rabbit in Italian cooking.*

Wash hare and cut into pieces, put into a bowl and prepare the marinade.

Fry the onion, carrot and celery in half the oil for about 5 minutes until the vegetables are soft. Add the garlic, bay leaves, cloves, rosemary and sage. Add the wine and boil off the alcohol for about 2 minutes. Season to taste with salt and pepper.

Strain marinade carefully, reserving vegetables and herbs. Let marinade cool completely. Pour it over the hare, cover and let it stand in a cool place for 24 hours.

Remove the pieces of hare from the marinade with a slotted spoon and coat them lightly in flour. Heat the remaining oil in a heavy casserole and brown the hare all over. Add the vegetables and herbs and continue to cook gently, turning the pieces of hare and basting with the marinade. After all the marinade has been added, season to taste with salt and pepper. Cover and simmer for about 1 hour until completely tender. Remove the pieces of hare with the slotted spoon and arrange them on a warm serving platter.

Stir the orange rind and red currant jelly into the casserole, scraping the bottom of the casserole with the spoon to be certain you have as much flavor as possible. Bring to a boil and then pour the sauce over the hot hare and serve at once.

Serves 6.

144

Jägerbraten Hubertus

(Hunter's Roast St. Hubertus)

MARINADE

1 onion, chopped coarsely

1 carrot, sliced finely

8 juniper berries, crushed

4 c. (1 l) red wine, dry

5 peppercorns, crushed

1 bay leaf

MEAT

1½ lb. (750 g) beef (topside)

salt and pepper

2 Tbsp. butter

3 strips of bacon, lean, well smoked

½ c. (125 ml) sour cream

1 Tbsp. red currant jelly

Mix all the ingredients for the marinade together in a large bowl. Put the meat into it and let it marinate for 24 hours in the refrigerator. Turn meat over a few times while marinating.

Remove meat and dry with a paper towel. Save marinade. Season with salt and pepper.

In a heavy casserole with a lid melt the butter and brown the meat thoroughly on all sides. Add 1 cup (250 ml) of the marinade, cover the meat with the bacon and braise in the covered casserole in a hot oven 375°F (190°C) for 1½ hours to 1 hour 40 minutes. During this time turn the meat over a couple of times and pour extra marinade over it.

When the meat is cooked, put the cooking juices through a sieve or purée them and put in a saucepan over low heat. Season sauce with salt and pepper, add the sour cream and red currant jelly.

This is best served with braised red cabbage, steamed apples and dumplings, spätzle or mashed potatoes.

Serves 4.

This recipe is somewhat unusual, since recipes with St. Hubert usually involve game meat. However, this recipe uses beef and prepares it as one would prepare a venison roast, by marinating it in red wine and spices and making a sour cream based sauce. It is an easy recipe that tastes exquisite.

145

St. Ignatius of Loyola

IGNATIUS was born in 1491 in the Basque hill country near Loyola as the youngest of eleven children of a nobleman. He was baptized Iñigo after a Spanish Benedictine saint. Iñigo was raised to be a soldier and fought in a war against the French. He was injured at the siege of Pamplona in 1521 by a cannonball. This injury and bad surgery left him with a permanent limp. During his recovery he was given as reading material a book on the life of Christ and one on lives of the saints. This reading inspired him to become a knight in the service of God.

After his recovery he made several pilgrimages, including one to the Holy Land. He returned to Spain, and at the age of 33 he began his studies, changing schools several times and finally ending up in Paris, where he received a master of arts degree in 1534.

It was in Paris that he attracted his first six like-minded disciples. In 1534 they took a vow of poverty and chastity and dedicated themselves to the service of God. Initially they intended to work in the Holy Land but were prevented from getting there. Iñigo decided to put his company in the service of the pope under the name the "Company [or Society] of Jesus". The Society moved to Rome, and Ignatius, who took this Latin name in 1537, drew up constitutions for the Society, which received papal approval in 1540. Against his will he was elected general of the Society in 1541.

Ignatius remained in Rome for the rest of his life and oversaw a miraculous expansion of the Society until his death in 1556. By then the Jesuits, as the new order was commonly called, numbered over a thousand and worked in many countries, especially the foreign missions in the Americas and the Far East. Ignatius was canonized in 1622.

The influence of St. Ignatius and his Jesuits is far-reaching. His book of *Spiritual Exercises* has had a profound influence on Catholics through the centuries.

Ignatius is the patron saint of retreats. In art he is generally shown in a black robe. His feast day is July 31.

146

Ignacio

(Cake for St. Ignatius Day)

6 egg whites
2½ c. (625 g) sugar
4 c. (400 g) almonds, ground
1½ c. (200 g) flour
1 c. (250 g) butter

In a large bowl beat the egg whites with an electric beater until quite firm. Slowly add the sugar while continuing to beat. After the sugar has been used up, fold in the ground almonds and the flour. Melt the butter; when cool, add it to the mixture, folding it in carefully.

Use an ungreased large round cake pan, about 10 inches (25 cm) in diameter and 5 inches high. Pour in the mixture. Preheat oven to 350°F (175°C) and bake on a low rack for about 1½ to 1¾ hours, or until a wooden skewer inserted comes out clean.

Makes 12 to 16 servings.

A Spanish Jesuit gave this recipe to a German friend of mine. This cake is baked in the Basque country for the feast day of St. Ignatius, but it is also known in other parts of Spain. It is very rich and somewhat similar to the "Tart of St. James".

147

St. James (Apostle)

JAMES, brother of St. John the Evangelist and the son of Zebedee, is called the Greater to distinguish him from the other apostle with the same name, who, because he was younger, is called James the Less. James the Greater was born in Galilee and was by trade a fisherman, working with his father and brother. James was among the first apostles, and he is mentioned several times in the Gospels, such as at the Transfiguration and at Gethsemane.

Where James preached after Jesus' Ascension cannot be determined from the early Christian writers. St. James was the first of the apostles to die. Around 43 he was beheaded at Jerusalem under King Herod Agrippa I, who started a persecution of Christians to increase his popularity.

Tradition in Spain, where he is called Iago, has it that St. James made a visit during his lifetime to that country. He was buried at Jerusalem, but again, according to Spanish tradition, his remains were transferred to Spain and found a permanent home in Santiago de Compostela. The relics are still there, and the cathedral at Compostela is even today the center of many pilgrimages.

The popularity of James in Spain increased tremendously in the twelfth century, when he was reportedly seen helping the Spanish in their battles against the Moors. His reputation as a defender of Christianity helped spread his fame all over Europe. In England alone 414 churches were dedicated to James. The feast day of James the Greater is July 25. It comes as no surprise that he is the sole patron saint of Spain. He is also patron of some of the former Spanish dominions, such as Guatemala and Nicaragua, and also of Chile. He is the patron saint of druggists and pilgrims. The pilgrim's hat and stick, and the scallop shell are all associated with James, and they can be seen in the paintings of many artists.

Scallops are called in French "Coquilles Saint-Jacques" and in German "Jakobsmuschel", and recipes containing scallops make up the majority of those associated with St. James. Scallop dishes and a special tart made in Compostela are included in the following recipes.

COQUILLES SAINT-JACQUES AU GRATIN
(Broiled Scallops with Cheese)

2 lbs. (900 g) scallops
salt and pepper
1 c. (250 ml) white wine
¾ lb. (350 g) mushrooms
4 Tbsp. butter
1 Tbsp. lemon juice
½ c. (125 ml) onion, chopped finely
6 Tbsp. flour
½ c. (125 ml) whipping cream
4 Tbsp. parsley, minced
1½ c. (200 g) Swiss cheese, grated

This is the classic scallop dish found in many cookbooks, but without the mashed potato border that is often added.

Wash scallops, and put in a saucepan with enough water to cover. Add a bit of salt and pepper and simmer gently for about 5 to 10 minutes until scallops are just opaque throughout. The cooking time depends on the size of the scallops. Remove from heat, let scallops cool in the liquid. Drain 1 cup (250 ml) of the cooking liquid into a measuring cup, add the wine to make 2 cups (500 ml) of liquid. Cover scallops and chill.

Wash and slice mushrooms. Melt half the butter in a pan and sauté the mushrooms, add the lemon juice and cook until mushrooms are golden brown and all liquid has evaporated. Set aside in a small bowl.

To the frying pan add the remaining butter and the onion. Cook over medium heat until onion is soft but not brown. Stir in flour and cook until bubbly. Remove pan from heat and whisk in the reserved liquid until no lumps are visible. Return to the heat and bring to a boil, stirring; cook until thickened. Add the mushrooms, cream and ⅓ of the cheese. Stir until well blended.

When the sauce is cold, stir in scallops with the parsley and adjust the seasoning with salt and pepper.

Divide scallop mixture evenly among 6 to 8 ramekins or scallop shells and sprinkle the top with the remaining cheese. Cover and chill (up to 24 hours maximum) until ready to bake.

To bake, preheat oven to 400°F (200°C). Bake uncovered until the sauce begins to bubble and the edges are beginning to brown, which should take about 12 to 15 minutes.

Serves 6 to 8.

St. Iago Pork Chops

6 pork loin chops, thick, ½ lb. each
1 Tbsp. oil
1 onion, finely chopped
2 Tbsp. rum, light
3 Tbsp. soy sauce
½ c. (125 ml) tomato catsup
1 c. (250 ml) chicken stock
1 tsp. pepper, freshly ground
2 c. (250 g) rice, cooked

Trim fat from the chops. Heat the oil in a large frying pan that can hold all the chops comfortably. Sauté chops on both sides until lightly browned. Remove and set aside.

In the remaining oil sauté the onion until lightly browned. Remove onion and set aside. Discard any leftover fat. Pour the rum into the pan and scrape off any brown bits. Add soy sauce, catsup, chicken stock and pepper and bring to a boil while stirring thoroughly to blend the ingredients. Add the onion and the chops. The chops should be close together but not overlapping.

Cover and simmer gently until the chops are tender, about 1 hour. If the sauce becomes too thick, add more stock or water.

Put 1 pork chop on a plate and heap 3 or 4 tablespoons of the hot cooked rice on top. Pour a little bit of sauce over the rice, some more around the meat and serve.

Serves 6 people.

This recipe from Jamaica is an easily prepared dinner with a Caribbean flavor.

Brochettes de Coquilles Saint-Jacques
(Broiled Scallops on a Skewer)

32 scallops, medium
½ c. (125 ml) dry white wine
salt and pepper
4 shallots
¾ c. (175 g) butter
2 Tbsp. parsley, chopped
16 thin slices of bacon
2 Tbsp. wine vinegar
1 Tbsp. chives, chopped
1 Tbsp. chervil, chopped

Wash and dry scallops thoroughly. Put the wine in a saucepan with a little salt and pepper, add the scallops and bring to a boil. Simmer for 5 minutes over low heat. Drain and reserve 2 tablespoons of the liquid.

Chop the shallots finely. Cook half of them gently in 2 tablespoons of butter without allowing them to change color. Add the chopped parsley, stir and remove from heat.

With a pastry brush, coat the scallops with that mixture. Cut the bacon slices in half lengthwise and wrap the scallops in them, then thread them onto skewers.

Melt 4 tablespoons of butter, brush the bacon-wrapped scallops with this and broil them under a medium grill for 14 minutes, basting them with more butter if necessary and turning them frequently.

While the scallops are under the grill, prepare the sauce. Put the remaining chopped shallots in a pan with the reserved poaching liquid and the vinegar. Bring to a boil and simmer until the liquid is reduced by half. Away from the heat whisk in the remaining butter, cut in small pieces, until it is perfectly blended and the sauce is smooth. Add the herbs and put the sauce in a warmed server.

Serve brochettes and sauce separately. Saffron rice or plain buttered rice go well with this dish.

Serves 4 to 6, depending on appetite.

This recipe is a Flemish dish from the Belgian Cookbook *and is a popular first course even for people who generally do not care for scallops.*

151

This is a simple, classic French dish from the Hotel Maxim in Paris.

Coquilles Saint-Jacques au Safran

(Scallops with Saffron Sauce)

2 lb. (1 kg) scallops
5 Tbsp. butter
1 shallot, chopped
2 pinches of saffron
salt and pepper
2 large tomatoes
½ tsp. brandy
½ tsp. dry vermouth
¼ lb. (125 g) mushrooms
1½ c. (400 ml) whipping cream
4 Tbsp. Hollandaise sauce

Wash the scallops and put them in a pan with a tightly fitting lid. Add half the butter, the shallot, saffron, and salt and pepper to taste and cook over medium heat for 4 minutes. Remove scallops and set aside.

Peel, seed and chop the tomatoes. Now add the tomatoes, brandy, vermouth and mushrooms to the pan and simmer for 15 minutes. Add the cream and remaining butter in small pieces, a piece at a time. Reduce this sauce while stirring constantly. When the sauce is smooth, add the scallops and reheat them. Bind the mixture with the Hollandaise sauce.

Serve at once with rice pilaf or French bread.

Serves 4 to 6.

152

Soufflé Saint-Jacques

SOUFFLÉ

16 scallops, small

1¼ c. (300 ml) milk

4 Tbsp. butter

7 Tbsp. flour

salt and pepper

½ c. (50 g) Cheddar cheese, grated

4 eggs

TOMATO SAUCE

4 Tbsp. onion, finely chopped

1¾ c. (400 g) tomatoes, canned

1 bay leaf

1 Tbsp. Worcestershire sauce

½ tsp. garlic, minced

pinch of thyme

sugar

salt and pepper

This light and easy-to-make first course is impressive in addition to tasting excellent.

First prepare the tomato sauce by combining the onion with the rest of the ingredients in a small sauce pan. Bring to the boil, then lower heat and simmer for about 20 minutes. Strain the sauce and put aside.

Over low heat gently poach scallops in the milk for about 5 minutes. Remove scallops from milk and set aside, but save milk. Melt butter in a small saucepan and, when completely liquid, remove from heat and stir in the flour. Add the reserved milk, return to the heat and, while stirring constantly, bring it to a boil. Continue stirring until it has thickened. Add salt and pepper and then stir in the grated cheese. Let cool slightly.

Separate eggs, beat the yolks and add them to the cheese sauce.

Butter 4 deep scallop shells or ramekins. Slice scallops through the middle horizontally and place 4 halves in the bottom of each ramekin. Beat egg whites until stiff and fold into the cheese mixture.

Divide soufflé mixture between the ramekins and place them on a baking sheet. Bake in a hot oven 400°F (200°C) for about 10 minutes, or until well risen.

Reheat tomato sauce. When the soufflé is ready, spoon some of the sauce over it, reserving the rest to serve separately.

Serves 4 persons.

A superb recipe from Keith Floyd's book FLOYD ON FRANCE. *This casserole is simple but delicious and makes an excellent hors d'oeuvre.*

CASSOLETTE DE SAINT-JACQUES À LA NORMANDE

(Normandy Casserole)

32 mussels
4 Tbsp. butter
¼ lb. (125 g) scallops
4 shallots
1 Tbsp. garlic, minced
2 Tbsp. calvados
60 shrimp, cooked
¼ tsp. paprika and thyme
salt and pepper
4 Tbsp. whipping cream

Steam mussels in a small amount of slightly salted water until they open. Reserve liquid.

In a pan melt the butter and gently heat the scallops with the finely chopped shallots and the garlic for 6 minutes.

Pour the calvados over the scallops and ignite. When flames die down, add the mussel juices, the shrimp, paprika, thyme, salt and pepper.

Reduce over medium heat for 3 minutes. Add the whipping cream and mussels and heat gently. Serve in ramekins with a slice of lemon and fried bread.

Serves 2.

154

Coquilles Saint-Jacques en Waterzooi

4 Tbsp. butter
4 Tbsp. carrot, chopped finely
4 Tbsp. onion, chopped finely
4 Tbsp. leek, chopped finely
4 Tbsp. celery, chopped
½ c. (125 ml) dry white wine
½ cup (125 ml) fish stock
1 bouquet garni
1½ lb. (675 g) scallops
2 egg yolks
6 Tbsp. cream

Melt the butter in a large saucepan and gently cook the finely chopped vegetables without browning them for 5 to 10 minutes.

Add the wine and simmer for 3 minutes. Add the hot fish stock and the bouquet garni and, with a lid on, simmer gently for 15 minutes.

In the meantime wash and dry the scallops. Slice them thickly if they are too large. Poach the scallops 8 to 10 minutes in the stock over low heat. Beat the egg yolks and cream together. Remove the bouquet garni from the liquid. Check that the scallops are done; they still should be firm, not mushy.

Remove from heat, stir in the egg and cream mixture and return to a gentle heat, stirring until the liquid thickens slightly. Do not boil or sauce will curdle.

Serve with crusty bread as an appetizer or with rice for a main dish.

Serves 6 as an appetizer or 4 if used as a main dish.

This is a Flemish dish less known than Lobster Waterzooi. It is an excellent appetizer, though it also makes a nice main course.

155

Coupe Saint-Jacques

(Ice Cream Cup St. James)

fresh fruit in season
lemon sherbet

Put any mixture of fresh fruits in season in a parfait glass. Pear, grapefruit, orange and dark grapes or strawberries make a delicious combination.

Spoon the lemon sherbet over the fruit. Top with a spoonful of chocolate syrup, if desired.

This is a quick and easy dessert for summer.

Tarta de Santiago

(Tart of St. James)

This is a famous Spanish recipe from Santiago de Compostela, the reputed burial place of St. James.

4 eggs
1 c. (240 g) sugar
1¼ c. (150 g) flour
½ c. (125 g) butter, softened
½ c. (125 ml) water
2½ c. (250 g) almonds, ground
1 tsp. lemon rind, grated
powdered sugar

Preheat oven to 350°F (175°C). Cream the eggs with the sugar until pale yellow, light and fluffy. Add flour, butter and water. Beat with an electric beater for 15 minutes. Add almonds and lemon rind. Pour the mixture into a round, greased cake pan 10 inches (25 cm) in diameter and bake in the preheated oven for 30 to 40 minutes until done. Test for doneness with a wooden skewer. Serve sprinkled with powdered sugar and cut into wedges.

Serves 6 to 8.

POTAGE SAINT-JACQUES

(Soup à la St. James)

¼ lb. (125 g) scallops
½ c. (125 ml) white wine
1 bay leaf
6 peppercorns
1 shallot, sliced
1¼ c. (300 ml) water
3 leeks; about 1 lb. (500 g)
⅓ lb. (170 g) potatoes sliced thinly
4 Tbsp. butter
2¼ c. (600 ml) milk
salt and pepper
2 egg yolks
½ c. (125 ml) cream
accompaniment: fried croutons

Wash the scallops and place in a pan with the wine, bay leaf, peppercorns, shallot and water, and poach gently for 5 to 7 minutes. Set aside.

Slice the white part of the leeks thinly and cut the green part of 2 leeks into shreds. Blanch the shreds in boiling salt water, refresh with cold water, drain and set aside for a garnish. Slice potatoes thinly.

Melt the butter in a stew pan, add the white leeks and potatoes. Cover and simmer gently for 6 to 7 minutes. Pour on the milk and bring to a boil. Simmer for 15 to 20 minutes. Add the strained liquid from the scallops and season to taste with salt and pepper. Put in a blender and purée.

Slice scallops thinly.

Return to a clean pan, blend egg yolks and cream together and add this mixture slowly to the soup. Stir over gentle heat until thickened, remove from heat, add scallops and the blanched green leek. Serve with fried croutons.

Serves 6 to 8.

This is an easy but elegant soup that makes the perfect start to a fancy dinner.

TIMBALES DE COQUILLES SAINT-JACQUES

(Scallop Timbales)

TIMBALES

1 lb. (500 g) white fish fillets

½ c. (125 ml) whipping cream

1 tsp. salt

½ tsp. pepper

3 egg whites

SCALLOPS

¾ lb. (300 g) scallops

4 Tbsp. butter

1 pinch (⅛ tsp.) cayenne pepper

1 tsp. garlic, minced

1 Tbsp. parsley, minced

1 Tbsp. tomato paste

¼ c. (60 ml) whipping cream

SHELLFISH SAUCE

2 Tbsp. onion, chopped fine

2 Tbsp. carrot, chopped fine

6 freshwater crayfish with shells on, or shell of one lobster

4 Tbsp. butter

1 c. (250 ml) brandy

4 Tbsp. dry white wine

2¼ c. (600 ml) fish stock

4 Tbsp. tomatoes, chopped

1 Tbsp. tomato paste

salt and pepper

3 Tbsp. flour

Here is a classic French recipe for fish served with a scallop in the center of a ramekin. Topped with a special sauce, this dish makes a good appetizer and it is not difficult to prepare. The fish and scallops should be very fresh.

If the fish fillets have skin on them remove it. Purée the fish fillets in a blender and put them into a cold mixing bowl. Stir in ½ cup (125 ml) of the cream, season with salt and pepper. Separately, beat egg whites until stiff.

Fold egg whites into the fish mixture. Butter the inside of 6 to 8 ramekins (timbales) and fill halfway with the mixture. Make a small depression in the middle of each for the scallops.

Fry the scallops gently in the butter with the cayenne, garlic and parsley and add the tomato paste and the remaining ¼ cup cream.

Divide this among the ramekins, putting it in the prepared depressions. Top with the remaining fish mixture. Poach in a bain-de-marie for 30 minutes at 300°F (150°C).

Tip out of the ramekins and serve with hot shellfish sauce.

Sauce: To make this sauce, fry the onion and carrot in half the butter until they turn golden. Add the crayfish or lobster shell. Flame with the brandy and pour in the white wine. Reduce this mixture by a third. Add fish stock and simmer gently. Next add the tomatoes and tomato paste, salt and pepper and cook for a further 30 minutes.

Pour this mixture through a very fine sieve to remove any pieces of shell. Put the sauce in a blender and liquidize. Melt the remaining butter, add the flour and cook it for 1 minute. Take off the heat and add the sieved liquid and stir thoroughly. Put back on heat and bring to simmer, stirring all the time. Adjust seasoning if necessary.

Serves 6 to 8 as an appetizer.

This is a recipe from a famous
NOUVELLE CUISINE *cookbook*
by the Troisgros brothers,
Jean and Pierre.

MACQUERAUX SAINT-JACQUES

(Mackerel with Scallops)

8 mackerel fillets

8 scallops, large

salt and pepper

2 tomatoes

4 Tbsp. butter

4 Tbsp. carrot, chopped fine

1 tsp. garlic, minced

2 shallots

32 coriander seeds

5 Tbsp. dry white wine

1 Tbsp. lemon juice

2 Tbsp. parsley, chopped

Make two slits in each fillet. Slice each scallop and season with salt and pepper. Insert scallop slices into the slits in the fillets.

Preheat oven to 400°F (200°C). Peel, remove seeds and chop tomatoes. Melt half of the butter in a gratin dish large enough to hold the fillets. Put in the carrots, garlic, shallots and tomatoes together with the coriander, let them soften over medium heat for 2 minutes. Put the mackerel into the dish, pour on the wine and lemon juice and dot with the rest of the butter. Cover with a sheet of waxed paper and bring to a boil.

Cook for 18 minutes in the hot oven. At the end of the cooking time, the sauce should be like a syrup lightly glazing the fish. If the sauce is too thin, pour the liquid into a saucepan and reduce until there are about 8 tablespoons of sauce left.

Taste for seasoning, coat the fish lightly with the sauce and sprinkle with the coarsely chopped parsley. Serve immediately.

Serves 8 persons.

Coquilles Saint-Jacques Aurore

(Scallops with Aurora Sauce)

1½ lb. (750 g) scallops
½ c. (125 ml) white wine
4 Tbsp. water
pinch of salt
1 shallot, sliced
1 bay leaf

SAUCE AURORE
½ lb. (250 g) ripe tomatoes
1 tsp. garlic, minced
pinch of sugar
3 Tbsp. butter, divided
salt and pepper
4 Tbsp. flour
½ c. (125 ml) milk
4 Tbsp. cream

A classic French dish for scallops that goes well with plain rice and vegetables, it can also be served as an hors d'oeuvre.

Rinse scallops and pat dry with a paper towel. Lay the scallops in a pan, and pour the wine and water over them. Add a pinch of salt, the shallot and bay leaf. Poach gently for 5 to 6 minutes. Set aside and prepare the sauce.

Wash tomatoes, but do not peel. Cut in half and squeeze to remove the seeds. Put in a small pan with the garlic, sugar and 1 tablespoon of butter. Season with salt and pepper, cover and cook gently to a thick pulp. Rub through a sieve or purée in a blender. You need about ½ cup (125 ml).

Melt the remaining 2 tablespoons butter, stir in the flour off the heat, strain the liquid from the scallops, blend and add the milk. Stir until boiling, season lightly and gradually add the tomato pulp. Simmer for 3 or 4 minutes, stir in the cream and continue to cook gently until a creamy consistency.

Cut scallops into two or three pieces and add to the sauce. Spoon into deep scallop shells or ramekins and serve immediately. If this is not possible, keep the pan warm in a bain-de-marie until serving time.

Serves 4 persons.

St. Januarius

Giovanni Battistello, 17th century, Certosa di S. Martino, Naples, Italy

St. Januarius, or Gennaro, as he is known in Italy, was the bishop of Benevento toward the end of the third century. Emperor Diocletian was persecuting Christians everywhere, and four of St. Januarius' flock were imprisoned. He went to visit them to encourage them in their faith. Informers subsequently denounced him, and he was imprisoned with his four companions. He was supposedly exposed to wild lions in an arena, but they would not touch him. Eventually he was beheaded in 305. At first his body was kept at Benevento, but because of the threat from the Norman Wars his body was transferred to Mount Vergine and in 1497 to Naples. The earliest reference to St. Januarius is from 431, when he supposedly protected Naples from a threatened eruption of the volcano Mount Vesuvius.

St. Januarius is quite famous for being the patron saint of Naples and for the miracle that occurs there annually. The cathedral in Naples has a flask that reputedly contains some of his blood. When on special occasions this flask is brought close to another relic, believed to be his head, the blood liquefies and changes color from brown to red. There has not yet been a scientific explanation for this phenomenon, which has been observed since the fifteenth century, though this may be due to the lack of an exhaustive scientific study.

Emigrating Neapolitans have brought their patron saint with them to the New World, and in New York the Feast of San Gennaro is celebrated in Little Italy with great fanfare.

The feast day of St. Januarius is September 19, but Naples celebrates its patron saint on December 16. This was the day Mount Vesuvius threatened the city in 1631, a disaster avoided, it is believed, through St. Januarius' intercession.

Pizzette di San Gennaro

(Little Pizzas of San Gennaro)

PIZZA DOUGH
pinch of sugar
½ c. (125 ml) water, lukewarm
1 tsp. dry yeast
1 Tbsp. olive oil
½ tsp. salt
2 c. (250 g) flour

TOPPING
3 tomatoes
4 anchovies
¼ c. (40 g) green olives
1 tsp. oregano, fresh
freshly ground pepper
3 Tbsp. olive oil

Add the pinch of sugar to the water, sprinkle the yeast on top and let stand for 5 minutes. Add the olive oil and salt, stir and pour into the flour. Work the mixture to a smooth dough. Let the dough rise for about 1 hour in a warm location. Preheat oven to 425°F (220°C).

Roll out the dough thinly and cut out circles about 3 inches (8 cm) in diameter. Brush each circle with oil and place on an oiled baking sheet.

Slice the tomatoes and arrange on the circles with the anchovy fillet and the green olives. Sprinkle with the fresh oregano and some freshly ground pepper and brush with oil. (Dried oregano may be used if fresh is not available.) Bake in the oven for about 10 minutes. Serve hot.

Makes about 30 little pizzas.

These small, spicy pizzas are easy to prepare and make good appetizers.

The name of this dish, with a detailed description of the ingredients and the cooking style, was found on the Internet. As I could not obtain the actual recipe, the version given here was created from the description of its ingredients.

It makes a good and healthy entrée that proved extremely popular with my family. One advantage is that it can be prepared easily in less than half an hour.

CHICKEN SAN GENNARO

4 chicken breasts, skinned
salt and pepper
4 Tbsp. olive oil, divided
2 tsp. garlic, minced
½ c. (125 ml) white wine, dry
1 tsp. oregano and basil
½ lb. (250 g) onion
½ lb. (250 g) red bell pepper
1 loaf of Italian bread—foccacia, ciabatta or Italian flatbread

Make sure chicken breasts are free of bones and have no skin. Lightly salt and pepper each chicken breast.

Put 2 tablespoons oil and the garlic into a heavy frying pan and sauté for a few minutes over low heat. Turn up the heat, put chicken breasts into the pan and cook until nicely browned. Turn down heat and remove chicken and keep warm on a plate. Pour the wine into the frying pan, removing all the scrapings from the bottom of the pan. Add the herbs and boil for 1 minute. Pour sauce onto chicken.

Slice onion thinly. Fry in 1 tablespoon oil over high heat until brown and soft. Set aside and keep warm.

Slice the red peppers and sauté in the remaining tablespoon of oil until softened but still crunchy.

Slice bread down the middle and brown in the oven under the broiler.

Cut a slice of the bread large enough to hold the chicken breast, top with a spoonful of the wine sauce, add a quarter of the sautéed peppers and onions. Cover with the top of the toasted bread and serve. Some nice Italian white wine goes well with this dish.

Serves 4.

164

St John the Baptist

ALL THE INFORMATION we have about St. John the Baptist comes from the Gospels. He was born six months before Jesus. His father was Zachariah, a priest of the Temple, and his mother was Elizabeth. According to Luke, an angel told Elizabeth he was to be named John (Lk 1:13). We are told of his birth, circumcision and naming. Then nothing more is reported about John until he started preaching and baptizing in the river Jordan around the year 27. The Gospel reports that he baptized Jesus and recognized him as the Messiah. John had a very austere life-style, living on a diet of locusts and wild honey. He preached repentance and told people to prepare for the coming of the Messiah.

John did not approve of the incestuous marriage of King Herod Antipas and said so publicly. For this he was thrown into prison, and, later, after the famous dance of Salome, he was beheaded, Salome receiving his head on a plate. (This occurred around A.D. 30.) It is believed that John the Baptist was buried at Sebaste in Samaria, but the tomb was destroyed in the fourth century.

St. John the Baptist is one of the earliest saints of the Church, and he is greatly venerated in both the Eastern and the Western Church. His solitary and austere life-style appealed especially to monks, who considered him one of them.

In the Western Church two feast days during the Church year are now celebrated in honor of John the Baptist. The most well-known one, his birthday, is celebrated on June 24, six months before Christmas. In the East his feast is celebrated on January 7 and his conception on September 23.

The figure and life of St. John the Baptist has captured the imagination of many artists. He is often painted as a recluse in the wilderness, or he is shown baptizing people in the river Jordan. His beheading is also the subject of several famous paintings. St. John the Baptist is the patron saint of Jordan.

165

Escalope de Veau San Juán

(Veal Escalopes St. John)

4 escalopes of veal
salt, pepper
3 Tbsp. flour
1 Tbsp. olive oil
16 asparagus tips
4 Tbsp. butter
1 lb. (500 g) cooked lobster tails

SAUCE
2 Tbsp. wine vinegar
1 Tbsp. fresh tarragon
3 Tbsp. onion, finely chopped
1 Tbsp. parsley, chopped
6 egg yolks
1½ c. (350 g) butter

This is a modern recipe from a German cookbook that contains dishes from around the world. This one, from Puerto Rico, combines tender veal with lobster tails, asparagus and a classic French sauce. Spanish tradition meets French cuisine!

Tenderize escalopes by gently knocking them with the back of a large knife. Salt and sprinkle one side with flour. Heat oil in a frying pan and brown each side on high heat, floured side first. Take out the meat and keep warm.

Cook asparagus tips in boiling salt water until tender but still firm. Drain.

Melt butter over low heat, add lobster tails and toss till heated through. Add asparagus tips and toss for a further minute.

To make the sauce, boil vinegar, tarragon, onion and parsley over high heat until reduced to a third. Cool.

In a double boiler gently heat the egg yolks and the cooled mixture. When it begins to thicken, slowly add the melted butter and stir constantly until it becomes a smooth sauce.

Put escalopes on a large serving plate, garnish with the lobster tails and asparagus, and pour the sauce over the servings. Leftover sauce may be served separately.

Serves 4 hungry people.

JOHANNISWEIBL

(St. John's Day Woman)

1 tsp. dry yeast
½ c. (125 ml) milk
4 Tbsp. sugar
3 c. (375 g) flour
4 Tbsp. butter
salt
1 lemon
2 eggs, separated

Dissolve yeast in the lukewarm milk with 1 teaspoon each of sugar and flour. Let stand for 15 minutes.

Put butter, remaining flour and sugar and a pinch of salt in a bowl. Grate the lemon rind and add. Separate the eggs and add the egg whites, reserving the yolks. Add the yeast mixture.

Work all this to a smooth dough. On a flat surface roll out the dough to a thickness of about ½ inch (12 mm). Cover with plastic wrap and let rest for 15 to 20 minutes.

Using a sharp knife, cut out 1 or more figures in the shape of a woman in a skirt, about 6 inches (15 cm) tall. Use the tip of a knife to make marks and indents for eyes, noses, buttons, belt and other decorations. Left-over dough may be worked together again, and more figures may be cut out, or other shapes may be created.

Mix the 2 egg yolks with a pinch of salt and brush the cutouts. Let them dry. Repeat twice more, letting them dry well between brushing.

Preheat oven to 400°F (200°C). Transfer shapes to a greased baking sheet. Bake in the oven for about 20 minutes.

Makes about 4 large figures.

In many parts of Europe it was an old custom to make special breads for the feast day of a saint and give it to the poor. Often these breads had unusual shapes. This is an example of such a bread that in Germany was given out on June 24, the feast of the Birth of St. John the Baptist.

The pods of the honey locust tree are called St. John's bread in some European countries. Because of their sweetness, these pods are ground and used as a chocolate replacement. In North America this is known as carob powder.

HONIG-JOHANNISBROT LAIB
(Loaf with St. John's Bread and Honey)

2 tsp. sesame oil
1 c. (300 g) honey
2 c. (300 g) whole wheat flour
2 tsp. baking powder
2 tsp. baking soda
pinch of salt
1 egg
½ c. (125 ml) water or milk
¼ c. (30 g) carob powder, for dough
1 Tbsp. orange rind, grated
¼ c. (30 g) carob powder, for dusting

Preheat oven to 300°F (150°C). In a large bowl mix the oil with the honey. Add the flour, baking powder, soda and salt to the mixture and stir until mixed thoroughly. Lightly beat egg with the water and add to mixture. Finally add ¼ cup carob powder and the orange rind and mix until well blended.

Butter a loaf pan and pour the dough into the pan. Dust the top with the remaining ¼ cup of carob powder.

Bake the bread for about 70 minutes. Test with a wooden skewer. The bread is done when the skewer comes out clean.

Makes 2 loaves.

Lasagne al Forno
(Baked Lasagna)

MEATBALLS
salt and pepper
½ lb. (250 g) ground beef
1 Tbsp. olive oil

TOMATO SAUCE
½ c. (125 ml) onion, chopped
2 tsp. garlic, minced
4 Tbsp. olive oil
3 c. (800 g) can of plum tomatoes
1 tsp. salt
1 tsp. sugar
1 tsp. basil
1 tsp. oregano

FILLING
¾ lb. (350 g) lasagna noodles
1 lb. (500 g) mozzarella cheese, diced
6 hard-boiled eggs
½ lb. (250 g) pepperoni sausage
1 lb. (500 g) ricotta cheese
1 c. (140 g) Parmesan cheese, grated

The feast day of St. John is celebrated with different meals in different regions of Italy. Here is a lasagna recipe from Abruzzi that is served there on St. John's Day. This lasagna proved quite popular with my family.

To make the meatballs, mix salt and pepper with the ground beef and shape into tiny meatballs about the size of a large pea. Put the oil in a frying pan and carefully brown the meatballs. Drain off any fat and set the meatballs aside. You may have to do this in batches, since the meatballs may fall apart when crowded.

To make the sauce, sauté the onion and garlic in the olive oil. Chop the tomatoes into chunks. Add tomatoes, their juice, salt, sugar and herbs to the onion and garlic. Let simmer for 30 minutes.

In the meantime, cook the lasagna noodles in plenty of boiling salt water until about half done.

In a well-buttered dish arrange about half of the noodles on the bottom. Cover with half the mozzarella, eggs, pepperoni, ricotta, Parmesan cheese, meatballs and sauce. Add second layer of noodles, ending with sauce.

Bake in moderately hot oven 375°F (190°C) for about 30 minutes.

Serves 8 to 10.

This is a very rich dish that is easy to prepare for a crowd.

CHICKEN ST. JOHN

2 chicken broilers, cut into pieces (the pieces may be skinned)
4 c. (1 l) water, hot
½ c. (125 ml) celery, chopped
3 Tbsp. onion, chopped
1 parsley sprig
3 Tbsp. carrot, chopped
1 Tbsp. salt
4 peppercorns
1 bay leaf

SAUCE
2 Tbsp. butter
3 Tbsp. flour
1 c. (250 ml) chicken broth
1 c. (250 ml) whipping cream
½ c. (60 g) Cheddar cheese, grated
1 tsp. salt
generous pinch each rosemary and basil
dash Tabasco sauce
2 Tbsp. butter
½ lb. (200 g) mushrooms, fresh, sliced
1 c. (175 g) almonds, toasted
2 avocados, sliced

170

Place chicken pieces into a heavy pot, add the hot water, celery, onion, parsley, carrot, salt, peppercorns and bay leaf. Bring to a boil; cover tightly and let simmer over low heat for 1 hour. Let chicken cool in the liquid. Strain and reserve 1 cup of broth for the sauce. The leftover broth can be used for other purposes.

To make the sauce, melt 2 tablespoons butter in a saucepan, blend in the flour and cook for 1 minute. Stir in broth and cream. Stir until thick but do not boil. Add cheese, salt, rosemary, basil and Tabasco sauce.

Preheat oven to 350°F (175°C).

Sauté the sliced mushrooms in 2 tablespoons of butter. Place sautéed mushrooms in bottom of a 9 x 13-inch (20 x 30 cm) baking pan, add chicken pieces, and pour the sauce on top. Bake covered for 40 minutes.

To toast the almonds, put them on a baking sheet in the oven until lightly brown, or brown them in a frying pan. No oil or butter is needed, as the almonds have enough natural oil.

During the last 10 minutes, remove cover and top with the sliced avocados and toasted almonds.

Serves 8 to 10.

Lumache con Salsa
(Snails in Sauce)

4 Tbsp. onion, chopped
1 tsp. garlic, minced
2 Tbsp. olive oil
7 oz. (200 g) snails, canned
1½ c. (400 g) can of plum tomatoes
½ tsp. salt
½ tsp. sugar
½ tsp. basil
½ tsp. oregano
pinch of black pepper and cayenne

One of the special delicacies in Rome is snails. This is the traditional Roman dish for St. John's Day.

In a heavy saucepan sauté the onion and garlic in the oil until golden brown. Add the snails and brown them.

Roughly chop the tomatoes and add them with their juice and salt, sugar and herbs to the pan. Cover and let simmer for 30 minutes.

Add the pepper and cayenne. Adjust seasoning if necessary.

Serve with cooked spaghettini.

Will serve about 4 as a main course and 6 as an antipasto.

St. Joseph

JOSEPH is the husband of Mary and foster-father of Jesus. All knowledge about him comes from the Gospels. He was of the House of David, but not wealthy, as evidenced by his carpenter trade. He looked after Jesus from the Child's birth, occasionally helped by angels who advised him in his sleep. Joseph is mentioned only in the early chapters of the Gospels of Matthew and Luke, and his absence in later chapters has led many to believe that he died early.

The cult of St. Joseph began in the East and by the eighth century had spread to the West. St. Teresa of Avila contributed greatly to the popularization of Joseph by naming her first monastery of reformed Carmelite nuns in Avila after him—and by her well-known advice to "Go to Joseph". His feast day, March 19, was until recently a holiday in many countries.

The center of veneration of Joseph in the New World is in Montreal.

Joseph's name is a common choice for a boy's first name, and there are many Josephs around, whether they are called Joe, Giuseppe, José or Sepp.

In art St. Joseph is rarely found alone, but he is easy to find in scenes of the Nativity or with the Child Jesus. The symbols shown with him on statues often depict his trade as a carpenter. St. Joseph is the patron saint of carpenters and of many countries, including Canada, China and Peru.

PAPPARDELLE DI SAN GIUSEPPE
(Noodles for St. Joseph's Day)

½ lb. (250 g) noodles, pappardelle or fettucini
salt
4 Tbsp. olive oil
1 c. (125 g) walnuts, chopped
1½ c. (150 g) fine fresh bread crumbs
4 Tbsp. sugar

Cook the pasta in salted water until tender and drain.

Place the remaining ingredients in a large frying pan over medium heat. Fry till delicately brown while stirring constantly. Remove from heat and toss the cooked and strained noodles in the mixture.

Serve.

As a dessert this will be enough for 6.

Most people associate pasta with savory dishes. Here is a recipe from the Lucania region of Italy for a sweet pasta dish that proved popular in our house. My children thought that adding a little maple syrup made it a tasty Canadian version of the dish.

TOTANO AL FORNO
(Baked Red Snapper)

1 red snapper 3–4 lb. (1.5 kg)

FILLING
2 c. (200 g) bread crumbs, fresh
2 Tbsp. Romano cheese, grated
4 Tbsp. parsley, chopped
2 tsp. garlic, minced
4 Tbsp. green onion, chopped
½ c. (125 ml) olive oil
2 Tbsp. currants

TOPPING
1 lemon, tomato, onion
2 Tbsp. garlic, minced
4 Tbsp. parsley, chopped
salt and pepper

This recipe from Sicily is served on the feast day of St. Joseph. It can be made with any large fish.

Clean the fish, wash well and pat dry. Mix the next 7 ingredients for the filling together and stuff the fish. Place fish on a rack in a large roasting pan. Place thin slices of fresh tomato, lemon and onion over fish. Sprinkle more chopped parsley and garlic all over the fish. Salt and pepper to taste.

Bake uncovered at 350°F (175°C) for about 1 to 1½ hours. If fish appears dry, add some water. (This dish can be made with other fish, such as trout or salmon.)

Serves about 6 persons.

173

On March 19 in Sicily the women of a parish prepare a big table of food for the poor, since St. Joseph is the patron saint of the needy. Thirteen places are set, and twelve poor boys are invited as guests to represent the apostles. The centerpiece of the table is the huge loaf of bread for which the recipe is given here.

The quantity here is half of the original recipe to allow the bread to fit into normal household ovens.

PANE DI SAN GIUSEPPE

(St. Joseph's Day Bread)

2 tsp. dry yeast
1½ tsp. salt
½ c. (125 g) sugar
½ c. (125 g) shortening
2 c. (500 ml) lukewarm water
4 c. (500 g) flour
6 eggs
2 Tbsp. sesame or anise seeds

Dissolve yeast, salt and sugar, and melt the shortening in the water. Pour flour into a bowl and make a well in the middle. Drop eggs and a few seeds into the well. Stir slowly, and gradually add the yeast mixture.

Knead mixture until you have a smooth elastic dough. It may be necessary to add some extra water or flour to achieve this.

Brush top with a bit of shortening, cover and leave in a warm place until doubled in bulk.

Punch dough down, and shape into a huge round flat doughnut. As the dough will rise and expand a lot, make sure the hole in the middle is quite large. Place on a large greased baking sheet and sprinkle the remaining seeds on top. Cover and let rest for half an hour. Bake in a preheated oven at 375°F (190°C) until done and golden brown. The bread is done when it sounds hollow when knocked on the bottom.

Serves 10 to 12.

CAPONATA
(Eggplant Appetizer)

1 lb. (500 g) eggplant
1 tsp. salt
½ c. (115 ml) olive oil, for frying eggplant
about ¼ c. (60 ml) olive oil, for frying onions, celery and garlic
1 c. (150 g) onions, chopped
½ c. (100 g) celery, chopped
3 Tbsp. garlic, minced
3 Tbsp. tomato paste
½ c. (100 g) green olives
½ c. (100 g) black olives
2 Tbsp. capers
½ c. (100 g) bell peppers, chopped
1 tsp. brown sugar
2 Tbsp. dry vermouth
2 Tbsp. balsamic vinegar
½ tsp. black pepper
¼ tsp. cayenne pepper
¼ tsp. white pepper
½ tsp. oregano
¼ tsp. thyme
½ tsp. basil
2 Tbsp. sweet wine

This is another recipe from Sicily for the St. Joseph's Day table. Though it is a must for that occasion, it is often served when 2 or more Sicilians get together.

Cut eggplant into ¾-inch (2 cm) cubes and sprinkle with the salt. Allow to sweat for 15 minutes. Wash the salt off with cold water, drain and pat dry with paper towels.

In a large saucepan with lid, cover the bottom with about ½ cup olive oil and fry the eggplant over high heat till lightly brown. Turn frequently. Remove eggplant.

Turn the heat to low, add some more olive oil and the onions. Simmer until onions are clear. Add the celery and garlic, simmer for 5 more minutes. Add the tomato paste and slow fry for 10 minutes, stirring constantly. Add the eggplant and remaining ingredients, except for the wine, and simmer for another 25 minutes. Stir occasionally.

When done, remove from heat, add the wine and allow to cool. Refrigerate.

Serve in small bowls with some crusty Italian bread. Goes well with a hearty red wine.

Serves 8.

175

This recipe from the Campagna region in Italy somewhat resembles its more famous cousin the "Sfingi di San Giuseppe".

ZEPPOLE DI SAN GIUSEPPE

(St. Joseph's Day Puffballs)

DOUGH
4 Tbsp. shortening
1 c. (250 ml) water
1 c. (125 g) flour
3 eggs, small
oil for deep frying

FILLING
4 Tbsp. sugar
6 egg yolks
3 Tbsp. flour
2 c. (500 ml) milk
optional: orange or lemon peel, grated; cherry brandy

Cut shortening into small pieces. Place it with water and flour in a double boiler over high heat, stirring constantly until the mixture thickens. Work into a big hard ball that leaves the side of the pan. Remove from heat. Add eggs one at a time, whisk until smooth. Put dough into a piping bag with a wide nozzle, ½ inch (1 cm).

Oil some waxed paper and pipe doughnut-sized circles onto the paper. Slide the circles off the paper into hot oil and deep fry until golden brown, turning over once. Drain on absorbent paper and cool.

To make the filling, beat sugar and egg yolks until creamy, blend in flour. Slowly add the milk, stirring well. Pour into a double boiler and add some flavoring. Grated orange or lemon peel or cherry brandy is good. Stir constantly with wooden spoon until thick. Remove from heat and whisk until glossy.

Take each doughnut and slice it in half. Put the filling in each half, put the top half back on and top with a candied cherry.

Makes about 15.

STRAUBINGER JOSEFITORTE

(St Joseph's Day Cake from Straubing)

DOUGH

1 lemon

⅔ c. (150 g) butter

¾ c. (100 g) sugar

3 eggs, small

6 Tbsp. milk

2 Tbsp. kirsch or brandy

4 c. (500 g) flour

2 tsp. baking powder

½ tsp. cinnamon

pinch of allspice and nutmeg

FILLING

1¼ lb. (600 g) apples

1 c. (150 g) hazelnuts, whole

3 Tbsp. milk

3 Tbsp. honey

4 Tbsp. sugar

1 c. (100 g) raisins

2 tsp. cinnamon

melted butter

In times past in Bavaria the feast day of St. Joseph was always celebrated in style. It was an official holiday until the 1960s. This recipe, as reported by Erna Horn, is from an old handwritten cookbook from 1835 that was found in Straubing, near Munich.

Grate the rind of the lemon. Mix all the dough ingredients together and work to a smooth dough. Choose a round cake pan about 8 inches (20 cm) in diameter. Roll out the dough and make 5 dough circles, so that they fit into your cake pan.

To make the filling, peel and core the apples and then grate them coarsely. Grate or chop hazelnuts finely. In a bowl mix all the ingredients for the filling together.

Put one of the dough circles into the pan and put a quarter of the filling on top of the dough circle. Distribute the filling evenly and then add the next dough circle. Repeat three more times, finishing with a circle of dough on the top. Brush with some melted butter.

Bake on the lowest rack in a preheated oven at 350°F (175°C) for about 1 to 1½ hours. Test the cake with a wooden skewer. While still warm, sprinkle the top with sugar.

When cool, remove from cake pan. Let the cake stand overnight and cut it the next day.

Serves 8 to 10 people.

This unusual dessert is reminiscent of a good mince pie. The dough is very crumbly, but the ravioli are easy to make and are baked in the oven.

RAVIOLI SAN GIUSEPPE

DOUGH
1 lb. (450 g) flour
½ c. (125 g) sugar
1 c. (225 g) butter
2 eggs
1 tsp. grated lemon rind
pinch of salt
powdered sugar
whipped cream

FILLING
10 prunes
½ c. (125 ml) tea
1 Tbsp. sugar (dissolve in the tea)
½ c. (100 g) pine nuts
1½ lb. (600 g) cooking apples
2 c. (450 g) sugar

To make the dough, put flour and sugar in a food processor. At full speed add the butter in small pieces till well blended. Then add the eggs, the lemon rind and the salt. The dough will be crumbly. Put it on a sheet of plastic wrap, form it into a cylinder and chill.

To make the filling, soak the prunes for a couple of hours in the tea sweetened with the tablespoon of sugar.

Toast the pine nuts under the grill or in a heavy frying pan, watching carefully not to burn them.

The apples should be fairly tart and should fall apart during cooking. Peel and core and slice the apples.

Put a few spoonfuls of water in a saucepan, add 2 cups sugar and dissolve it over low heat, stirring from time to time. After the sugar has been dissolved, add the apples and increase the heat to medium. Do not stir. The mixture should be ready in 15 minutes when the apples have fallen apart and the filling becomes quite dry. During the time the apples are cooking, remove the pits from the prunes and chop the prunes finely. Remove the apple-sugar mixture from the heat, and stir in the prunes and pine nuts. Allow to cool.

Preheat oven to 350°F (175°C). Butter a cookie sheet.

Cut slices of dough off the end of the cylinder, and roll out slightly. Cut out as many 3-inch (8 cm) circles as possible. Put a spoonful of the candied filling in each circle, slightly off center.

Brushing the edges with a little bit of water, fold over to make a half circle and crimp the edges to make a firm seal.

Arrange ravioli on the greased cookie sheet and bake for 10 to 12 minutes. Turn over after 5 minutes. Dust with powdered sugar and serve with a dollop of whipped cream.

Makes 32 to 36 ravioli.

Covezun' di San Giuseppe
(Filled Cookie for St. Joseph's Day)

DOUGH
1½ c. (350 g) sugar
5 c. (625 g) flour
1 c. (250 ml) milk
2 tsp. baking powder
4 eggs

FILLING
½ c. (50 g) bread crumbs, fine
3 Tbsp. grape jelly
¼ tsp. baking powder
2 tsp. cocoa powder
6 Tbsp. cream
¾ c. (150 g) walnuts, chopped
1 Tbsp. grated orange rind
powdered sugar for dusting

From the Abruzzi region of Italy comes this delicacy that is baked for St. Joseph's Day.

To make the filling, put all the ingredients in a saucepan and cook over low heat for about 10 minutes. Stir constantly. Cool.

To make the dough, mix all ingredients and work them by hand into a smooth noodle dough. On a floured surface roll out the dough thinly, about as thick as the back of a knife. Cut out circles about 3 inches (8 cm) in diameter. Place a tablespoon of filling on each circle of the dough, fold over and pinch together the edges of the dough with a fork. Prick each cookie with the fork.

Transfer cookies to a greased baking sheet and bake in a preheated oven 425°F (220°C) for about 8 minutes, till light brown. Dust with powdered sugar.

Makes about 40 cookies.

Charlotte à la St. José

CHARLOTTE
lemon gelatin dessert sufficient to make 2 c. (500 ml)
candied pineapple
20 ladyfingers

PINEAPPLE CREAM
pineapple gelatin dessert sufficient to make 3 c. (750 ml)
½ c. (125 ml) hot water
½ c. (125 ml) pineapple juice
2 c. (500 ml) thick custard
7 oz. (200 ml) can of pineapple
½ c. (125 ml) whipping cream
additional whipped cream for decoration

This variation of a charlotte is a recipe that appeared in one of the many editions of Mrs. Beeton's cookbook.

Use a mold that has straight sides. Prepare the lemon gelatin dessert, and line the bottom of the mold with some of it. When set, decorate with fancily cut pieces of the candied pineapple dipped in the liquid gelatin.

Cover with another layer of cold liquid gelatin. This can be easily done by preparing all of the lemon gelatin at once and putting the mold in the refrigerator while keeping the rest at room temperature.

While the jelly is setting in the refrigerator, make the pineapple cream.

First, dissolve the pineapple gelatin in the hot water and pineapple juice, following the instructions on the gelatin package.

Prepare the custard. (Packaged custard powder is easy to use for this.) When slightly cooled, stir the custard into the pineapple gelatin. Chop pineapple and stir into the mixture. Whip the cream and fold in.

After the gelatin in the mold has set, line the sides of the mold with the ladyfingers. The ends should be trimmed so that they fit closely to the gelatin. Avoid getting crumbs on the gelatin.

Now pour the pineapple cream into the lined mold and allow to set. You may have to push the ladyfingers down a couple of times as they tend to rise. When the cream is fully set, trim the fingers level with the rim. Dip mold into boiling hot water and turn out. Decorate with some piped whipped cream.

Serves 8 to 10 persons.

Note: If you do not like the taste of packaged gelatin dessert, you can prepare the gelatins with lemon and canned pineapple juice with the correct amounts of gelatin for setting the given amounts of liquid. (Do not use fresh pineapple or juice.)

St. Lawrence

FACTS about St. Lawrence are sparse. He was a deacon in Rome who was responsible for giving alms to the poor. Lawrence was killed a few days after Pope Sixtus II was martyred in 258 in the persecution of Valerian. Lawrence's tomb is in Rome in a church called St. Lawrence-Outside-the-Walls.

Although we know few facts, legend has a lot more to contribute. *The Golden Legend* has about five pages devoted to St. Lawrence. It states that he was a native of Spain and that he was killed by being burned on a gridiron. He is said to have performed many miracles before he was put to death.

He was placed on the list of saints very early on and has been a popular saint in many countries. His feast day is August 10, in the heat of the summer in the Northern Hemisphere.

He is the patron saint of Sri Lanka and of students and brewers. In art he is usually shown in his martyrdom on the gridiron, but it is not uncommon to see paintings of him in his role as deacon giving alms to the poor.

St. Lawrence Fried Fish

4 medium onions
4 medium potatoes
½ c. (65 g) flour
1 Tbsp. crushed dried rosemary
1 Tbsp. dill, fresh
1 lb. (400 g) side bacon
4 fish fillets, 6oz. (150 g)
butter
1 c. (125 g) Cheddar cheese, grated

Remove stem and root end of each onion, but do not peel. Wash potatoes and prick with a fork. Wrap each onion and potato in heavy foil and bake at 400°F (200°C) until soft to the touch, 20 to 30 minutes.

Ten minutes before serving, combine flour and herbs on a plate. In a heavy skillet fry bacon until crisp. Set bacon aside.

Roll fillets in flour-herb mixture. Put gently in the hot pan and fry each side for 2 to 3 minutes or until golden brown and encrusted with small bits of bacon.

Serve 1 potato and 1 onion in the foil along with 1 fried fish fillet and some of the bacon. Each guest unwraps his own parcel and butters the vegetables to taste. Provide grated Cheddar cheese for sprinkling on potatoes and onions.

Serves 4.

This recipe comes from a Canadian country inn in Ontario and is really an outdoor recipe to be cooked over a campfire. It has been adapted for the kitchen.

The name comes from fish that were caught in the St. Lawrence River and fried on the banks in lots of bacon drippings.

*This unusual recipe is
from E. B. Vitz' cookbook
A CONTINUAL FEAST*

Bizcocho de San Lorenzo

(St. Lawrence Sweets)

½ lb. (250 g) fresh chestnuts or 6 oz. (200 g) canned chestnut purée
milk, if using fresh chestnuts
¾ c. (200 g) sugar
2 Tbsp. grated orange rind
2 Tbsp. fresh orange juice
6 eggs
1 c. (100 g) cornstarch
orange marmalade
powdered sugar

If you are using fresh chestnuts, cut an X into the shell of each. Cover the chestnuts with cold water in a saucepan and bring them to a boil. Boil for 2 to 3 minutes. Remove from heat. Peel the chestnuts one at a time by removing the hard shell as well as the skin.

Return the peeled chestnuts to the saucepan. Cover with milk and cook them gently until they are soft. Purée them in a blender or push them through a sieve. (All this may be skipped if you use canned puréed chestnuts.)

Combine the sugar, orange juice, orange rind and eggs in a large saucepan. Beat vigorously with a whisk over low heat until the mixture is light and spongy. (This step can be done with an electric mixer.)

Add the chestnut purée and then the cornstarch, a little at a time. Blend thoroughly, then pour the mixture into a generously buttered ring mold.

Place the mold in a pan of hot water (bain-de-marie) in the oven and bake at 350°F (175°C) until the chestnut mixture is set, about 1 hour.

Remove from oven and let cool. When the bizcocho has cooled, turn it out of the mold, and cut it into slices about ¾ inch (2 cm) thick. If you like, spread the slices with orange marmalade. Sprinkle with powdered sugar.

Makes about 20 slices.

PORK LOIN ST. LAURENT

2 5–7 lbs. (2½–3½ kg) pork loins, boneless
3 garlic heads, with cloves peeled
½ bunch shallots
1 c. (250 ml) creole mustard
½ c. light soy sauce
½ Tbsp. ground ginger, or 4 Tbsp. fresh ginger root, minced
½ c. (125 ml) olive oil, extra virgin preferred
½ tsp. white pepper
2 Tbsp. tarragon vinegar
4 Tbsp. fresh basil (optional)
1 c. (250 ml) white wine
¼ tsp. liquid mesquite smoke

Clean the pork loins with a sharp chef's knife, remove most of the excess fat and silver skin. With a fillet knife, punch holes in the loin. Stuff each hole in the pork with a garlic clove, then push a shallot into the same hole, cut the shallot flush with the surface of the meat. Continue with the remaining garlic and shallots. Rub the creole mustard all over the meat.

Use cotton twine to tie the two loins together with the fat side out and the small side of the first loin facing the large side of the second loin, to insure even cooking.

Mix the remaining ingredients in a stainless steel bowl. Marinate the pork loins for at least 6 hours but not more than 24 hours. Turn the loins at least twice during this time.

Preheat a gas barbecue to the highest setting. Cook the loins until they have griddle marks, then insert a meat thermometer and place the meat in a roasting pan. Cover with foil and slow roast in a 275°F (130°C) oven for 2 to 2¼ hours, or until the temperature reads 150°F (65°C). Remove twine and allow meat to cool about 15 minutes, and then slice the meat about ¼ inch thick. Retain drippings from the pan to serve with the meat. Serve with warmed pistolettes. (Pistolettes are small loaves of French bread about 4 inches long.)

Serves 30 to 36 people.

This is one of the few recipes for which there is an explanation of the name: it was created by Chef Émile Laurent Stieffel of Custom Catering in honor of his patron saint. A delicious dish that feeds a large crowd, it can easily be adjusted for smaller quantities.

St. Louis

Louis IX, the son of King Louis VIII and his wife, Blanche, was born in Poissy, France, in 1214. His mother raised him in a religious atmosphere. After his father's death in 1226, his mother became regent of France until Louis came of age in 1234. The same year he married Margaret of Provence, and the couple had eleven children.

The first few years of his reign were spent quelling revolts and consolidating his power in France. In 1248 he went on a crusade, but after initial successes he and his men were taken prisoner and had to be ransomed. He stayed in the Holy Land until his mother died in 1254 and then returned to France. He settled many territorial claims through treaties rather than war. In 1270 he set out on a new crusade but contracted typhoid soon after landing in Tunisia and died near Tunis on August 25.

St. Louis was noted for his personal piety, justice, ability and charity. He founded many religious and educational institutions and supported the establishment of the Sorbonne. During the forty-four-year reign of Louis, France gained many cultural achievements, cathedrals were built and the use of Roman law became standard. Louis was pronounced a saint by Pope Boniface VII, and his feast day is August 25. In art he is shown in royal attire, often with a crusader's cross.

Saint-Louis Nierchen

(Kidneys St. Louis)

1¼ lb. (600 g) kidneys, calf or lamb
6 Tbsp. butter
salt
freshly ground pepper
2 Tbsp. Dijon mustard
1 tsp. lemon juice

Cut kidneys in half, remove white parts. Wash kidneys thoroughly under running water and pat dry.

Melt half the butter in a pan and brown kidneys all over for 5 to 6 minutes. Remove from pan, let juices drip off, then cut off any remaining fat or sinews. Cut kidneys into slices about ½ inch (1 cm) thick.

Heat rest of the butter in a flameproof casserole dish, add kidneys, salt and pepper. Mix mustard with lemon juice and add. Cook over high heat for 2 minutes, stirring constantly. Check seasoning and serve immediately. Best served with pan-fried potatoes and some dry red wine.

Serves 3 or 4 persons, depending on appetite.

This is a recipe from the German cookbook Recipes Collected during a Lifetime, *by A. Burda. This recipe originated in a gourmet restaurant and should appeal to all those who like kidneys and other variety meats.*

St. Lucy

LUCY was a Sicilian lady who died in 304 in Syracuse during the persecution of the emperor Diocletian. The earliest reference to her is an inscription in Syracuse that dates to the year 400. These are the only known facts about St. Lucy.

According to legend, St. Lucy was a wealthy Sicilian who gave her goods to the poor and refused offers of marriage. One of the rejected suitors denounced her to the authorities as being a Christian. The detailed legend of her death, too long to be included here, involved the removal of her eyes and death by burning at the stake.

St. Lucy is a popular saint in Sicily and in Sweden. Her feast day, on December 13, is probably celebrated more in Sweden than elsewhere. This may be due to the existence of a pre-Christian celebration on that day.

In early representation St. Lucy is shown as a virgin, and later the story of her death became the main focus for artists.

Eisbecher Santa Lucia

(Ice Cup Santa Lucia)

½ lb. (250 g) blue grapes
5 Tbsp. Bénédictine liqueur
2 Tbsp. powdered sugar
4 almond macaroons
1 c. (250 ml) whipping cream
a few drops of vanilla
4 c. (1 l) vanilla ice cream
8 Tbsp. chocolate syrup

Wash grapes, cut in half and remove the seeds. Mix the liqueur with powdered sugar, pour over grapes and let stand for a few minutes. Use a rolling pin to break the macaroons into fine crumbs. Whip the cream, add a few drops of vanilla and whip again.

Cut ice cream into 16 cubes, or use an ice cream scoop to make 16 scoops. Distribute half of the ice cream among 8 dessert glasses. Spread grapes and their marinade on top. Cover with remaining vanilla ice cream. Sprinkle the crushed macaroons on top. Distribute the whipped cream over the 8 glasses and put a tablespoon of chocolate sauce on top of the whipped cream. A glacé or maraschino cherry on top will make it look pretty. Serve immediately.

This will serve 8 people.

Santa Lucia Leves

(Saint Lucy's Soup)

½ c. (125 g) rice, uncooked
8 c. (2 l) water
1 tsp. salt
½ c. (125 g) butter
1 c. (200 g) ham, cooked
4 Tbsp. onion, chopped
½ c. (65 g) flour

This Hungarian recipe is very similar to the Italian soup recipes on page 193. However, instead of whole grains, it calls for rice. The rice is used only to flavor the water; it is not put into the soup itself.

In a saucepan with a lid boil the rice in the water with the salt until the rice is quite soft. In another saucepan melt the butter, and fry the finely chopped ham and the onion until glossy. Add the flour and cook for 1 minute.

Remove from heat and strain the water from the rice into the ham-onion-flour mixture. Do not use the rice in this soup. Stir until all lumps have disappeared. Return saucepan to the heat and bring to a boil. Adjust seasoning and serve.

This amount will serve about 8.

189

Santa Lucia Crown

CROWN
½ c. (125 ml) warm water
2 tsp. dry yeast
½ c. (125 ml) warm milk
½ c. (120 g) sugar
4 Tbsp. butter, softened
1 tsp. salt
⅛ tsp. saffron powder
4 c. (500 g) flour
3 eggs, small

ICING AND DECORATION
1 c. (125 g) powdered sugar
4 tsp. milk
½ tsp. vanilla
red and green glacé cherries

In Sweden the feast day of the Sicilian saint Lucy is celebrated with many different customs. One of these is to serve a special bread with candles. Lucy means light, and light is of special importance in Sweden, where the winter is long and dark. There the feast day of St. Lucy is a celebration in the otherwise uneventful Advent season.

Pour half the warm water into a large warm bowl. Sprinkle in the yeast; stir until dissolved. Add remaining water, warm milk, sugar, butter, salt, saffron and half the flour; blend well. Stir in 2 eggs and enough remaining flour to make a soft dough. Add more flour if the dough is too sticky.

Knead on lightly floured surface until smooth and elastic, about 6 to 8 minutes. Place in greased bowl, turning to grease top. Cover; let rise in warm, draft-free place until doubled in size, about 1 hour.

Punch dough down. Remove dough to lightly floured surface; reserve ⅓ of dough for top of crown. Divide remaining dough into 3 equal pieces; roll each to 25-inch (75 cm) rope. Braid ropes. Place braid on greased baking sheet. Form braid into circle; pinch ends together to seal.

To shape top of crown, divide reserved dough into 3 equal pieces; roll each to 16-inch (40 cm) rope. Braid ropes. Place braid on separate greased baking sheet. Form braid into circle; pinch ends together to seal. Cover both braids; let rise in warm, draft-free place until doubled in size, about 1 hour.

Lightly beat remaining egg; brush on braids. Bake in a moderately hot oven at 375°F (190°C) for 15 minutes or until done (small braid) and 25 minutes or until done (large braid). Cover large braid with foil during the last 10 minutes to prevent excess browning. Remove braids from baking sheets; let cool on wire racks.

To make the icing, combine the sifted powdered sugar, milk and vanilla in a small bowl. Stir until smooth.

To decorate the bread, make 6 holes for candles in the small braid. Place small braid on top of large braid and use toothpicks or icing to fasten it. If desired, drizzle with icing and garnish with candied cherry halves. Insert candles in prepared holes.

Serves about 12.

COOKING WITH THE SAINTS

LUSSEKATTOR

(Saint Lucia Cats)

½ c. (125 g) butter
1¼ c. (300 ml) milk
¼ tsp. saffron
1 Tbsp. dry yeast
½ c. (150 g) sugar
5¾ c. (700 g) flour
raisins
1 egg
salt

Melt butter in a pan and add the milk and the saffron. Warm the mixture to body temperature, 98.6°F (37°C). Use a cooking thermometer, because the correct temperature is important. Sprinkle the yeast over the mixture, let stand for three minutes, then add the remaining ingredients (except for the egg and the raisins), which should be at room temperature. Mix into a smooth dough.

Cover the dough with a piece of cloth and let it rise for 30 minutes. Knead the dough, divide it into 25 to 30 pieces and form each piece into a round bun. Let the buns rest for a few minutes, covered by a piece of cloth.

Form each bun into a string, 6 to 8 inches (15–20 cm) long, then arrange the string in a suitable shape, e.g., a figure eight or a double S. Regardless of the shape, the ends of the string should meet. Press a few raisins into the dough. Cover the "Lucia cats" with a piece of cloth and let them rise for 40 minutes. Whip the egg together with a few grains of salt, and paint the "Lucia cats" with the mixture. Bake them for 5 to 10 minutes in a very hot oven at 475°F (250°C) until golden brown.

Makes 25 to 30 buns.

In Sweden the feast of St. Lucy is celebrated with much cooking and baking. One of the foods present this day in every household is the St. Lucia buns or, as they are often called, St. Lucia cats. The design for this yeast bun goes back several centuries.

COOKING WITH THE SAINTS

Cucia

(St. Lucy's Day Soup)

POTENZE STYLE

2 c. (200 g) corn
2 c. (200 g) chick-peas
2 c. (200 g) lentils
2 c. (200 g) whole wheat
water to cover
salt and pepper

Put all ingredients except salt and pepper in a large pot and cover completely with cold water. Bring to a boil and simmer slowly, adding water as necessary and stirring occasionally, until tender. When done, season with salt and pepper to taste. Serve as a snack in small bowls.

Serves 8 to 10.

SICILIAN STYLE

1 c. (100 g) whole grain wheat
1c. (100g) chick-peas
2 bay leaves
4 c. (1 l) water
¼ tsp. salt

Place all ingredients in a large kettle and let simmer slowly for 12 hours, stirring occasionally. Serve with honey and sugar.

Serves 8 to 10.

CALABRIAN STYLE

2 c. (200 g) whole grain wheat
4 c. (1 l) water
salt

Place in a large kettle and boil over low heat for 12 hours, stirring occasionally. Serve with milk and sugar.

Serves 8 to 10.

Cucia is an Italian dialect word meaning "eyesight". Whole grains are supposed to give strength to eyes. This soup is supposed to be the only food taken on December 13, the feast day of St. Lucy. Different regions in Italy have different recipes.

193

St. Luke

St. Luke the Evangelist and author of the third Gospel is known to us from the New Testament. He was born most likely in Antioch (now in Syria) of Greek parents. A physician, he was one of the first non-Jewish converts to Christianity. He may have known St. Paul before his conversion, and we know from his own writings in the New Testament that he accompanied Paul on many of his missionary journeys. Eventually they both ended up in Rome, where Luke started to write his Gospel. It was based on various existing accounts, oral or written, about the life of Jesus. It seems that Luke set out to write a Gospel specifically designed for the non-Jewish Christians. This Gospel may have been finished in Rome sometime between A.D. 61 and 70, and it contains an account of Jesus' birth in Bethlehem and some of the best-known Gospel stories, such as the Prodigal Son.

Tradition holds that St. Luke was unmarried and died at the age of eighty-four. He may have known Mary, and some material in his Gospel may have come from her.

Luke was an artist—and not only with words, because according to tradition he painted an icon of Mary. For this reason he is the patron saint of artists, and because of his profession he is also patron of physicians. His relics are supposedly in Padua or Constantinople, and his feast day is October 18. Artists have depicted him as an evangelist writing or as a painter of Mary.

194

LUKASHERINGE

(Herrings St. Luke)

4 salt herrings
milk
2 c. (500 ml) mayonnaise
1 tsp. mustard, prepared
1 tsp. shallots, chopped
1 tsp. pickles, chopped
1 tsp. parsley, fresh, chopped

Soak herrings in water to cover fish for about 6 hours, changing the water 2 or 3 times. Fillet the fish and put the fillets in a bowl and cover with milk for about 2 hours.

Mix mayonnaise, mustard, shallots, pickles and parsley to a thick sauce. Remove fish from milk and pat dry. Put fillets into the mayonnaise mixture and let marinate for at least 24 hours.

Serve as an hors d'oeuvre. If it is eaten as a meal, serve it with crusty bread and a glass of beer.

Serves 4 as a meal or about 8 as an appetizer.

This is a recipe from a cookbook published in 1924 for salt herrings marinated in a special sauce. It is good for New Year's Eve parties.

195

St. Margaret of Antioch

MARGARET OF ANTIOCH was one of the most popular saints in medieval times. However, because of the lack of historical evidence, in 1969 Rome removed her name from the list of saints whose feasts are universally celebrated, a fate that she shared with St. Catherine of Alexandria and others.

According to legend, Margaret was the daughter of a pagan priest. When she became a Christian, her father turned her out of the house and she became a shepherdess. The governor of Antioch saw her and wanted to marry her, but she refused because she was a Christian. She was then tortured and, according to legend, swallowed by a dragon and eventually beheaded.

The legend reports that she promised before her death that those who invoke her would receive heavenly rewards. This assurance was a powerful incentive to her cult and helped spread her popularity.

Margaret was a favorite subject of artists, especially because of her martyrdom and the dragon legend. Many English churches have a stained-glass window dedicated to Margaret. Margaret is still a very common Christian name for girls. The feast day of Margaret was July 20, and she was a patroness of childbirth.

Margariten Lebkuchen

(St. Margaret's Lebkuchen)

¾ c. (200 ml) sour cream
¾ c. (200 ml) plain yogurt
¾ c. (180 g) sugar
pinch of salt
1½ tsp. coriander
1½ tsp. cinnamon
½ tsp. each cardamom, nutmeg, cloves, allspice
2 tsp. baking soda
3 Tbsp. milk
1 c. (100 g) whole-meal spelt flour
2¼ c. (300 g) spelt flour

Mix the first 4 ingredients together and whisk until foamy. Add spices. Mix baking soda with milk and add to mixture. Finally, add the 2 flours and stir well with wooden spoon until blended nicely.

Grease and flour a 10-inch (25 cm) round cake pan and fill with mixture.

Bake in bottom half of a moderately hot oven at 375°F (190°C) for 35 to 45 minutes. Serve when cool.

Serves 8.

This recipe is from the cookbook of St. Hildegard of Bingen (1098–1179), who believed that spelt was a cure for many ailments. Spelt is an old-fashioned form of wheat that is now available in many health food or natural food stores. If spelt cannot be found, regular whole-wheat flour may be substituted.

COOKING WITH THE SAINTS

AVOCADO SAINTE-MARGUERITE

1 lb. (450 g) fresh cod
2 lemons
salt and pepper
3 avocados
2 onions, medium-sized
3 tomatoes, small
1 Tbsp. sweet pickles, chopped
1 Tbsp. capers
2 egg yolks
2 tsp. hot mustard
¾ c. (180 ml) olive oil
1 Tbsp. Worcestershire sauce

Remove any bone and any skin from the fish. Slice fish thinly, sprinkle with the juice of 1 lemon and some salt and let it sit and marinate for an hour in the refrigerator.

Cut the avocados in half, remove the pit. Hollow out the flesh, leaving a thin layer of flesh on the skin. Rub with the juice from the other lemon to prevent it from darkening. Chop the removed flesh. Chop the fish finely, preferably in a food processor. Chop all other ingredients finely.

Put the egg yolks in a blender with the mustard and, while it is spinning, slowly add the olive oil and the Worcestershire sauce to make a flavored mayonnaise. If you are in a hurry, mustard and Worcestershire sauce may be added to regular mayonnaise to speed up the process, but the taste will suffer somewhat.

Mix the cod flesh, the mayonnaise and the other ingredients with the diced avocado. Taste. The mixture must be well seasoned. Fill the avocado with this mixture. Let it sit in the refrigerator for another 2 to 3 hours before serving.

Before serving, decorate with slices of tomatoes. Serve with butter and slices of rye bread.

Serves 6 as an appetizer and up to 16 if used as an hors d'oeuvre.

This recipe from a gourmet magazine blends fresh fish with an avocado mixture and brings out the best in both. It may be served as a substantial appetizer in the avocado shell or as an hors d'oeuvre spread on crackers or rye bread.

St. Mark

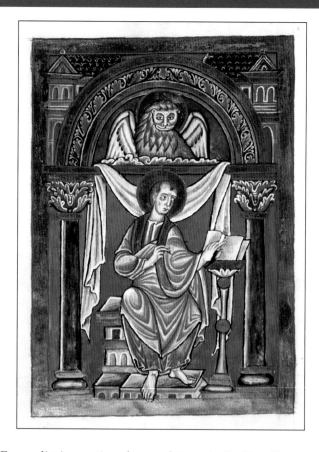

MARK the Evangelist is mentioned several times in the New Testament, either as Mark or John Mark. After the Ascension Mark became a traveling companion of St. Peter, St. Paul and St. Barnabas. The latter was his cousin, and they preached together in Cyprus. Later Mark was in Rome when St. Paul was held captive. He also was held in special affection by St. Peter, who referred to him in one of his letters as his "son". Mark's Gospel was probably written while he was in Italy, and it represents Peter's version of the events.

There is a persistent tradition that Mark went to Alexandria, but other than the date of his martyrdom in "the eighth year of Nero" in 74, very little else is known besides what is in the New Testament.

Early in the ninth century his "body" was moved from Alexandria to Venice, and his relics are still to be found in the famous Venetian Basilica San Marco. Many miracles are said to have occurred during the transfer of his body to Venice, and legends are very numerous.

Mark became the patron saint of Venice, and the symbol that is shown with him as evangelist, the lion, is very prominent in Venice. In art he is usually shown writing the Gospel with the lion at his feet. Many paintings deal with the miracles that occurred during the transport of his relics to Venice.

His feast day is April 25. He is not only the patron saint of Venice, but, because of the connection with Alexandria, he is also the patron saint of Egypt. He is the patron saint of notaries.

Pasta San Marco

SAN MARCO SAUCE

3 Tbsp. olive oil

2 lb. (900 g) chicken meat, skinned, boned and cubed

1 c. (250 ml) onion, diced

1 c. (250 ml) carrot, diced

1 Tbsp. garlic, minced

1 c. (250 ml) chicken stock

3½ c. (875 ml) can of plum tomatoes

1 tsp. oregano

1 tsp. rosemary

¾ tsp. salt

½ tsp. black pepper

1 Tbsp. flour

PASTA

1½ lb. (675 g) fettuccini

1 Tbsp. olive oil

VEGETABLES

1 c. (150 g) green pepper, in julienne strips

1 c. (150 g) red pepper, in julienne strips

2 c. (300 g) broccoli florets

1 c. (150 g) zucchini, sliced

1 c. (150 g) yellow squash, sliced

3 Tbsp. olive oil

This recipe from the Internet is a delightful light pasta dish. Without the chicken it is quite suitable for vegetarians.

To make the sauce, preheat a large, heavy pot over moderately high heat and add the oil. When the oil is fragrant, add the chicken pieces and sauté, turning frequently for 5 minutes till lightly browned on all sides. Add the onions and carrots and sauté, stirring constantly until translucent. Add the garlic and sauté for 30 seconds. Add the chicken stock to the pot, and loosen all ingredients sticking to the bottom. Add all other ingredients, lower the heat to a gentle simmer and cover. Stir occasionally until the chicken is tender but not soft, about 10 minutes. Adjust seasoning.

In the meantime cook the pasta. When finished, toss in the oil to prevent it from sticking.

At the same time prepare the vegetables. Cut the peppers into julienne strips, the broccoli into small florets. Slice the zucchini and squash into ¼-inch (6 mm) thick slices and then halve them.

Add the oil to a heavy saucepan and sauté the vegetables until just crisp-tender.

Mix together pasta, sautéed vegetables and sauce in a large bowl. Serve immediately.

This recipe will easily feed 8 people.

This old Bavarian recipe certainly uses a lot of marzipan in the dough and the icing. Marzipan is sometimes sold as almond icing. If you can find some imported marzipan, the almond flavor will not be as strong as with almond icing.

MARKUSBROT
(St. Mark's Bread)

St. Mark is supposedly associated with marzipan, which comes from the Latin marci panis, meaning "bread of Mark". More a cake than a bread, it was traditionally cooked for St. Mark's Day.

CAKE

1 Tbsp. dry yeast

4 Tbsp. milk

⅔ c. (150 g) butter

4 c. (500 g) flour

½ c. (120 g) sugar

4 eggs

1 c. (100 g) raisins

½ c. (100 g) mixed peel

½ c. (100 g) almonds, chopped

3 Tbsp. rum

½ c. (100 g) marzipan

ICING (optional)

1 c. (200 g) marzipan

1 egg white

1 tsp. sugar

1¾ c. (200 g) powdered sugar

water

Soak the yeast in the lukewarm milk for 10 minutes until frothy. Melt the butter. In a large bowl mix all the ingredients together and knead to a smooth dough, adding more milk as needed. The dough should be soft. Turn out on a pastry board and knead dough for about 5 minutes. The long kneading time will make the dough smooth without large air bubbles.

Shape the dough into a loaf, or put it in a bread pan. Let stand in a warm place until doubled in bulk.

Bake in a preheated oven on a low shelf at 350°F (180°C) for about 45 minutes or until done. Test with a wooden skewer by inserting it in the middle of the cake.

If you want to put on the icing, roll out the marzipan so it fits on the top of the cake. Lightly beat the egg white with the sugar and brush the cake while still slightly warm with it and put the rolled-out marzipan on top. Mix powdered sugar with water to make a thick paste and cover the marzipan with this mixture.

Serves 8 to 10 people.

San Marco Roast

2 Tbsp. olive oil
½ c. (125 ml) onion, chopped
1 tsp. garlic, minced
1 c. (250 ml) meat stock
3½ lb. (1.5 kg) beef roast, boneless
3 Tbsp. flour
3½ c. (875 ml) canned tomatoes, crushed
1 tsp. salt
1 tsp. black pepper
2 Tbsp. wine vinegar
1 Tbsp. dill weed

Heat the olive oil in a large pan that can be covered. Add chopped onion and garlic and sauté until translucent and slightly brown. Add meat stock and simmer for 10 minutes.

In the meantime cut the meat into large 3-inch (8 cm) cubes. Sprinkle the meat with the flour. When the meat stock has finished simmering, add the meat, tomatoes, salt, pepper, vinegar and the dill to the pan. Simmer over low heat for 2 to 3 hours, until meat is tender. Adjust seasoning and serve with noodles or mashed potatoes.

Serves 6 to 8.

A simple recipe found on the Internet from the kitchen of Carole Woodard. (This recipe has been slightly modified.) Great for a slow cooker.

St. Martha

MARTHA, her sister Mary and their brother Lazarus are mentioned in the Gospels of Luke and John. When Jesus visited their house at Bethany, Mary listened to his teaching. Martha rebuked Jesus for not asking Mary to help her prepare the meal. Jesus reproved Martha, saying that Mary was doing the one necessary thing.

Martha is mentioned again in the Gospel of Luke in connection with the raising of Lazarus, when she recognized Jesus as the Son of God. Martha received little recognition until about 1200, when the relics of a Persian nun named Martha, who had been martyred about 347, appeared in Provence. These relics gave rise to the legend that Martha and the two Marys and Lazarus evangelized Provence and that Lazarus was the first bishop of Marseille. This legend, without any historical foundations, gave the cult of Martha great support, especially since it was also reported in the 13th-century collection titled *The Golden Legend*.

Martha is the patron saint of housewives and lay sisters. She is usually shown with her attributes, a ladle, a broom or a ring of keys. Artists painted her in the house preparing the meal or at the raising of Lazarus. Her feast day in the West is July 29.

204

Tarte à la Citrouille Sainte-Marthe

(Pumpkin Pie St. Martha)

3 eggs
¾ c. (200 g) sugar
1½ c. (375 g) pumpkin purée
½ c. (125 ml) milk
½ tsp. salt
½ tsp. ginger
½ tsp. nutmeg
½ tsp. cinnamon
4 Tbsp. cold water
1 Tbsp. gelatin (1½ envelopes)
1 pre-baked piecrust

If you have to use sweetened pumpkin purée, reduce the amount of sugar in the recipe by half.

Separate the eggs. Beat the egg whites until fluffy, add half the sugar and continue beating until smooth. Set aside.

In another bowl beat the egg yolks with the other half of the sugar until the mixture thickens and becomes pale. Add the pumpkin purée, milk, salt, ginger, nutmeg and cinnamon. Continue beating until mixture is smooth.

Transfer mixture to the top of a double boiler and cook it for 7 to 8 minutes until it thickens.

Sprinkle the gelatin on top of the cold water and let it soak for 5 minutes. Add gelatin to the contents of the double boiler and stir until it is dissolved.

Let the pumpkin mixture cool to room temperature, then carefully fold in the beaten egg whites with a spatula.

Pour into the pre-baked piecrust and refrigerate for 4 hours or until firm and set.

Serves 6.

This recipe from Quebec is for a quick no-bake pumpkin pie that firms in only 4 hours in the refrigerator.

St. Martin of Tours

A. van Dyck,
16th century,
Staatsgallerie,
Stuttgart, Germany

MARTIN OF TOURS was born around A.D. 316 in Hungary, where his father was a pagan Roman officer. He was sent to Pavia, Italy, for his education and at the age of 15 joined the Imperial cavalry. He wanted to become a Christian and joined the catechumens, but he soon realized that his commitment to Christ would prevent him from serving as a soldier. After protesting and objecting to military service, he was imprisoned and eventually discharged. From that time stems the famous episode about cutting his cloak in half and giving half to a naked beggar, who in a dream revealed himself to be Jesus.

Martin became a disciple of St. Hilary at Poitiers, was baptized and traveled to Hungary and Italy. After Hilary's return to Poitiers, Martin joined him, living as a monk. Many disciples joined him in what was effectively the first monastery in France. He remained there until 372, when by acclamation he became bishop of Tours. Even as a bishop he continued to live as a monk, and he founded many other monasteries. His influence on Western monasticism and on the development of the Church in Britain and Ireland is far-reaching, because of the many priests who came under his influence.

Martin died in 397, after having been bishop of Tours for twenty-five years. He was one of the most popular saints in Europe during the Middle Ages. His feast day is November 11; he is the patron saint of soldiers and one of the patron saints of France. In art the most common image of Martin is as a soldier on horseback giving his cloak to the beggar, but other images can also be found in early stained-glass windows.

MARTINSHÖRNCHEN

(St. Martin's Day Croissants)

¾ c. (200 ml) milk
1 tsp. dry yeast
4 c. (500 g) flour
3 Tbsp. sugar
¼ tsp. salt
3 eggs
¾ c. (200 g) butter
2 egg yolks
½ c. (125 g) coarse sugar

Heat milk to lukewarm and dissolve the yeast. Sift the flour into a bowl, make a well in the middle and add the yeast mixture and sugar and salt. Work to a smooth dough and let rest for 1 hour in a warm place.

Add the eggs and half the butter and work it back into a smooth dough. Some flour may have to be added if the dough is too sticky. Melt remaining butter.

If you cannot get coarse sugar, crush sugar cubes with a rolling pin. On a floured surface roll out the dough to a thickness of about ⅛ inch (3 mm). Cut into 8-inch (20 cm) squares. Brush with butter and sprinkle with the coarse sugar.

Starting from one corner, roll up each square and turn in the ends to make croissant shapes. Brush with egg yolks and sprinkle with more sugar. Preheat oven to 400°F (200°C). Transfer croissants to a buttered baking sheet and bake for about 25 minutes.

Makes 12 to 16 large croissants.

This is a recipe from Saxony in Germany for sugared croissants that were given out to children as a special treat on St. Martin's Day.

This is a recipe for a coffeecake served in the Abruzzi region of Italy on the feast day of St. Martin. It is popular with children because of the special trinket that is supposed to be found under each serving.

Pizza di San Martino

(St. Martin's Day Cake)

2 tsp. dried yeast
1 c. (250 ml) lukewarm water
5 c. (625 g) flour
1 lemon or orange
2 eggs
1 c. (250 ml) lukewarm milk
1 tsp. salt
½ c. (125 g) melted butter
1½ c. (150 g) seedless raisins

Dissolve the yeast in water. When it begins to bubble, stir in about ¼ of the flour and let rise for an hour.

Grind the rind of the orange or lemon. After 1 hour, add the remaining ingredients and stir until well blended. Let rise in a warm place for 1 hour. Preheat oven to 400°F (200°C).

Punch down the dough and beat for about 3 minutes. Place in a large well-buttered round cake pan. Bake in the oven for about 45 minutes.

Before serving the cake, place a wrapped trinket, such as a coin or a ring, under each piece.

Serves 8 to 10.

St. Martin's Torte

(Gateau Saint-Martin)

4 eggs
½ c. (120 g) sugar
3 Tbsp. hot water
1 c. (125 g) flour
½ tsp. baking powder
2 c. (500 ml) whipping cream
4 Tbsp. powdered sugar
1 tsp. vanilla
¾ c. (75 g) ground almonds
4 Tbsp. brandy
1½ lb. (700 g) blue grapes

Separate eggs. In a bowl whisk egg yolks, sugar and water until creamy. Beat egg whites until stiff. Fold the flour and baking powder into the egg-yolk mixture and then fold in the egg whites. Grease a 10-inch (25 cm) round cake pan, cover the bottom with waxed paper. Pour in the mixture and bake in a preheated hot oven at 350°F (180°C) for about 35 minutes. When cool, remove paper at the bottom and cut cake into 2 layers.

Whip the cream until stiff peaks form, then add the powdered sugar, vanilla and ground almonds.

Sprinkle the brandy over the top and bottom layers of the cake. Cut the grapes in half, remove seeds. Spread half the cream mixture and half the grapes over bottom layer of cake. Put on the top. Garnish the outside of the cake with the remaining cream and grapes.

Serves 8 to 10.

This recipe, from a German cookbook published in the early 1970s, combines cream flavored with almonds and sugar with the tartness of blue grapes.

209

This recipe from Chef John Folse is available on the Internet.

CRABMEAT ST. MARTIN

½ c. (125 g) butter
4 Tbsp. onions, chopped
4 Tbsp. celery, chopped
4 Tbsp. green onions, chopped
1 Tbsp. garlic, minced
2 Tbsp. flour
3½ c. (875 ml) whipping cream
2 Tbsp. dry white wine
1 Tbsp. lemon juice
Tabasco sauce
4 Tbsp. Parmesan cheese
salt
cayenne pepper
4 Tbsp. red pepper, diced
1 lb. (500 g) crabmeat
4 Tbsp. parsley, chopped

In a heavy-bottomed saucepan, melt butter over medium heat. Add onions, celery, green onions and garlic. Sauté 3 to 5 minutes until vegetables are soft, but do not brown them. Sprinkle in the flour, blending well into the mixture. Heat cream in a separate saucepan, but do not boil. Whisk hot cream into the vegetable mixture and stir constantly until a thick sauce is achieved. Reduce heat to simmer, add white wine, lemon juice and a dash of Tabasco sauce. Add Parmesan cheese, stirring constantly, so mixture will not scorch. Season to taste using salt and cayenne pepper. Add red pepper. If mixture is too thick, some more cream may be added. Remove from heat and fold in the crabmeat.

Place in ramekins, garnish with parsley and serve with garlic croutons or crackers.

Serves 6 for lunch and about 10 if served as an hors d'oeuvre.

MARTINSENTE
(St. Martin's Day Duck)

1 duck about 4 lbs. (1.8 kg)
1 tsp. salt
1 tsp. marjoram
pinch of ground caraway
½ c. (125 g) butter
1 Tbsp. brandy

STUFFING

6 (100 g) slices of stale white bread
2 Tbsp. milk
1 duck liver
½ c. (100 g) bacon, finely chopped
2 cans (100 g) anchovies
½ c. (50 g) mushrooms, chopped
pinch of nutmeg
pinch of thyme
2 bay leaves

In Germany, Sweden and other European countries, a goose or duck was the standard dish for the feast of St. Martin. Ducks and geese are supposed to be best between the end of September and the beginning of February. This is a modern German recipe for an old, traditional dish.

Clean and wash duck, remove giblets if necessary and keep the liver for the stuffing. Prick the skin with a fork if the duck appears to be very fatty.

Mix salt, marjoram and ground caraway and rub it over the inside of the duck.

Drain oil from anchovy fillets, pour milk over anchovies, and let them soak for 5 minutes. Drain but reserve the milk.

Prepare stuffing by chopping the bread into large cubes. Soak these with the milk. Mix in the chopped liver, the chopped anchovies, chopped mushrooms, chopped bacon and the remaining spices. Stuff duck with this mixture.

Melt butter in a roasting pan on the stovetop and brown the duck on all sides. When it has been browned sufficiently, turn the duck breast-side down, cover the roasting pan and transfer it into a preheated 350°F (175°C) oven. Roast for 15 minutes and then turn the duck over. Baste with the juices.

Repeat this procedure every 15 minutes until the duck is done. Total cooking time is 2½ to 3 hours. Before serving, brush duck with the brandy and return to the oven for 5 minutes.

Serves 4 to 6.

St. Mary Magdalen

MARY MAGDALEN is mentioned several times in the Gospels, first as a sinner who was possessed by "seven devils". After becoming a follower of Jesus, she stood by the Cross during the crucifixion. She went to anoint Jesus in the tomb, and he appeared to her on Easter morning.

A legend in the East tells us that Mary Magdalen went to Ephesus with Mary and John the Evangelist and died there. In the West, especially in France, there is a legend that Mary Magdalen, Mary and her sister Martha, and their brother Lazarus arrived in Provence and evangelized that area.

Mary Magdalen's role in the Gospels and her presence at the important moments in Jesus' life made her a very popular and easily recognizable saint over all of Europe in the Middle Ages. Almost every artist's painting of the crucifixion shows Mary Magdalen at the side of the Cross. She can also be found in scenes of the Resurrection. Individual paintings show her often with a jar of ointment. Her feast day is July 22.

MAGDALENENSTRIEZELN
(St. Magdalen Fingers)

½ c. (140 g) butter
½ c. (140 g) sugar
3 eggs
3 Tbsp. sour cream
2 c. (280 g) flour
½ c. (100 g) almonds, slivered
½ c. (50 g) cube sugar

Use an electric beater to cream butter and sugar until light. Add eggs 1 at a time and continue beating. Add sour cream. Finally, fold in flour.

Butter baking sheet and spread mixture finger-thick onto it.

To make coarse sugar, crush sugar cubes with a rolling pin. Cover dough with slivered almonds and the coarse sugar.

Bake until golden brown at 350°C (175°F) for about 35 minutes.

While still warm, cut into pieces as long and as wide as a finger.

Makes about 30.

This is an old German recipe for almond-covered cookies. There are quite a few German recipes that associate almonds with Mary Magdalen.

Rindsbraten St. Magdalena mit Kartoffelnudeln

(Braised Beef St. Magdalena with Potato Noodles)

MEAT
½ lb. (200 g) fatty salted bacon
4½ lb. (2 kg) beef, topside, boneless
salt and pepper
5 Tbsp. oil
4½ lb. (2 kg) beef or veal bones
5 Tbsp. carrot, chopped
5 Tbsp. celery, chopped
5 Tbsp. leek, chopped
4 c. (1 l) dry white wine
1 c. (250 ml) beef stock
1 tsp. thyme
1 tsp. sage and savory
5 Tbsp. gherkins, chopped
½ c. (50 g) dried mushrooms
1 Tbsp. tomato paste
1 Tbsp. flour

POTATO NOODLES
2¼ lb. (1 kg) potatoes, mashed
2½ c. (300 g) flour
2 egg yolks
salt, nutmeg
4 Tbsp. butter
1 Tbsp. fine bread crumbs

This Austrian recipe, which is named for the wine the beef is braised in, St. Magdalena, is a good example of one of Austria's favorite dishes, braised beef.

Cut bacon into thin strips and with a larding needle thread the bacon into the meat. Salt and pepper the meat all over.

Pour the oil in a pan and fry the meat on all sides till nicely brown.

Transfer to a large casserole. In the same pan brown the bones; add them to the casserole. In the same pan soften the vegetables for a few minutes and then transfer them to the casserole.

Heat oven to 400°F (200°C) and put the covered casserole in it for about 20 minutes. Remove casserole from oven, then add the wine, stock, herbs, gherkins, dried mushrooms and tomato paste.

Cover and return to the oven for 1½ to 2 hours.

Remove the bones and take out meat. Skim off any fat from the juice, add the flour and bring to a boil. Purée the sauce or put it through a sieve. Cut meat into slices and serve with some sauce poured over the meat.

To make the potato noodles, mix all the ingredients together to a smooth dough. If the potatoes are fairly new or not very starchy, more flour (½ c. [50 g]) may have to be added. Shape dough into little noodles.

Drop a batch of noodles into boiling salt water and cook briefly for about 1 minute. Be careful not to overcook them. Remove with a slotted spoon and drain. Repeat until all noodles are done. Melt butter, add bread crumbs and brown slightly. Toss noodles in the butter before serving. This, too, should be done in several batches.

Serves 8 to 10 persons.

Magdalenenkuchen
(Magdalen Cake)

This is a German recipe for an interesting 2-layer cake using 2 kinds of dough.

DOUGH (BOTTOM LAYER)
5 Tbsp. butter
1¼ c. (150 g) flour
1 egg, small
5 Tbsp. sugar
1 tsp. vanilla

BETWEEN LAYERS
8 Tbsp. orange marmalade

DOUGH (TOP LAYER)
2 eggs
6 egg yolks
¾ c. (150 g) sugar
1 tsp. lemon rind, grated
1¼ c. (150 g) flour
½ c. (120 g) butter, melted

DECORATION
¾ c. (80 g) powdered sugar
2 Tbsp. Cointreau
1 Tbsp. orange juice
2 Tbsp. butter
¼ c. (50 g) almonds, flaked

To make the bottom layer, cut the butter into small pieces and work all ingredients with your hands to a smooth dough. Refrigerate for 30 minutes.

Butter a 10-inch (25 cm) round cake pan. On a lightly floured surface, roll out the dough into a circle so it fits into the pan. Spread the orange marmalade on top. Preheat oven to 350°F (175°C).

To make the second dough, beat the eggs, egg yolks, and extra sugar in a large bowl until creamy. The best results are achieved when the bowl is heated over a pot with steaming hot water while you beat the mixture. Remove the pan from the heat and continue until the mixture is cool. Add grated lemon rind.

Carefully fold in the flour and then the cooled butter. Pour this on top of the dough in the cake pan.

Put pan on the lowest rack in the oven and bake for 40 minutes. Remove from oven and let cool for 10 minutes. Remove from the pan.

To make the icing, mix the powdered sugar and Cointreau with the orange juice. Spread this over the top of the still warm cake.

In a small frying pan melt the 2 tablespoons butter, and brown the flaked almonds. Let them cool and then spread them on the top of the cake.

Serves 12 persons.

COOKING WITH THE SAINTS

St. Maurice

St. Maurice was an officer in the Roman army, in the Theban legion, which consisted of soldiers recruited in Upper Egypt. Tradition has it that almost the entire legion was made up of Christians. This legion was sent in 287 to a part of Gaul (now Switzerland) and was asked to put down a revolt of the natives. Emperor Maximinian asked all the soldiers to sacrifice to the gods for the military success of the mission.

The Theban legion, because of its Christian members, refused, and Maurice as their officer and spokesman withdrew the legion from the area. According to legend, Maurice and all Christians in the legion were killed for their refusal to participate in the sacrifice. The legend mentions the death of several thousand men. There appears to be a historical basis for the legend of Maurice, but the details written in the fifth century are questionable. Because of the many soldiers put to death with him, his feast is usually referred to as the feast of Maurice and Companions. A church to house their relics was built in the fourth century at what is now Saint-Maurice-en-Valois.

His feast day is September 22, and he is one of the patron saints of soldiers, weavers and dyers. He is the patron saint of Sardinia, Savoy and Piedmont in northern Italy. His name is Moritz in the German-speaking countries and was at times quite a popular boy's name.

In art Maurice is usually shown as a dark-skinned foot soldier escorted by many of his companions.

St. Moritz

DOUGH
2½ c. (300 g) butter
¼ c. (60 g) sugar
3 c. (350 g) flour
½ c. (50 g) almonds, ground
¼ lb. (100 g) chocolate, grated

FILLING
¼ lb. (200 g) chocolate, good quality, melted

To make the dough, blend together butter and sugar until smooth. Add all other ingredients and knead until a smooth ball.

Refrigerate for 10 minutes.

Roll dough into a rectangle with a thickness of ½ inch (12 mm) and put onto a buttered baking sheet. Bake in a moderate oven at 350°F (175°C) for 15 to 20 minutes, till firm and colored but not too brown.

To make the filling, melt chocolate in a double boiler or microwave oven. Cut rectangle in half, spread 1 half with the melted chocolate and place other half on top. Let cool for about 15 minutes until the chocolate has hardened somewhat. With a very sharp knife cut finger-sized pieces. When completely cold, dust with powdered sugar.

Makes 24 to 30 cookies that tend to disappear very quickly.

This recipe is from André Simon's Concise Encyclopedia of Gastronomy, *published in 1952.*

This recipe comes from a hotel in Saint Moritz, Switzerland. The chef who originated it presented it as an entry in the Culinary Olympics of 1960, held in Frankfurt, Germany. This recipe was so special it was awarded a gold medal.

ÉMINCÉ DE VEAU ST. MORITZ

(Curried Veal St. Moritz)

1½ lb. (750 g) veal, sliced thinly
1 c. (250 ml) onion, chopped
4 Tbsp. butter
garlic salt
1–2 Tbsp. curry powder
2 Tbsp. cornstarch
3 c. (750 ml) veal or chicken stock
salt and pepper
4 Tbsp. white wine

The meat should be cut about ⅛ inch (3 mm) thick and into bite-sized pieces.

Chop the onions very fine and sauté in half the butter until transparent. Add a dash of garlic salt. Mix desired amount of curry powder with cornstarch and add to the onions. Stir and cook slowly until blended. Slowly add the stock, stirring constantly until sauce is slightly thickened. Season to taste with salt and pepper. Stir in wine and additional curry powder if desired. Transfer sauce to a baking dish that has a lid.

Season veal with salt and pepper. Sauté in the rest of the butter until lightly brown on both sides.

Add meat to curry sauce and place in preheated 325°F (160°C) oven for at least 1 hour or until ready to serve. Baste occasionally. If necessary, add some more stock or wine in order to have sufficient sauce. Serve over plain rice or rice pilaf with small dishes of coconut, chopped peanuts, or almonds and chutney.

Serves 6.

Zucchini St. Moritz

1 zucchini, about 3 inches (8 cm) in diameter, 12 inches (30 cm) long

1 c. (250 ml) onion, finely chopped

2 c. (200 g) mushrooms, chopped

4 Tbsp. olive oil

2½ c. (300 g) Swiss cheese, grated

1 c. (125 g) brown rice, cooked

1 c. (175 g) walnuts, finely chopped

3 eggs, large, well-beaten

¾ tsp. curry powder

salt and pepper to taste

Boil zucchini in enough water to cover until tender but not mushy, approximately 7 to 8 minutes. Drain, cut off the top third lengthwise and let cool. It is important that the ends of the zucchini are not cut off, otherwise the liquid in the stuffing will run out. Scoop out the seeds first and discard. Scoop out the flesh inside, leaving about ¼ inch (6 mm) of flesh on the shell. Retain 1 cup of pulp. Preheat oven to 325°F (160°C). Sauté the onions and mushrooms in oil about 5 minutes. Drain off excess liquid and transfer to bowl. Blend in zucchini pulp, half of the cheese, the rice, nuts and eggs. Add curry, and salt and pepper to taste.

Heap this mixture into the zucchini shell and sprinkle with remaining cheese. Place in baking dish with a little water and cover with foil. Bake 20 to 30 minutes or until stuffing is set and cheese is melted.

Serves about 6 as a side dish.

This recipe for the ubiquitous zucchini does not use much of the zucchini itself, instead utilizing the shell for baking a rice-cheese mixture.

Stained-glass window,
17th century,
Église Notre-Dame,
Ste-Ménéhould, France

MÉNÉHOULD, or Manechildis, as she is sometimes called, was born in Perthois, France, sometime in the sixth century. She was one of seven daughters of Sigmar, Count of Perthois, all of whom are honored as saints in Champagne. Ménéhould became a nun and received the veil from St. Alpinus. She then lived as a hermitess at Bienville on the Marne, devoting herself to the care of the poor and sick. The village that was next to one of the castles of Sigmar adopted the name Sainte-Ménéhould in the ninth century in honor of her. Her feast day is October 14.

Recipes that bear her name are very similar in the way they are prepared: meat is first poached, then breaded and grilled.

Salmon Sainte-Ménéhould

2 lbs. (900 g) salmon fillets, thick
½ c. (125 ml) white wine
½ c. (125 ml) water
½ c. (125 g) butter
1 Tbsp. onion, chopped
1 tsp. chives, chopped
½ tsp. garlic, minced
½ tsp. thyme
¼ tsp. basil
1 bay leaf
1 clove
½ tsp. pepper
½ tsp. salt

2 egg yolks
1 c. (100 g) fine, fresh bread crumbs
½ c. (125 ml) butter, melted
1 Tbsp. cream

This recipe is a variation on Eel St. Ménéhould, because eel is not easily available and many people have an aversion to eating it. Salmon is widely available, and with some careful handling this makes a lovely dinner.

The salmon fillets should be between 1 inch to 1½ inches (3 to 4 cm) thick. For this recipe the best pieces are those from the tail end of the fish.

Remove the skin from the salmon. Put the pieces in a large, heavy, shallow frying pan with a lid. Add the next 12 ingredients and poach slowly for about a half hour. After the half hour, turn the heat off and let the salmon absorb more of the flavor.

When ready to cook the dish, remove the fillets carefully and put them on a broiler pan. When the fish has dried from its own heat, brush with the egg yolks and sprinkle with bread crumbs. Carefully drizzle with the melted butter, then brush with eggs again and sprinkle with more bread crumbs. (There is no need to turn the fish over when putting on the eggs and bread crumbs—it might easily fall apart.)

Put the broiler pan under the broiler and brown the salmon, but be careful not to burn the bread crumbs.

To make the sauce, reduce the cooking juices until they have the consistency of a sauce. Add the cream and adjust seasoning.

Serves 6 to 8.

COOKING WITH THE SAINTS

This way of cooking various meats was popularized by Elizabeth David, who attempted to introduce new methods into English cooking.

Poulet à Sainte-Ménéhould

(Chicken St. Ménéhould)

3 lb. (1.3 kg) chicken
½ c. (125 ml) white wine
½ c. (125 g) butter
1 Tbsp. onion, chopped
1 tsp. chives, chopped
½ tsp. garlic, minced
½ tsp. thyme
¼ tsp. basil
1 bay leaf
1 clove
½ tsp. pepper
½ tsp. salt
2 egg yolks
2 c. (100 g) breadcrumbs, fine, fresh
½ c. (125 g) butter, melted
1 Tbsp. cream

Cut the chicken in half lengthwise. Put the pieces in a heavy braising pan with a lid. Add the next 11 ingredients and simmer in the oven slowly at 300°F (150°C) for about 30 minutes to 1 hour. Spoon sauce over the chicken frequently so it absorbs the flavor. When the chicken is done, remove carefully and put it on a broiler pan. When it has dried from its own heat, brush with the egg yolks and sprinkle with bread crumbs. Carefully drizzle with the melted butter, then brush with eggs again and sprinkle with more bread crumbs.

Put the broiler pan under the broiler and brown the chicken, but be careful not to burn the bread crumbs.

To make the sauce, reduce the cooking juices (from braising) until they have the consistency of a sauce. Add the cream and adjust seasoning.

This dish can be made with different cuts of meat, such as breast of lamb, pigs' trotters (pigs' feet), pork or turkey.

Serves 4 to 6.

St. Michael the Archangel

MICHAEL THE ARCHANGEL is mentioned in the Old Testament in the Book of Daniel as "one of the chief princes" and as the special protector and guardian of Israel. St. John the Evangelist in Relevation portrays Michael as the principal fighter against the devil, who is in the form of a dragon (Rev 12:7–9). This passage led to the popular image of St. Michael slaying the dragon.

Emperor Constantine built a church dedicated to Michael near Constantinople, but an apparition of Michael on Monte Gargano in Southern Italy in the fifth century and later on at Mont-Saint-Michel in Brittany in the eighth century spread his popularity in the West. The famous Benedictine monastery built at Mont-Saint-Michel in the tenth century commemorates that apparition. The Norman Conquest brought to England abbots and monks who imported their devotion to Michael with them.

The image of the soldier angel fighting for the good cause was a popular one, especially during the crusades. In England many churches are dedicated to St. Michael, and his name is still a very common Christian name.

Artists have found great inspiration in painting the angel Michael fighting the dragon, and this scene is the most predominant representation of him. He has also been painted as the angel handing out judgment by weighing souls.

Michael's feast day traditionally has been celebrated on September 29, and in 1969 Rome combined the archangels' feasts. The feast day is now known as the feast of Ss. Michael, Gabriel and Raphael, Archangels.

Piero della Francesca,
15th century,
National Gallery, London

COOKING WITH THE SAINTS

*This is a French recipe from a
1930 cookbook that specializes in
seafood of all forms.*

Moules Saint-Michel

(Mussels St. Michael)

2 lb. (1 kg) mussels
½ c. (125 ml) white wine, dry
4 Tbsp. onion, chopped
1 shallot, chopped
3 parsley stalks
1 sprig of thyme
1 bay leaf
pinch of pepper
3 Tbsp. butter

SAUCE
1 Tbsp. butter
1 Tbsp. flour
1 Tbsp. parsley, chopped
1 Tbsp. chervil, chopped
1 tsp. prepared mustard

Clean the mussels by scraping off the beard and washing away any
dirt. Put wine and all the other ingredients in a large saucepan with a
lid and bring to a boil over high heat. After 2 minutes shake the pan
and repeat 2 or 3 times until the mussels have been cooked for about 6
minutes. This should open all the mussels. Discard those that did not
open. Drain liquid from the mussels and use for the sauce. Keep
mussels warm in the pan until sauce is finished.

In a small saucepan melt the butter, add the flour and cook for 1
minute. Add the liquid from the mussels and stir until smooth. Add
herbs and remove from heat.

Remove half of each mussel shell and arrange the full halves in a
pyramid shape on a plate. Pour the sauce over the pyramid. Serve with
white wine and crusty French bread.

Serves 4 to 6 as an hors d'oeuvre.

226

TINTENFISCH SAN MIGUEL
(Octopus San Miguel)

MAIN DISH

4½ lb. (2 kg) octopus
1 c. (250 ml) onion, chopped
1 Tbsp. garlic, minced
1 c. (250 ml) olive oil
1 Tbsp. butter
1 tsp. salt
1 tsp. pepper
2 bay leaves
3 c. (750 ml) white wine

SIDE DISH

6 large potatoes
1 green pepper

Wash octopus thoroughly, pat dry and cut into strips. Chop onions and mince garlic and put in a heavy casserole dish. Put octopus strips on top with the oil and butter.

Gently salt and pepper the fish. Cover the dish and bring to a simmer. Let it cook for 30 minutes. Crush bay leaves and add with the wine. Simmer for another 30 minutes. Before serving, check and adjust seasoning.

To make the side dish, clean the potatoes, but do not peel. Cut the seeded pepper lengthwise into thin strips. With a small knife or a skewer make holes in the potato all the way through and fill it with a strip of pepper. Boil the potatoes in salt water and serve as accompaniment to the octopus.

As a main course, this recipe is sufficient for 6.
As an appetizer, it will be enough for 12.

Here is a dish from San Miguel, the largest island in the Azores. It makes a flavorful first course if served with crusty bread.

227

STRUAN MICHEIL

(St. Michael's Bannock)

1¼ c. (200 g) barley meal
1¼ c. (200 g) oat meal
1¼ c. (200 g) rye meal
1 c. (125 g) flour
½ tsp. salt
2 tsp. baking soda
2½–3 c. (750 ml) buttermilk
3 Tbsp. honey or molasses
½ c. (100 g) blueberries (optional)
2 eggs
1 c. (250 ml) cream
4 Tbsp. butter, melted

On the islands of Scotland St. Michael is a very popular saint, and it is an ancient tradition to eat this cake on his feast day. On that day, everyone in the household, family member or visitor, must eat a piece of this large cake baked on a griddle.

Put the barley, oat and rye meal into a large bowl. Add the flour and the salt. Mix well. Stir the baking soda into 2½ cups (625 ml) of the buttermilk, and add to the flour mixture. Stir in the honey, and the berries if desired.

Turn the mixture onto a well-floured board. Mix the ingredients to make a soft dough. Add more flour or buttermilk depending on the consistency of the dough.

Divide the dough into 3, 4 or 5 equal-sized balls, so that each ball when flattened to ¾ inch (2 cm) will fit into a frying pan or griddle. (A heavy frying pan can be substituted for the griddle.) On a sheet of floured waxed paper or foil, roll out 1 ball to about ¾ inch (2 cm) thickness.

Mix together the eggs, cream and melted butter.

Heat the griddle and grease it lightly. Paint the top surface of the bannock with the egg mixture, and put this side on the griddle. Remove the paper.

Cook the bannock over moderate heat, and while this is in progress paint the upper surface of the bannock with the egg mixture. Turn the bannock over and cook. Experienced pancake cooks may want to try flipping it. Repeat this until each side has been cooked and painted with the egg mixture 3 times.

The other dough balls are treated in exactly the same way. The bannocks may be served with butter.

This recipe will serve a lot of friends and neighbors—probably about 18.

Roast Michaelmas Goose with Apples and Prunes

9–11 lb. (4–5 kg) goose, with giblets
salt and pepper
1 Tbsp. butter
½ c. (125 ml) onion, chopped
1 lb. (450 g) prunes, pitted
4 Tbsp. port wine
¼ lb. (100 g) fresh whole meal bread
1 tsp. dried sage
1½ lb. (700 g) apples (Cox, Gala)
1 c. (300 ml) dry white wine

Prick the skin of the goose all over with a fork and pull any fat inside the bird out and reserve it. Rub salt over the skin.

To make the stuffing, melt the butter in a large frying pan, add the chopped onion and cook for 5 or 6 minutes, until softened. Separate the goose liver from the giblets, chop finely and add to the onion, and cook for 2 or 3 minutes.

If the prunes are dry, soak for about 2 hours in slightly sweetened water. Chop one half of the prunes roughly, and stir into the onion with the port. Cover and simmer gently for 5 to 6 minutes. Chop bread coarsely and put into a blender to make fresh bread crumbs. Now add the sage and bread crumbs to the mixture and stir until well blended. Season the stuffing mixture to taste with salt and pepper. Spoon the stuffing into the neck end of the goose, then truss with strong cotton or fine string. Weigh the bird.

Put on a wire rack in a roasting pan. Cover the breast with the reserved fat and then with foil. Roast in a preheated oven at 400°F (200°C) for 17 minutes per pound (40 minutes per kilo) plus an extra 20 minutes. Baste goose frequently during this time.

One and a half hours before the end of the cooking time, remove the foil from the goose. An hour later (30 minutes before the end of the cooking time) drain off the fat and discard. Core the apples and cut into eighths, then add to the pan with the remaining prunes and the white wine. Place bird on top, standing on the roasting rack, and cook uncovered for the last 30 minutes.

Serve the goose with the cooking juices and the apples and prunes. Mashed potatoes and braised red cabbage are the traditional accompaniments.

Serves 8 to 10.

In much of Europe, goose was the traditional fare and was always accompanied by apples, as there were plenty of windfalls at that time.

This is a recipe from Ireland and the north of England. Green geese—those fed on grass rather than grain—were less fatty than Christmas geese, who were fed grain in the last few months before Christmas.

Michaelmas, falling in late September, was throughout Europe a special holiday on which seasonal farm laborers were laid off until the spring. A special feast was served on that occasion.

Gâteau Saint-Michel

GENOESE SPONGE CAKE
6 eggs
¾ c. (200 g) sugar
1 c. (125 g) flour
6 Tbsp. (90 g) melted butter

FILLING
½ c. (100 g) butter, unsalted
1 Tbsp. coffee liqueur

BUTTER CREAM
4 egg yolks
½ c. (125 g) sugar
1 c. (250 ml) milk
¾ c. (200 g) unsalted butter
2 tsp. coffee liqueur
1 tsp. vanilla

DECORATIONS
½ c. (100 g) almonds
coffee beans

This is a recipe for a classic French cake with a subtle coffee flavoring topped with crunchy roasted almonds.

Grease a square 8-inch (20 cm) pan, and line the base with greased waxed paper. Preheat oven to 350°F (175°C).

Combine eggs and sugar in a large bowl, place over a saucepan of simmering water, but do not allow bowl to touch water. Using an electric beater, beat until mixture is thick and creamy, about 10 minutes. Remove the bowl from the hot water, beat the mixture until it returns to room temperature. Sift half the flour over the egg mixture and carefully fold it in. Repeat with remaining flour.

Quickly fold in the cooled melted butter.

Pour mixture into the pan and bake for about 20 minutes until sponge feels elastic to the touch. Turn cake onto wire rack to cool. When cool, remove paper at the bottom and split cake into 3 layers.

To make the filling, soften the butter and blend it with the coffee liqueur. Spread bottom and next layer of cake with this mixture. Assemble cake.

To make the butter cream, put egg yolks, sugar and milk into a double boiler and stir until the mixture has become like a custard.

Let cool to room temperature. Make sure butter is also at room temperature. Add butter in small dollops to the custard and whisk well.

230

Remove ¼ of the cream and flavor with the coffee liqueur. Add the vanilla to the remaining cream and whisk well.

Roast almonds in the oven and chop finely.

Cover top and bottom of cake with the vanilla-flavored cream and smooth it. Sprinkle the cake with the roasted almonds. Pipe the coffee-flavored butter cream for decoration around the cake. To the piped decoration add the coffee beans; use chocolate-covered ones if you can get them.

Serves 8 to 12.

231

Croustilles Saint-Michel

(Fish Sandwich Saint-Michel)

FILLING

1 lb. (500 g) fish, white (fillets)

2 c. (500 ml) fish stock

4 Tbsp. butter

½ c. (125 ml) carrot, chopped

½ c. (125 ml) celery, chopped

4 Tbsp. onion, chopped

4 Tbsp. flour

1 bay leaf

½ c. (125 ml) dry white wine

1 tsp. paprika

salt and pepper

SANDWICH

12 slices of white bread

4 eggs

½ c. (125 g) butter

This is a French hors-d'oeuvre that can be prepared easily for a crowd once the fish sauce has been made. This recipe is from a French fish cookbook of the 1930s.

The fish sauce can be made the day before it is needed; it just has to be reheated before use.

Poach fish in the stock over low heat until it is white and cooked completely. Remove fish and break into small pieces. Reserve liquid.

Melt the butter in a pan and fry the finely chopped carrot, celery and onion until golden brown. Add flour and cook for 1 more minute. Add the stock and bay leaf. Reduce stock to 1½ cups (375 ml).

Add the wine and paprika, and adjust the seasoning with salt and pepper. Remove bay leaf and purée in a blender or put through a fine sieve. The sauce should be quite thick. Put fish into the sauce and keep it warm.

Remove crust from the bread slices. Put some of the fish sauce on one half, but do not make it too thick. Cover with the other bread slice and dip the sandwich into the beaten eggs. Fry this egg-covered sandwich in a pan where the butter is hot and foaming until the sandwich is nicely browned. Serve immediately.

Serves 6 to 8 for lunch.

Côtelettes d'Agneau Saint-Michel

(Lamb Chops St. Michel)

SAUCE

1 bay leaf
parsley stalk
sprig of thyme (¼ tsp. dried)
1 onion, small
6 peppercorns
1 c. (250 ml) milk
1 Tbsp. butter
1 Tbsp. flour
salt and pepper

MEAT

12 lamb chops, rib or loin
salt and pepper
flour
4 Tbsp. butter
½ c. (125 ml) onion, finely chopped
6 artichoke bottoms, parboiled
6 pastry tart shells, pre-baked
lemon for garnishing

This is a recipe from the famous French chef Paul Bocuse. It is fairly easy to make and has an unusual combination of flavors.

To make the sauce, put the bay leaf, parsley, thyme, sliced onion and peppercorns into a small saucepan together with the milk. Bring slowly to a boil, remove from heat and let stand for a few minutes. Strain the milk into a container.

Melt the butter in the saucepan, add the flour and stir until smooth. Remove pan from heat, gradually add the milk while stirring constantly. When well blended, return to heat and stir until sauce thickens. Season with salt and pepper.

Sprinkle chops with salt and pepper, dredge in flour and brown on both sides in 3 tablespoons of the butter. Put chops on serving dish and keep warm. Boil onion for 3 minutes in hot water, drain well. Cook the onion in the remaining tablespoon of butter, along with the quartered artichoke bottoms, but do not brown.

Add this mixture to the sauce. Spoon into the tart shells and arrange them on the serving platter with the chops. Garnish with a lemon.

Serves 6.

St. Nicholas

NICHOLAS lived in the fourth century and was bishop of Myra, now in southwestern Turkey. Nothing else is of historical certainty, though his veneration in the East can be traced to the sixth century. A fictitious biography written by Methodius in the ninth century contains all the miracles and legends we now associate with St. Nicholas.

Before Myra fell to the Moslems in 1087, Nicholas' relics were taken to Bari, in Italy, where a large church was built in his honor and consecrated by Pope Urban II. For this reason he is sometimes referred to as Nicholas of Bari. From that time his cult spread all over Europe and was especially strong in Holland and Belgium. In Holland he has a helper who hands out cookies before the arrival of St. Nicholas on December 6.

The invention of Santa Claus can be traced back to the legend of Nicholas and his love for children. The custom of the Dutch Protestants who founded New York of giving presents on his feast day was combined with Nordic folktales about a magician punishing naughty children while rewarding good ones. This gave us the present-day image of Santa Claus.

The legends as written by Methodius are responsible for the many different images of St. Nicholas found in art, showing the many miracles attributed to him. Nicholas is one of the patron saints of Greece and Russia. In addition, his duties include being patron saint of children, sailors, perfumiers and pawnbrokers. Each of these patronages can be traced to a specific legend.

The feast day of Nicholas is December 6, a day celebrated widely in continental Europe, especially among the Dutch.

Speculaas

1 c. (240 g) sugar
1 c. (160 g) brown sugar
1 c. (250 ml) shortening
½ c. (125 g) butter
½ c. (125 ml) condensed milk
4 Tbsp. cinnamon
1 pinch each nutmeg, cloves, salt
4 c. (500 g) flour
1 tsp. baking soda
½ c. (100 g) slivered almonds, crushed

Mix together the sugars, the shortening and the butter. Add the condensed milk and spices and gradually blend in the flour and baking soda. Crush the almonds with a rolling pin and mix in. The dough will be somewhat stiff. Roll into logs covered with plastic or waxed paper.

Leave in refrigerator overnight.

Cut into slices and place on a lightly greased cookie sheet. Bake in preheated oven at 375°F (190°C) for around 10 minutes. Traditionally Speculaas are imprinted with some pattern created by a wooden mold. If you imprint the cookies with such a mold, they will look better.

Makes about 80 cookies.

This is an old Dutch recipe for the special cookies that St. Nicholas brings and that are consumed between December 6 and Christmas.

235

This traditional recipe from
Poland was originally associated
with St. Nicholas' Day.
Nowadays it is connected with
the entire Christmas period.

CIASTKA MIODOWE
(Honey Cakes)

½ c. (125 ml) honey
½ c. (125 ml) sugar
3 eggs (1 whole, two separated)
4 c. (500 g) flour
1 tsp. baking soda
½ tsp. cinnamon
½ tsp. nutmeg
¼ tsp. cloves, ground
¼ tsp. ginger
50 almond halves, blanched

Warm the honey slightly and combine with the sugar. Separate 2 eggs
and set the white of one aside to use on the following day. To the
honey mixture add 1 whole egg and 2 egg yolks and beat well. Sift the
flour with the soda and spices and stir into the honey batter
thoroughly. Let the dough rest overnight.

Roll dough to ¼-inch (6 mm) thickness; cut out shapes with a cookie
cutter. Brush with the slightly beaten white of an egg and press half a
blanched almond into each cookie. Bake at 375°F (190°C) for about 15
minutes.

Makes about 50 cookies.

St. Nicholas Pudding

PUDDING
½ c. (125 g) butter
½ c. (120 g) sugar
1 orange
2 eggs
¾ c. (90 g) flour
½ tsp. baking powder
½ c. (50 g) bread crumbs
½ lb. (200 g) plums, pitted
4 Tbsp. prunes, pitted, chopped
1 tsp. cinnamon
2 Tbsp. golden syrup
6 plums or prunes, halved and pitted (for decoration)

PLUM SAUCE
1½ lb. (750 g) plums
1 c. (240 g) sugar

A typical English pudding that is subtly flavored with orange, this recipe uses fresh plums in the dough and is steamed for several hours. This may have been what Jack Horner of nursery rhyme fame ate at Christmas.

Cream the butter and sugar together until light and fluffy, then add the grated orange rind. Add the eggs gradually to the butter mixture. Sift the flour with the baking powder, mix with the bread crumbs and fold into the mixture. Stir in the juice of the orange, the plums and prunes and the cinnamon.

Grease a bowl with butter, coat the bottom of the bowl with golden syrup and arrange the halves of the 6 plums or prunes on top in a circle. Carefully spoon the pudding mixture into the bowl.

Cover with foil and waxed paper, secure with string and steam for approximately 2 hours.

To make the sauce, cover the bottom of a saucepan with a little water and slice the plums into it.

Simmer gently to prevent sticking. Remove pits, then purée the cooked plums in a blender before straining.

In a separate pan dissolve the sugar slowly with 4 or 5 tablespoons of water. When the sugar is dissolved, stop stirring and turn the heat up to full. Boil until golden brown, then remove from heat. Carefully stir in 6 tablespoons of water—the caramel can spatter. Put back on low heat until the lumps have dissolved. Add the puréed plums and cool a little.

Turn the pudding out and serve with its special plum sauce poured over it.

Serves 6 to 8.

Nikolausstiefel

(Boots of St. Nicholas)

This recipe makes a gift for the children; it used to be handed to them on St. Nicholas Day in Germany.

DOUGH
1 tsp. dry yeast
1 tsp. sugar
¾ c. (150 ml) milk, lukewarm
4 c. (500 g) flour
5 Tbsp. butter
5 Tbsp. sugar
½ tsp. vanilla
1 egg
1 pinch salt

EGG WASH
1 egg yolk
1 Tbsp. milk

DECORATION
Sesame and poppy seed, almonds, sunflower seeds, or nuts
powdered sugar, licorice, sweets, etc.

Mix yeast, sugar and milk in a bowl until yeast is dissolved and let it stand for 15 minutes.

Add the flour to the bowl, melt the butter. Add sugar, vanilla, egg, salt, and melted butter to the flour. Work to a smooth dough first by stirring, then kneading. Put in a warm place until doubled in bulk.

In the meantime take some cardboard and cut a template for a boot about 14 inches (40 cm) high. Roll out the dough about ½ inch (1 cm) thick in the shape of an L. Put the template on top and cut the dough into the shape of the boot. Transfer the boot to a greased baking sheet.

Make the egg wash by mixing the egg yolk and milk. Brush the boot with the egg wash. Shape the rest of the dough into the rim and heel of a boot and put on top. Brush again with egg wash and put on the seeds, almonds or nuts.

Preheat oven to 400°F (200°C) and bake the boot about 25 minutes until golden brown.

After it is cool, you may want to decorate the boot further by mixing some powdered sugar with water and sticking on extra sweets.

PEPERNOTEN

(Peppernuts)

2½ c. (300 g) flour
1½ tsp. baking powder
½ c. (75 g) brown sugar
1 egg yolk
4 Tbsp. water
¼ tsp. cinnamon
¼ tsp. nutmeg
¼ tsp. cloves
pinch of salt
¼ tsp. anise seeds

Knead all ingredients into a soft ball. Butter two baking sheets. Form about 50 marble-sized balls. Place them on the two sheets, so that they are the same distance from each other. Flatten each ball slightly.

Bake at 350°F (175°C) 20 minutes or until done. The cookies will be very hard, but they will get softer as they get older.

Makes about 50 peppernuts.

In Holland St. Nicholas visits the children on December 6 accompanied by his faithful helper "Black Peter". He, or a black gloved hand, distributes the pepernoten to the children by throwing them through the door before the arrival of St. Nicholas.

Tarte Normande Saint-Nicolas

(St. Nicholas Apple Tart)

SWEET SHORTCRUST PASTRY
2 c. (250 g) flour
1 Tbsp. sugar
pinch of salt
4 Tbsp. butter
4 Tbsp. shortening
5 Tbsp. ice water
1 tsp. lemon juice

FILLING
½ lb. (250 g) apples, tart
1 c. (240 g) sugar
1½ tsp. cinnamon
1½ lb. (750 g) apples, sweet
½ c. (150 g) butter
½ tsp. vanilla
2 eggs
¾ c. (90 g) flour
½ tsp. baking powder
2 Tbsp. apricot jam
½ c. (50 g) raisins

This is a recipe from Normandy for an apple and raisin tart flavored with cinnamon. It is best eaten while slightly warm.

First make the pastry. In a medium bowl combine flour, sugar and salt. Cut in butter and shortening until mixture resembles coarse bread crumbs.

In a measuring cup whisk together ice water and lemon juice. Sprinkle over flour mixture until moistened all over. Gather dough into a ball, wrap and refrigerate for at least 1 hour.

Line a 10-inch (25 cm) flan ring or pan with the dough to about 1½ inches (4 cm) high. Keep dough cool while preparing the filling.

Peel and quarter the tart apples. Make applesauce by simmering the apples with 2½ tablespoons sugar, 2 tablespoons of water and the cinnamon.

Peel, core and dice the sweet apples and sauté in a frying pan with 2½ tablespoons butter, 5 tablespoons sugar and vanilla. Cook for 10 minutes on low heat, then allow to cool. Beat the remaining butter with the remaining sugar until creamy. Add the eggs 1 after another, then add the applesauce, the sifted flour and the baking powder.

Preheat oven to 400°F (200°C).

Spread the apricot jam over the bottom of the dough, then place the raisins on top. Cover with the diced sautéed apples. Fill a pastry bag with the applesauce-egg mixture and pipe a spiral on the top to cover the diced apples completely. Bake for 30 minutes, remove from oven and allow to cool for 15 to 20 minutes. While still warm, remove from mold and serve.

Serves 8 to 10.

St. Ninian

T. Apollonio, 19th century,
St. Ninian's Cathedral,
Antigonish, Nova Scotia

St. Ninian is a saint not well known outside of Scotland and Nova Scotia. A bishop and a missionary in the fifth century, he worked in Scotland among the Picts. According to Bede, on whom we rely for much of early British Church history, he was instructed in Rome in "the faith and mystery of the truth".

St. Ninian established a church at what is now Whithorn probably around the year 420. It was built of stone, something perceived as unusual by the Britons of the time. Archeological excavations near Whithorn have found the remains of an early church whose masonry was in fact painted white, which explains the name "Whithorn".

Ninian was sufficiently important in Scotland that an eighth-century author penned a poem about him and his accomplishments. In the twelfth century a story of his life written by an abbot gives a good indication of how Ninian was revered in Scotland.

His burial place was a popular spot for pilgrimages and survived until the sixteenth century. With the emigration of the Scots in the eighteenth and nineteenth centuries, his name was brought to the New World, and there are some churches dedicated to him in Nova Scotia. In art St. Ninian is usually shown as a bishop or priest. His feast day is September 16.

COOKING WITH THE SAINTS

St. Ninian's Gingery Muffins

1½ c. (200 g) flour
1 tsp. baking soda
¼ tsp. salt
¼ tsp. cinnamon
¼ tsp. nutmeg
¼ tsp. cardamom
1 tsp. ground ginger
½ c. (175 g) molasses
¼ c. (65 g) brown sugar
4 Tbsp. butter
½ c. (125 ml) boiling water
1 egg

Preheat oven to 400°F (200°C). Sift together into a large bowl the flour, baking soda, salt and spices. In another bowl combine the molasses, brown sugar, butter and boiling water. Add the liquid mixture to the dry mixture a little at a time. Beat in the egg. Do not overbeat. The batter may be lumpy. Leave it that way for best results.

Pour into buttered muffin pans and bake in the middle of the preheated oven for 20 to 25 minutes.

Makes about 12 muffins.

This recipe comes from a cookbook published in 1971. The association between St. Ninian and this recipe is not known.

243

St. Patrick

Stained-glass window, parish church, Magheralin, Northern Ireland

PATRICK was born around 390, probably somewhere on the west coast of Britain. His father was a deacon, and his grandfather a priest. In his youth he was captured by Irish pirates, taken to Ireland and kept there in slavery as a shepherd. He used this time to pray and after six years was told in a dream that he soon would return to his own country. He escaped or was freed and made his way to a port, probably on the southeast coast of Ireland. Eventually he convinced some sailors to take him with them on their boat. After an adventurous trip, which may have even landed him in France, Patrick returned to his family in Britain, a much-changed person from when he was abducted.

He trained to be a priest, was ordained, probably in Britain, and may have visited France at some point in his life. Patrick was appointed successor to Palladius as bishop of the Irish Christians and returned to Ireland around 435. He worked principally in the north, establishing his see at Armagh, and organized the Irish Church into diocese-like structures, as had been done elsewhere in the Western Church.

Patrick died probably around 461. Three of his writings survive and are the oldest known writings of the British Church. All our knowledge about Patrick comes from these three writings, mainly the very personal *Confessions*. This book shows Patrick as a sincere, humble man with great concern for his Irish flock and a complete trust in God.

Many legends exist about St. Patrick. He is supposedly the saint who expelled snakes from Ireland, who explained the Trinity by using a shamrock, who single-handedly converted Ireland to Christianity and performed other miracles. However, these stories may well be the invention of later monastic writers, mostly from the eighth or ninth century, who used St. Patrick to further the political cause of their bishops. His connection with the shamrock and the green are of even later date, namely, the fifteenth or sixteenth century. The Patrick in artists' representations is generally the Patrick of the legends.

As the patron saint of Ireland, St. Patrick is well known in Europe and all English-speaking countries. Irish immigrants took their favorite saint with them wherever they went. St. Patrick became a symbol of the immigrants' love for Ireland and the Church.

The feast of St. Patrick is March 17.

The recipes associated with St. Patrick fall into two groups. The first considers anything green as appropriate for St. Patrick's Day. This includes mousse or cheesecake colored green with crème de menthe. The second consists of recipes for traditional Irish food, such as corned beef and cabbage, boxty pancakes or recipes whose ingredients are traditionally thought to be Irish. These are potatoes, fish, bacon and, last but not least, Irish ale and Irish whisky. The recipes given here are from this second category and use simple, easily available ingredients

244

St. Patrick's Bacon

1¼ lb. (500 g) potatoes
½ lb. (200 g) onions
salt and pepper
1 egg
1 c. (250 ml) milk
2 Tbsp. butter
4 slices (300 g) bacon (back bacon preferred)

Peel potatoes and cut them into thin slices. Slice onions thinly. Butter a casserole dish and put in alternate layers of potatoes and onions, while seasoning with salt and pepper. The top layer should be potatoes. Beat egg and milk together and pour over the potatoes and onions. Dot with flakes of butter. Put bacon slices on top of potatoes.

Cover casserole and cook in moderate oven 350°F (175°C) for 1 hour. Remove cover and continue cooking for a further 15 minutes.

Serves 4.

Here is a simple recipe with ingredients we now consider standard Irish staples, such as potatoes, onions and bacon. This combination makes a nice light lunch.

Porter Cake

1 c. (250 g) butter
1½ c. (250 g) brown sugar
1¼ c. (300 ml) stout
½ tsp. grated orange peel
2 c. (200 g) raisins
4 c. (500 g) flour
½ tsp. baking soda
2 tsp. allspice
½ c. (100 g) mixed peel
½ c. (100 g) glacé cherries
3 eggs

Over low heat melt the butter and sugar in a pan with the stout. Add orange peel and raisins and boil for 3 minutes. Cool until slightly warm.

Sift the flour, baking soda and spice into a bowl, add fruit mixture and cherries. Whip eggs lightly and then add them gradually to the bowl, mixing well each time. Put mixture into a round greased cake pan. Bake on the bottom rack of a preheated oven at 350°F (175°C) for 1½ hours. Remove from the pan when cooled. Let stand for 24 hours before cutting.

Serves 8 to 10 persons.

This recipe is for an easy-to-make fruitcake that gets better with age. The stout gives the cake a nice brown color and a unique flavor. Though a cake that is often eaten in Ireland for St. Patrick's Day, it is good for any occasion.

245

St. Patrick's Drunken Fisherman's Pie

1 bottle (12 oz.; 350 ml) Irish ale
1 Tbsp. mustard
1¼ lb. (500 g) seafood (a mixture of fish, shrimp, scallops, mussels)
½ lb. (200 g) smoked salmon
1½ c. (150 g) leeks
1½ c. (125 g) mushrooms
4 Tbsp. parsley, finely chopped
3 Tbsp. butter
1 c. (125 g) parsnips
4 Tbsp. onion, chopped finely
1½ c. (375 ml) milk
4 cloves
1 bay leaf
3 Tbsp. flour
1 Tbsp. lemon juice
salt and pepper

TOPPING
1½ lb. (750 g) potatoes, preferably new ones
2 Tbsp. butter
½ c. (125 ml) milk
1 tsp. salt
½ tsp. pepper
1 c. (125 g) cheddar cheese, grated

This is a recipe for a most delicious seafood casserole. It can be prepared in advance, kept in the refrigerator and put in the oven an hour before serving.

As this dish contains fish, vegetables and a topping of mashed potatoes, it is a one-dish meal.

The Irish ale provides a good marinade for the seafood, and the smoked salmon adds some smoky flavor to this dish.

Mix beer with mustard and pour over seafood (except smoked salmon). Marinate for about 45 minutes.

Wash potatoes thoroughly and boil in their skins until perfect for mashing.

Clean and trim leeks into pieces about ½ inch (1 cm) long. Wash mushrooms and slice thinly. Peel parsnips, quarter, and slice thinly like the mushrooms. Chop parsley finely. Melt half the butter in a sauté pan over medium heat, add leeks and mushrooms. Sauté until they just begin to brown, then add parsnips and cook 2 more minutes. Set aside.

Drain seafood from marinade, saving ½ cup (125 ml) of the marinade. Chop onion finely. Steep milk and saved marinade with the cloves, bay leaf and onion for 25 minutes. Strain into a bowl.

Melt the rest of the butter over medium heat, add flour and slowly whisk in the strained liquid. Add all the seafood (including salmon) and cook for further 2 minutes. Add sautéed vegetables, parsley and lemon juice. Season with salt and pepper to taste. Pour mixture into greased casserole dish 13 x 9 inches (30 x 25 cm).

Mash potatoes with the skins on and add butter, milk, salt and pepper.
Pipe or spread this mashed potato mixture over top of casserole.
Sprinkle the grated cheese on top.

Preheat oven to 350°F (175°C). Place casserole in lower half of the oven
and bake for 45 minutes until top is golden brown.

Serves 4 to 6 persons.

247

St. Peter (Apostle)

PETER was a fisherman from Galilee, a native of Bethsaida, who was originally called Simon. His brother Andrew introduced him to Jesus, who gave him the

Jean Ingres, 19th century,
Musée Ingres, Montauban,
France

name Peter. Both Peter and Andrew became Jesus' disciples. In the list of apostles Peter is always in first place, and he was one of the three privileged apostles to witness special events. Jesus gave Peter the "keys of the kingdom of heaven" and told him he was the rock on which the Church would be built. Despite Peter's subsequent betrayal, Jesus always singled him out and later gave him the mission "to look after his flock".

After the Ascension, Peter had the lead role in the development of the early Church and was always present when critical decisions had to be made. The New Testament says many things about Peter, but does not say explicitly that he preached and died in Rome. However, many early witnesses, such as St. Clement and St. Irenaeus, explicitly affirm his presence in Rome. These references and tradition authenticate that he was the first pope; he was martyred under Emperor Nero around A.D. 64.

It is likely that Peter was buried on the Vatican hill at the site now occupied by St. Peter's basilica. His cult became very popular after the Christians were given more freedom to worship under Emperor Constantine, and he was revered greatly by the Church in the West as well as in the East. He is a universal saint, the gatekeeper to heaven, the patron of the Church and the papacy. His main feast day is June 29, a feast he shares with the Apostle Paul, because it is believed that they were put to death on the same day. St. Peter is the patron saint of fishermen.

Peter has been a favorite subject of artists, as there are many images and legends that can be represented: Peter with the keys of heaven, Peter the fisherman, Peter's denials, Peter as bishop and leader of the Church, and finally his martyrdom and other legends.

Peter is a common Christian name throughout the world. In France there is a fish named St. Pierre; in Italy it is San Pietro; in England it has the more prosaic name "John Dory".

Filetti di San Pietro in Salsa di Broccoli

(John Dory Fillets with Broccoli Sauce)

4 Tbsp. butter
2 shallots, finely chopped
1¼ lb. (600 g) broccoli
1 c. (250 ml) fish stock
2 lb. (1 kg) John Dory fillets
salt and pepper
4 Tbsp. whipping cream

If no John Dory fillets are available, sole may be used. Preheat oven to 375°F (190°C). Put half the butter in a pan, add the shallots and a little salt and sauté until soft.

Wash broccoli thoroughly, peel the tough stalks, cut into small pieces and add to the shallots with half the fish stock. Cook until quite tender, adding some more stock whenever the broccoli is cooking without liquid. This should take about 20 minutes. Season with salt and pepper. While the broccoli is cooking, butter an ovenproof dish with the remaining butter and lay the fillets in it. Season with salt and pepper, cover the dish with foil. Bake for 10 minutes.

When the broccoli is done, put it in a food processor with all its juices and purée them. Spoon the purée into a saucepan and add the cream. Bring slowly to a boil and cook over very low heat for 5 minutes, stirring frequently. Taste and adjust seasoning. Keep sauce warm.

Transfer the fillets to a serving dish and surround with the broccoli sauce. Pour the cooking juices from the fish over it and serve at once.

Serves 4 to 6 people.

This is a dish from Italy, very easy to make, for a light and healthy dinner.

249

This is a modern German recipe that is healthy and easy to prepare. Most of this dish cooks in one casserole dish, so there are not many pots to clean.

PETERS FISCHTOPF MIT LIMETTENSAUCE

(Peter's Fish Stew with Limesauce)

STEW

1 lb. (450 g) firm fish fillets
½ lb. (250 g) potatoes
¾ lb. (300 g) cauliflower florets
½ lb. (250 g) asparagus, canned
½ lb. (250 g) shrimp
2 Tbsp. (30 ml) cream or yogurt
5 Tbsp. dry white wine
salt and pepper
2 Tbsp. fresh tarragon chopped
2 Tbsp. fresh chervil chopped

SAUCE

¾ c. (200 ml) yogurt or crème fraîche
2 Tbsp. cream
2 Tbsp. lime juice
1 Tbsp. honey
salt and pepper

Firm fish such as cod or halibut should be used. Wash fish fillets and cut into small cubes. Peel potatoes and cut into slices. Wash cauliflower florets. First blanch the potatoes, then the cauliflower in boiling salt water for 4 minutes. Drain the asparagus. (If desired, fresh asparagus can be used, in which case it should be blanched for 3 to 5 minutes in boiling water.)

In a casserole dish, arrange fish, shrimp, potatoes, cauliflower and asparagus. Mix cream with wine, salt and pepper and the chopped fresh spices and pour into the casserole. It needs no additional liquid.

Cover with foil and bake at 425°F (220°C) for about 20 minutes. Remove foil. If the cooking juice is too thin and a thicker sauce is wanted, some cornstarch mixed with cold water may be added at this point. Brown for further 5 minutes.

Make the lime sauce during this time. Put the yogurt or crème fraîche in a bowl, add the cream, lime juice and honey. Season with salt and freshly ground pepper. Sauce is served on the side.

Best with a simple green salad.

This serves 4 to 6 persons.

Ryba Sw. Piotra z Ziolami
(St. Peter's Fish with Herbs)

1 lemon
6 medium-sized fillets of a firm fish with skin on
2 Tbsp. ground herb mixture (thyme, oregano, basil, tarragon)
4 Tbsp. butter
salt and pepper

Squeeze juice from the lemon. Pat non-skin side of fish fillets dry. Cut a diamond-shaped pattern in the skin or the fish will curl when cooked. Rub the fish with lemon juice, and rub in the herbs.

In a large frying pan melt butter over medium heat and fry the fish on the herbed side for 1 to 2 minutes.

Turn fish over and fry for 2 more minutes on the skin side. Before serving, sprinkle the fish with salt and pepper.

Serves 6.

Although this Polish recipe is simple to prepare, the result is quite tasty. It originally calls for John Dory, but since this fish is hard to come by, cod, sole or other fish may be used.

251

SAINT-PIERRE À L'OSEILLE

(John Dory in a Cream Sorrel Sauce)

½ c. (125 ml) dry white wine
½ c. (125 ml) cider
1 lb. (500 g) sorrel, chopped
2 onions, chopped
2 shallots, minced
1 bay leaf
1 tsp. thyme
1 tsp. parsley
salt and pepper
2 lbs. (1 kg) John Dory fillets
2 Tbsp. butter
½ c. (125 ml) whipping cream
pinch of paprika
garlic croutons

First make the court bouillon. In a large saucepan put the wine, cider, ½ cup (125 ml) of water, a handful of sorrel, the onions, shallots and herbs. Season with salt and pepper. Bring to a boil and simmer for 15 minutes. Strain carefully.

Place the fillets in a large frying pan and cover with the court bouillon. Bring to a boil and simmer for 10 minutes. When the fillets are cooked, keep them warm on a serving platter.

To make the sauce, sweat the remaining sorrel in the butter. When it has become a green purée, add ½ cup (125 ml) of the court bouillon and the cream. Season with salt, pepper and paprika before pouring over the fillets. Serve with garlic croutons.

If John Dory is unavailable, sole may be used. If you cannot find sorrel, use spinach, but some of the unique flavor will be lost.

Serves 6.

Torta Garfagnana

(Cake for St. Peter's Day from Garfagnana)

¾ c. (175 g) butter, unsalted

1 lemon

2¾ c. (350 g) flour

1 c. (240 g) sugar

¾ c. (75 g) almonds, ground

1 Tbsp. anise seed

3 eggs

5 Tbsp. cherry brandy

⅔ c. (160 ml) milk

1 Tbsp. cream of tartar

1 tsp. baking soda

Grease and flour a 10-inch (25 cm) square pan. Melt the butter and let it cool. Grate the rind of the lemon and set aside. Preheat oven to 375°F (190°C).

Put the flour, sugar, almonds, anise seed and lemon rind into a large bowl. Mix thoroughly. Make a well in the middle and break the eggs into it. Add the melted butter and cherry brandy. Work everything together until the mixture is smooth.

Warm the milk slightly and add the cream of tartar and baking soda. When the milk foams, add it to the flour mixture. Stir until well blended. Pour into the cake pan.

Bake for 1 hour or until a wooden skewer stuck into the center comes out clean. Remove from oven. Sprinkle with powdered sugar, if desired. This cake may be served warm or cold.

Serves 8 to 10 people.

This cake from the Garfagnana region of Tuscany in Italy is the finale to the big meal served on St. Peter's Day, for Peter is the patron saint of this mountain region. This description and the recipe are from Wilma Pezzini's Tuscan Cookbook.

St. Peter's Pie

PIE FILLING
1¾ c. (425 ml) milk
salt and pepper
1 pinch mace
1 bay leaf
½ lb. (250 g) cod fillet
½ lb. (250 g) haddock fillet, smoked
2 Tbsp. butter
2 Tbsp. olive oil
2 Tbsp. whipping cream
1 tsp. garlic, minced
2 eggs, hard-boiled

CHEESE SAUCE
2 Tbsp. butter, melted
1 Tbsp. flour
1 pinch nutmeg
4 Tbsp. cheese, grated (Swiss and Parmesan mixed)

In a large saucepan, season the milk with salt, pepper, mace and bay leaf. Bring to a boil, put in the fish, turn the heat down and simmer it, covered, for about 20 minutes.

When the fish is cooked, strain off the cooking liquid and set aside 1 cup (250 ml) for the cheese sauce. Keep the rest of the liquid.

Flake the fillets carefully into a bowl, removing any bones and skin pieces. Mash with a fork and gradually work in the 2 tablespoons of

254

melted butter, olive oil, the cream and the minced garlic and 3 to 4 tablespoons of the cooking liquid. When everything is well blended, adjust the seasoning with salt and pepper. Transfer the mixture to a pie dish and cover with slices of hard-boiled egg.

Preheat oven to 425°F (220°C).

To make the cheese sauce, melt the butter in a heavy saucepan. When the butter starts to froth, remove pan from heat and stir in the flour. Add enough of the warm milk to make a thick paste. Return pan to heat and slowly stir in the rest of the measured milk. Season with salt, pepper and nutmeg and simmer for 5 minutes. Fold the grated cheese into the sauce and pour the cheese sauce over the eggs and put into the preheated oven. Leave for a few minutes until the top starts to brown. Serve with chips or mashed potatoes and a green vegetable.

Serves 4 to 6.

St. Peter's Pudding

3 envelopes of gelatin, unflavored
2 Tbsp. sugar
6 oranges
2 c. (500 ml) orange juice
½ c. (125 ml) lemon juice, fresh
2 c. (450 g) sugar
1 c. (100 g) grapes, green, seedless and halved
½ c. (80 g) walnuts, chopped
½ c. (50 g) raisins, golden
12 dates, pitted and chopped finely
12 maraschino cherries, quartered
½ c. (125 ml) whipping cream

This recipe is for a pudding that is popular with children and is a great summertime dessert. It must be prepared a day before serving.

In a small saucepan, combine gelatin and 2 tablespoons of sugar; add 1 cup (250 ml) of water. Stir over low heat until gelatin is dissolved. Set aside.

Peel oranges; cut into sections, holding over bowl to catch juice. Measure juice; add enough of the orange juice to make 2 cups (500 ml). Pour orange juice into large bowl. Add lemon juice, the sugar and the gelatin mixture; stir until sugar is dissolved. Refrigerate, stirring occasionally, until it has the consistency of unbeaten egg white. Fold in orange sections, grapes, walnuts, raisins, dates and cherries. Turn into a large serving bowl. Refrigerate at least 12 hours.

Garnish with the whipped cream and serve right from the bowl.

Makes 12 to 16 servings.

St. Regis

JOHN FRANCIS REGIS was born on January 31, 1597, at Fontcouverte, France, the son of a rich merchant. He studied at the Jesuit College of Béziers and joined the Jesuits in 1615, pursuing his studies and being ordained in 1631. He was assigned to do missionary work in southeastern France and became famous for his fervor, his preaching ability and as a confessor. John Francis spent considerable energy to organize a ministry to help the imprisoned, poor, destitute and sick. He founded a refuge for wayward women and girls, and, with gifts given to him, he set up a granary so that he could feed the hungry.

He had great success in turning the life of the region back into a more Christian direction. This success may explain why his repeated applications to become a missionary to the Indians in Canada were never granted. He considered the denial of his applications a punishment for his sins and pursued his activities in France with greater vigor, seeking out the most remote and isolated villages to spread the gospel and risking his health more and more.

His fame as a preacher always attracted large crowds from every class, peasants and nobility alike.

John Francis Regis seemed to have anticipated his death, for he told his superiors he would not be back to renew his vows. He died on December 31, 1640, at Louvesc and is buried there, where his tomb became the center for many pilgrimages.

John Francis Regis is aptly the patron saint of social workers and of illegitimate children. His feast day is June 16.

In art he is usually depicted as feeding and helping the poor.

Icon,
William H. McNichols, S.J.,
20th century,
Regis University,
Denver, Colorado.
(St. Regis is standing.)

Salad St. Regis

VEGETABLES
½ c. (125 ml) diced potatoes
½ c. (125 ml) asparagus heads
½ c. (125 ml) pineapple chunks
½ c. (125 ml) grapefruit chunks
½ c. (125 ml) celery chunks

Boil diced potatoes until tender. Drain.

Blanch asparagus tips in boiling salt water for 3 minutes and drain.

Mix all vegetables together.

VINAIGRETTE
2 Tbsp. vinegar
6 Tbsp. olive oil
2 Tbsp. cream
salt and pepper

Prepare vinaigrette by mixing all ingredients together and seasoning with salt and pepper. Pour vinaigrette over salad and serve.

Serves 6 persons.

This is an unusual salad recipe from an English cookbook.

257

Jacopo Tintoretto,
16th century,
S. Rocco, Venice

Roch, or Rocco, as he is known in Italy, was probably born in Montpellier in France around 1295, the son of a rich merchant family. Roch later became a hermit and spent much of his life on pilgrimages. One of these led him to Rome in 1368, and there he devoted himself to caring for the victims of the plague that was rampant in Italy at that time. He stayed for three years, but after leaving Rome he himself caught the plague in Piacenza. Legend has it that he was fed in the woods by a dog. He recovered from the plague and continued his work. Roch supposedly cured many afflicted by the deadly disease.

In Angleria in Lombardy he was thrown into prison as a suspected spy and died there in 1378. Miracles were claimed at his tomb, and his fame spread to the plague-stricken countries of Germany and France. His popularity subsided in the sixteenth century but had a revival during disastrous outbreaks of cholera in the nineteenth century.

His feast day is August 16, and he is one of the patron saints of physicians and surgeons. In art he is sometimes shown as a pilgrim with a sore on his leg and accompanied by a dog with a loaf of bread in its mouth.

St. Roch's Fingers

4 egg yolks
4 Tbsp. sugar
pinch of salt
2 c. (500 ml) milk, scalded and cooled to lukewarm
1 Tbsp. brandy
ladyfingers

Beat the egg yolks slightly and add the sugar and salt. Pour in the scalded milk slowly, stirring all the time, and place over a low heat. Cook until mixture begins to thicken, but do not allow it to boil. (It is safer to use a double boiler.)

Strain and, when cool, flavor with the brandy.

Arrange ladyfingers on the bottom and around the sides of a glass serving dish, pour in the custard, and serve when thoroughly chilled. May be sprinkled with grated chocolate.

Serves 4.

This recipe is an English version of a Spanish dish for which the source could not be located. It is an easy dessert.

St. Sebastian

ACCORDING to the sparse facts, Sebastian was a martyr in Rome in the late third century during the persecution of Emperor Diocletian. He was also connected to Milan either by birth or by education.

The legend does supply more, but it is believed to be entirely fictitious. According to this legend, Sebastian was a Christian who enlisted in the army to strengthen other Christians who were in prison or condemned to die. He was created captain of the guard by Diocletian, who did not know that Sebastian was a Christian. When the emperor found out, he condemned Sebastian to death by having a group of archers shoot at him until he was believed to be dead.

His body was recovered by St. Irene, and he was nursed back to health. Sebastian, from an open window during a parade, then took the liberty to rebuke the emperor publicly for his persecution of the Christians. As this came from a man who was supposed to be dead, the emperor was enraged and had Sebastian clubbed to death and thrown into the Tiber. His body was retrieved and buried in a cemetery on the Appian Way in Rome, close to where his basilica stands today.

In Renaissance paintings Sebastian's death is the prevailing theme of representation, but older pictures show him as an elderly bearded man holding the crown of martyrdom.

Sebastian's feast day is February 20, and he is the patron saint of policemen, archers and physicians.

Truchas al Horno à la Donostiarra

(Baked Trout à la San Sebastian—Basque Style)

6 trout, cleaned

1 onion, chopped

1 lemon

2 Tbsp. olive oil

2 Tbsp. parsley, chopped

1 tsp. salt

¼ tsp. pepper

1 Tbsp. butter

Wash and wipe the fish. Put into an ovenproof dish, together with the oil, onion, half the parsley and the seasoning. Squeeze lemon and pour half of the juice on the fish. Reserve rest of juice. Let fish sit in this mixture for 1 hour.

Bake fish in a preheated moderate oven 350°F (175°C) for 20 minutes. In a frying pan melt the butter and fry the remaining parsley for a few seconds, then add the rest of the lemon juice. Pour over the trout and serve.

Serves 6.

This recipe and the translation of its title are from The Home Book of Spanish Cooking, *by M. Pereira and N. Froud. The recipe is named after San Sebastian, a city in the Basque region of Spain.*

St. Stephen (Martyr)

Adam Elsheimer, 16th century,
National Gallery, Edinburgh

STEPHEN, who died around the year 35, was the first Christian martyr. His death is reported in the Acts of the Apostles. He was one of seven deacons appointed by the apostles to look after the distribution of alms to the faithful, especially the widows, and to help in the ministry of preaching.

A gifted speaker, he defended Christianity forcefully against Judaism and was stoned, without a trial, for blasphemy. His feast has been celebrated since the third century and received additional impetus from the discovery of his supposed tomb in the year 415. Subsequent transfer of his relics to Constantinople and Rome helped to spread his popularity.

Stephen always has been the patron saint of deacons, and many medieval churches have been named after him, including famous cathedrals in Bourges, Toulouse and Vienna.

In art he is shown as a deacon, often holding a book with a stone. Representations with a palm are also common. In the West his feast day is December 26, a day often overlooked in the Christmas excitement.

St. Stephen's Pudding

¾ c. (75 g) suet, shredded
1 c. (100 g) bread crumbs, fresh
½ c. (60 g) flour
½ c. (60 g) brown sugar
¼ tsp. baking powder
1 c. (100 g) raisins
1 egg
3 Tbsp. milk
1 pinch salt
3 cooking apples, small
1 lemon

Combine the suet and the dry ingredients. Peel and grate the apples and add them to the dry ingredients. Grate the rind of the lemon and add to this mixture. Beat egg into milk, add salt and add to previous ingredients. Stir with fork until well blended.

Pack the mixture into a 1-quart (1 l) bowl, cover with foil and tie it up with a string. Steam for 2 hours.

Serve warm with brandy butter.

Serves 6 to 8 persons.

A recipe from an English cookbook for a light steamed pudding.

263

STEPHEN'S BEIGLI
(St. Stephen's Roll)

DOUGH
¾ c. (200 ml) milk
1 tsp. sugar
1 Tbsp. dry yeast
4 c. (500 g) flour
7 Tbsp. powdered sugar
1 c. (250 g) butter
2 eggs
pinch of salt

WALNUT FILLING
¾ c. (200 g) sugar
2 Tbsp. water
3 c. (300 g) walnuts, ground
1 c. (100 g) seedless raisins
1 lemon

POPPY SEED FILLING
10 oz. (300 g) poppy seed
¾ c. (200 ml) milk, boiling
¾ c. (200 g) sugar
4 Tbsp. apricot jam
1 c. (100 g) seedless raisins
1 lemon

This is a famous Hungarian recipe that includes 2 kinds of filling, both of which are very good. The cake keeps and freezes well.

Warm ¾ of the milk to lukewarm and add sugar, yeast and ½ c. (60 g) of the flour. Stir and set aside to let it bubble.

Beat the powdered sugar and butter with an electric beater until light and fluffy, then whisk in the eggs 1 at a time. Sift the rest of the flour with the salt into a bowl, make a well and pour the butter mixture into it, stir a bit, then add the yeast mixture. Stir and knead, when the mixture is no longer sticky. More milk may be added if the dough is too hard, but it should not become too soft, otherwise the cake will crack. Continue kneading until the dough becomes very elastic and throws large air bubbles. Cover the bowl and put it in a warm place for about 2 hours or until the dough doubles its bulk. Knock the dough back and divide into 2 pieces.

Roll each piece of dough into a rectangle ¼ inch (6 mm) thick. Cover with damp cloth and let rise for another half hour. In the meantime, make either the walnut or poppy seed filling.

The walnuts for the filling should be fresh, otherwise an off flavor will occur. To make the walnut filling, dissolve the sugar in 2 tablespoons water over low heat, then add the ground walnuts and cook for 5 minutes. Remove from heat, stir in the raisins and the grated rind of the lemon. Cool, then beat until creamy before using.

264

To make the poppy seed filling, grind the poppy seed and then pour the boiling milk over it and let it stand for a while to swell. Dissolve the sugar over low heat in 2 tablespoons of water, stir in the sieved poppy seed and draw off the heat. Stir in the apricot jam, raisins and the grated lemon rind. Leave to cool, then beat until creamy before using.

Spread the filling over the yeast pastry base to within ¾ inch (2 cm) of the edge (taking care not to overfill or the roll will crack as it bakes). Roll the dough up carefully and set it on a greased baking sheet with the open edge underneath. Brush surface all over with beaten egg, which will give it a marbled effect when it is baked.

Set the roll to rise again, this time in a cool place for 30 minutes or more. Prick the roll on the outside with a fork several times to prevent it from cracking. Brush again with egg and bake in a preheated hot oven, 400°F (200°C). Do not open the oven door for at least 15 minutes if you want to check it. Total baking time will be about 25 minutes.

The beigli can be left for up to a week before it is cut; the flavor improves as it matures.

Sufficient for 8 to 10 people.

On the day of St. Stephen, special breads are traditionally baked in Poland and other Slavic countries. They are in the shape of horseshoes and are filled with chopped nuts and sugar.

PODKOVY
(St. Stephen's Horseshoes)

DOUGH

1 Tbsp. dry yeast

½ c. (125 ml) milk, lukewarm

3 eggs, small

1 c. (250 ml) sour cream

2 tsp. lemon juice

2 Tbsp. lemon rind, grated

1 c. (200 g) butter

5 c. (625 g) flour

½ c. (125 g) sugar

½ tsp. salt

½ c. (100 g) shortening

FILLING

1½ c. (300 g) walnuts, finely chopped

¾ c. (125 g) brown sugar

1 egg

½ tsp. vanilla

grated rind of 1 orange

grated rind of 1 lemon

Sprinkle the yeast into the lukewarm milk and let stand for 10 minutes.

Beat the eggs until light and fluffy. Stir in the sour cream, yeast mixture, lemon juice and rind.

Cut the cold butter into small pieces. Combine the flour, sugar and salt in a large bowl. Work the butter and shortening into the flour mixture using 2 knives or your fingers. The mixture should resemble coarse bread crumbs. Add the moist ingredients to the dry ones in the bowl and beat well. If necessary, add a little more flour, just enough to make a fairly soft and non-sticky dough. This may require a fair amount of additional flour, since it depends on the size of the eggs.

Knead dough briefly and wrap it in waxed paper or plastic wrap. Chill for 1 hour.

While the dough is chilling, prepare the filling. Chop the nuts finely (walnuts, hazelnuts or almonds can be used). Combine the brown sugar with the egg, vanilla and rinds. Stir in the nuts.

On a lightly floured surface, roll the dough out to about ⅛ inch (3 mm) thickness and cut into rectangles about 4 x 6 inches (10 x 15 cm).

Brush the rectangles with some melted butter and sprinkle lightly with the filling. Roll each rectangle up, starting on the long side. Form the roll into a horseshoe and place on a lightly greased baking sheet. You may want to brush the dough with cream, but this is not essential.

Bake in a preheated oven at 375°F (190°C) for about 15 minutes or until the horseshoes are nicely browned.

After they are taken from the oven, they may be sprinkled with powdered sugar or glazed with a mixture of lemon juice and powdered sugar.

Makes 2 to 3 dozen horseshoes.

St. Sylvester

Maso di Bianco, 15th century,
Santa Croce, Florence

SYLVESTER, the son of a Roman named Rufinus, became bishop of Rome in 314. The edict of Milan by Emperor Constantine had just recognized Christianity and ended the persecution by declaring tolerance for all religions. Sylvester was the first pope in charge of a Church that was at peace with the empire, and he benefited from Constantine's goodwill. Constantine gave him the Lateran Palace, which became the cathedral church of Rome.

Sylvester built other churches in Rome, too, probably the first St. Peter's, Holy Cross and St. Lawrence-Outside-the-Walls. He sent his legates to the Council of Nicaea and to a synod in Arles. He died in 335 and was buried in a church that he had built, though in the eighth century his relics were transferred to the present church of St. Sylvester.

Many legends exist about Sylvester. He supposedly cured Constantine from leprosy and later baptized him on his deathbed. The latter is a common image painted by artists, although sometimes Sylvester is seen in bishop's robes with a chained bull and a tiara. His feast day in the West is the last day of the year, December 31.

268

Caprice Saint-Sylvestre

(Cake of St. Sylvester)

CAKE
½ c. (125 g) sugar
4 eggs
1 c. (125 g) flour
4 Tbsp. unsweetened cocoa
½ c. (125 g) melted butter
½ c. (50 g) almonds, ground

GARNISH AND FILLING
3 Tbsp. Jamaican rum
3 Tbsp. vanilla flavored syrup
1 c. (250 ml) whipping cream
2 Tbsp. sugar
¼ tsp. (1 ml) vanilla
8 candied chestnuts
¼ lb. (125 g) chocolate, semisweet

This is a recipe for a classic cake from one of Robert Carrier's books.

Place sugar and eggs in a large mixing bowl. Beat with an electric mixer for 4 minutes. Sift flour and cocoa together, then fold into the egg mixture followed by the cooled melted butter.

Generously butter a round cake pan 10 inches (25 cm) in diameter, and sprinkle well with the ground almonds. Pour in the mixture and bake in a preheated oven at 400°F (200°C) for 25 to 30 minutes. When the cake detaches itself slightly from the sides of the pan, it is done. Remove from oven and let cool.

Split the cake horizontally so you have 2 circles, then moisten the cut sides with equal quantities of rum and vanilla syrup. (Vanilla syrup can be made by taking 3 tablespoons of syrup from the candied chestnuts and mixing it with ¼ teaspoon vanilla.)

Whip the cream until soft peaks form, add the sugar and vanilla. Chop half the candied chestnuts and add to whipped cream. Spread this mixture on the bottom half of the cake and cover with the top half. Melt the chocolate and ice the cake with it. Use the remaining candied chestnuts to decorate the cake.

Serves 8 to 10 persons.

269

COLLERETTE DE LA SAINT-SYLVESTRE AUX TROIS CHOCOLATS

(Three Chocolate Collar for St. Sylvester)

CAKE
6 eggs
1½ c. (200 g) powdered sugar
1 c. (125 g) flour
1 c. (100 g) cocoa
pinch of salt
1 c. (150 g) sour cherries

FILLING
½ lb. (200 g) milk chocolate
½ c. (100 ml) cream

DECORATION
½ lb. (200 g) dark bitter chocolate
½ lb. (200 g) white chocolate
red currant jelly, optional

This is a recipe for a dessert suitable for the last day of the year, the feast day of St. Sylvester. It is a cake that will delight all those who love chocolate.

Preheat oven to 350°F (175°C). Thoroughly grease a spring-form pan with butter and sprinkle it with flour. Shake off any excess flour that does not stick to the butter.

Separate the eggs. Beat the egg yolks together with the powdered sugar until light and fluffy. Sift together flour and cocoa and add to the mixture a tablespoon at a time.

Beat the egg whites with the pinch of salt until stiff but not dry. Fold gently into the batter.

Pour batter into the prepared spring-form pan and smooth the surface. Bake in the middle of the oven for 30 or 40 minutes or until a wooden skewer inserted in the middle comes out clean. Turn cake out onto a rack and let it cool completely.

Meanwhile, make the chocolate shavings for the decoration. First melt the white chocolate in a double boiler and pour it on a marble or pastry board. A baking pan covered with waxed paper will do also. Spread chocolate very thin with a knife or spatula and let it cool.

When the chocolate begins to set—it still should be somewhat soft— take a chef's knife or spatula and, holding the blade at an angle to the chocolate, scrape off shavings. They will be all different shapes and lengths. Set aside and keep cool. Repeat this process with the dark chocolate.

Cut the cooled cake horizontally in the middle to form 2 circles. Drain the cherries. Some of the juice may be sprinkled on the cut side of the

top layer of the cake, if desired. Distribute cherries over bottom layer of the cake.

To make the filling, melt the milk chocolate in a double boiler. Heat the cream and pour it, boiling hot, into the chocolate. Stir and distribute this mixture over the cherries.

Cover with top half of the cake.

Decorate cake with the chocolate shavings in an arbitrary pattern, but alternating dark and white chocolate.

If the chocolate shavings do not stay on top, brush the cake first with red currant jelly.

This cake will serve 8 to 10 people for dessert, unless you have a group of chocolate lovers, in which case it will be enough for 6.

271

St. Teresa of Avila

TERESA, born into an aristocratic Castilian family in 1515, showed an early interest in religious life. Educated by Augustinian nuns, but forced to leave due to ill health, she joined the Carmelite order in 1535. Again forced to leave for health reasons, she returned to the monastery in 1540. From 1555 on she experienced visions and heard voices that proved quite unsettling to her until a spiritual adviser convinced her that they were authentic.

Unhappy about the relaxed life-style in the Carmelite monastery, she founded in 1562 in Avila a new house for nuns. St. Joseph's convent was for women who wanted to follow a stricter rule of poverty, austerity and solitude than practiced in the other Carmelite monasteries. Despite bitter opposition from Church and civil authorities, Teresa continued to found more convents and, with St. John of the Cross, she reformed the Carmelite friars. In 1580 Rome recognized the Reformed Carmelites as a separate order.

Teresa was not only active in organizing her convents, but she was also a prolific writer, putting her experiences, visions and insights into words. Her writings are still spiritual classics. She was one of those rare souls who manage to blend a highly active life with one of deep contemplation.

Teresa died in 1582 at the age of sixty-seven, was canonized in 1622 by Pope Gregory XV and proclaimed a Doctor of the Church in 1970 by Pope Paul VI. She and Catherine of Siena were the first women to be so honored. Teresa's ideals survive today in small Carmelite communities living a contemplative life-style.

In art Teresa of Avila is usually shown having a vision and with a dove or fiery arrow above her head. Her feast day is October 15.

Yemas de Santa Teresa

(St. Teresa's Candied Egg Yolks)

½ c. (125 g) sugar
½ c. (125 ml) water
½ tsp. grated lemon rind
1 cinnamon stick
4 egg yolks

Put sugar, water, lemon rind and cinnamon stick into a heavy saucepan and boil to soft ball stage 238°F (115°C). Beat egg yolks and pour into a saucepan.

Remove the cinnamon stick from the sugar mixture and pour the hot syrup into the egg yolks, stirring constantly.

Cook this mixture over low heat until it thickens slightly. This may take about 10 minutes. Remove from heat and stir until quite thick and the egg yolk-syrup mixture no longer sticks to the side of the pan. Pour mixture onto a greased jelly-roll pan and let cool.

While still warm, shape into patties or small balls and roll in sugar. The balls may be placed into little paper cups.

Makes about 24 yemas.

These yemas, an unusual dessert or a nice snack, are taken from an old Spanish recipe. They are very popular in the Avila region of Spain, though similar candied egg yolks can be found in other parts of the country.

273

This dish, which makes a tasty breakfast especially for children, is a cousin to French toast.

Pan de Santa Teresa
(St. Teresa's Bread)

2 c. (500 ml) milk
3 Tbsp. sugar
1 cinnamon stick
1 lemon peel, piece
12 pieces of Italian or French bread ¾ inch (2 cm) thick
3 eggs
pinch of salt
olive oil
cinnamon sugar

If it is possible, cut the bread into slices the night before you are planning to make this dish so that the slices are slightly stale. Do not use regular white bread, as it is too soft for this recipe and the soaked bread will be mushy.

Combine the milk with the sugar, cinnamon and lemon peel. Simmer gently for 5 to 10 minutes or until you think the milk is well flavored. If desired, this can also be prepared the night before.

Place the bread in a large dish or pan and strain the milk over it.

Beat the eggs in a shallow bowl with a pinch of salt. With a spatula, lay the slices of bread in the egg, turning them over to coat both sides. Beat additional eggs and salt together if necessary to finish coating the slices. Fry the bread in the olive oil until it is browned and crusty on both sides.

Sprinkle with cinnamon sugar before serving.

Serves 3 to 4.

St. Thomas (Apostle)

THOMAS THE APOSTLE is mentioned by all four evangelists. He is remembered by most for his refusal to believe in the Resurrection unless he could actually touch the wounds of the risen Jesus. Many generations of churchmen have blamed Thomas for his lack of faith, but at the same time have praised him for the skepticism that helped to reassure many believers.

Much uncertainty exists regarding Thomas' missionary work. One tradition places it among the Parthians, but it is generally believed that he preached in India. The Christians of the Syro-Malabar rite claim that Thomas evangelized them.

A spear reputedly killed him in A.D. 72, and an ancient cross marks the place where this took place.

The story of the transfer of his remains is quite complex. According to one source, they have made their way to Ortona in Northern Italy, while another tradition claims that they are still buried at St. Tome in India.

In art Thomas is usually shown examining the wounds of Jesus, though images with a spear are not uncommon.

Thomas is the patron saint of India and Portugal and also the patron of architects and theologians. Formerly in the West his feast day was December 21, but this has now been changed to July 3. In the East his feast is celebrated on October 6.

*This is an old German recipe
from an 1894 cookbook.*

THOMASSTRIEZELN

(St. Thomas Fingers)

1 Tbsp. dry yeast
½ c. (125 ml) sour cream
1 lemon
2 c. (250 g) flour
½ c. (125 g) sugar
6 egg yolks
4 Tbsp. butter
½ c. (60 g) powdered sugar
1 Tbsp. cinnamon

Mix yeast with the sour cream and let stand for 5 minutes. Wash lemon and grate peel finely into a bowl. Add all other ingredients and stir them together. When the dough becomes only slightly sticky, knead for 5 minutes. (More flour may have to be added to make sure that the dough is firm.)

Butter a baking sheet 14 x 6 inches (40 x 16 cm) and roll dough out on it. With a pastry cutter cut dough into long fingers. Brush with melted butter. Mix powdered sugar with cinnamon and dust fingers thoroughly with the mixture.

Cover with a towel and let fingers rest in a warm place for about 40 minutes. Bake at 350°F (175°C) until golden. This should take about 30 minutes.

Makes about 40 fingers.

276

St. Valentine

Bartolomeus Zeitblom,
15th century, Staatsgallerie,
Augsburg, Germany.
(St. Valentine is the bishop
in both panels.)

VALENTINE is one of the more familiar saints, connected to the custom of sending "Valentines" on his feast day. Unfortunately, historical facts about Valentine are few. The Roman Calendar until 1969 listed two St. Valentines for February 14.

The first was supposedly a Roman priest martyred under Emperor Claudius about A.D. 270. Because of many doubts about his existence, Rome removed him from the universal calendar.

The other Valentine, reputedly a bishop of Terni in the third century, was martyred in Rome. He was beheaded, and his relics were transferred back to Terni. It is quite possible that the two martyred Valentines are one and the same person.

One possible explanations for the connection of this feast with lovers is that it falls near the time of the old Roman festival of Lupercalia, a pagan fertility celebration held in mid February.

In art Valentine of Terni is shown in the robes of a bishop, though few representations of him exist. Valentine is the patron of lovers, travelers and beekeepers. This strange mixture of patronages may be explained by there having originally been two different saints. Valentine is the patron saint of cripples and epileptics, since a legend reports his curing of an epileptic.

Baking a cake with pink icing on Valentine's Day is a widespread custom in the English-speaking world.

COOKING WITH THE SAINTS

Though this recipe is from a book on French cooking, the author reports that she came across it in Austria, where it was prepared by a local cook.

POULET SAINT-VALENTIN

(Chicken St. Valentine)

1 roasting chicken
½ c. (100 g) butter
1 tsp. each salt, pepper, nutmeg and paprika
1 Tbsp. flour
½ c. (125 ml) dry white wine
1 c. (250 ml) milk
½ c. (125 g) rice
2 c. (500 ml) chicken stock
4 Tbsp. ham, diced
2 Tbsp. parsley, chopped
1 Tbsp. lemon juice

Cut chicken into neat pieces and brown all sides in half the butter. Season with the paprika, nutmeg and salt. Pour away half the fat and sprinkle the chicken pieces with the flour. Add the wine and milk and cook covered over medium heat until done.

In another saucepan put the rice and chicken stock and cook until the rice has absorbed all the stock. Now mix in the ham, the parsley and the remaining butter.

Arrange chicken pieces in the center of a dish with the rice as a border. Add the lemon juice to the sauce the chicken was cooked in, let it boil for 2 minutes to reduce it, stir in a teaspoon of butter and strain over the chicken. Serve with a plain green salad.

Serves about 6 people.

St. Valentine's Day Cake

CAKE
3 eggs
¾ c. (175 g) sugar
2 Tbsp. strong black coffee
1¼ c. (150 g) flour

ICING
½ c. (125 g) butter
2 c. (225 g) powdered sugar
3 Tbsp. strong black coffee

CARAMEL
½ c. (100 g) sugar
½ c. (125 ml) water

Separate the eggs and put the yolks into a bowl with the sugar and coffee. Put the bowl over a pan of hot water and whisk until thick and fluffy. Remove bowl from pan and whisk for another minute.

Whisk the egg whites until stiff peaks form.

Sift the flour into the yolk mixture and fold it in. Fold in egg whites and put mixture into a well-greased heart-shaped pan and bake at 350°F (175°C) for 45 minutes. Turn out and cool.

To make the icing, cream the butter until soft and fluffy. Sift the powdered sugar into the butter, and whisk it while slowly adding the cooled coffee. If a traditional pink cake is wanted, some drops of red food coloring may be added at this time.

Cut the cake in half and sandwich top and bottom together with some of the icing. Spread most of the remaining icing over top and sides of the cake. Use the remaining icing to pipe small stars around the top of the cake.

To make the caramel, dissolve the sugar in the water and then boil rapidly until a dark golden brown. Pour from pan onto a sheet of waxed paper and let cool. Crack into small pieces with a rolling pin and use them to decorate the top of the cake.

Serves 8.

It is a tradition in the English-speaking world to bake a cake on Valentine's day for one's beloved. It is thought by some that the association between Valentine and lovers comes from the birds—February 14, St. Valentine's feast day, is when birds supposedly choose their mates and build their nests.

St. Valéry

VALÉRY, also known as Walaricus, was born in the Auvergne region of France, into a peasant family, though he learned to read early in life. Dissatisfied with being a shepherd, he became a monk. First he moved to the monastery of St. Germain near Auxerre and later to the monastery run by St. Columban near Luxeuil.

When the whole monastery was expelled by King Theodoric, St. Valéry became a missionary in Neustria and was successful in converting many to Christ.

However, the promises he saw in the eremitical life drew him to became a hermit at the mouth of the Somme. There, Valéry attracted numerous disciples and organized them into Leuconans Abbey around A.D. 614 and became their abbot. He is reputed to have evangelized first the Pas-de-Calais area and then the whole eastern area of the English channel. He died in 622.

Miracles occurred at his tomb, and his fame was spread with the Normans to England. The Norman troops in 1066 sailed from Saint-Valéry-sur-Somme.

In art he is usually shown as an abbot, and his feast day is April 1.

Kartoffeltorte St. Valery

(Potato Pie St. Valery)

½ c. (125 g) butter
2 c. (250 g) flour
1 pinch salt
1¼ lb. (600 g) potatoes
¾ lb. (300 g) leek
6 Tbsp. onion, chopped
½ c. (100 g) lean bacon, chopped
1 Tbsp. parsley, chopped
2 tsp. herbs de Provence
4 Tbsp. white wine
salt and pepper
3 egg yolks
½ c. (125 ml) cream

This recipe is from a fairly recent German cookbook, Gut gekocht für meine Gäste.

First, put aside 2 tablespoons of the butter. Sift flour into a bowl, add a pinch of salt and cut the rest of the butter into small cubes. Rub butter into flour until it resembles coarse bread crumbs. Add 4 tablespoons of water and shape everything into a dough ball. Let rest for 1 to 2 hours.

Peel potatoes and cut into thin slices. Clean the leek and cut into thin rings. Chop onion and bacon. In a medium-sized saucepan sauté the bacon, onion and leek with the reserved butter. Add the sliced potatoes, sprinkle with the herbs, turn over a few times and then add the white wine. Cover and cook over medium heat for about 5 minutes while stirring occasionally. Season with salt and pepper.

Use a round baking pan about 10 inches (25 cm) in diameter. The pan should have removable sides, so that later the pie can be served and sliced easily. Roll dough to a thickness of about ⅛ inch (4 mm) and line the round pan with ⅔ of the dough about 2 inches (5 cm) high on the side. Put cooled potato mixture into the dough-lined pan. With the rest of the dough make a lid. Be sure you mark a small circle for a steam vent.

Put the lid on top of filling and seal top with sides and brush with 1 egg yolk. Cut any remaining dough into decorations and put on top. Brush twice more with egg yolk.

Bake pie in preheated oven at 425°F (220°C) for 10 minutes. Take out and cut out steam vent. Mix cream with remaining 2 egg yolks, some salt and pepper and pour mixture through the steam vent into the pie. Return the pie to oven and bake for further 30 minutes.

Serve hot.

This pie will feed about 8 as a side dish and 6 for a light lunch.

St. Vitus

THE ONLY certain fact known about Vitus is that he was martyred around A.D. 303 in Lucania in southern Italy. His cult is quite ancient.

According to legend, he was the only son of a senator from Sicily and at the age of twelve became a Christian. The local governor tried to shake his faith, but he fled to Rome. There he supposedly cured the son of Emperor Diocletian from an unclean spirit, but when it was discovered he was a Christian, he was tortured. With the help of an angel he got back to Lucania, where he eventually died.

In the legend these sufferings were also endured by his tutor, Modestus, and his nurse, Crescentia. Nowadays it is believed that there were two different groups of martyrs and that Vitus was alone. The feast day for all three saints is the same, June 15.

Vitus' relics have been moved many times, and now both Corvey in Saxony and Saint-Denis in Paris claim his relics. As the transfer to Saxony took place in 836, a local cult of Vitus developed and spread into neighboring areas. The main cathedral in Prague is dedicated to St. Vitus, and his name was popular in Germany during the Middle Ages as a boy's Christian name. His name is also attached to the illness St. Vitus' dance, now known as Sydenham's chorea.

In art Vitus is most often shown suffering martyrdom, together with Modestus and Crescentia. He is a patron saint of dancers, of actors, and of Bohemia.

SFINCIONE DI SAN VITO

(Snack for St. Vitus' Day)

DOUGH

1 Tbsp. dry yeast
1 tsp. salt
1 tsp. sugar
4 tsp. olive oil
1½ c. (375 ml) lukewarm water
4 c. (500 g) flour

FILLING I

½ lb. (250 g) cooked pork, minced
2 c. (250 g) mozarella cheese, grated
1 c. (125 g) Romano cheese, grated
½ lb. (250 g) salami, chopped
salt and pepper

FILLING II

1 c. (250 ml) onion, minced
1 Tbsp. olive oil
1 can anchovies (50 g)
½ c. (125 ml) tomato sauce
2 c. (250 g) mozarella cheese, diced

The recipe for this rather substantial snack originates in Sicily, where it is served on the feast of St. Vitus. It comes from W. R. LaSasso's excellent 1958 cookbook THE ALL-ITALIAN COOKBOOK, *later published as* REGIONAL ITALIAN COOKING. *This dish is popular with people who like pizza. The second filling creates a Sicilian version of a French onion tart.*

Dissolve yeast, salt, sugar with the olive oil in lukewarm water. Mix in enough flour to make a smooth dough. Knead until dough is not sticky. Brush top with some olive oil, and let rest in a warm place until it doubles in bulk. Punch down and let rise a second time.

Decide which filling you want to use. To make the first filling, mix all ingredients together.

Or, to make the second filling, brown the onions in a bit of olive oil and then chop the anchovies. Mix all ingredients together.

Roll out ½ of the dough and place in a greased Dutch oven and add one of the fillings. Roll out the rest of the dough and cover the filling, pressing edges together as in a pie. Cut several slits as steam vents in the top. Cover with a towel and let rest for 45 minutes. Bake at 400°F (200°F) for about 30 minutes or until golden brown.

Serves 6 to 8.

St. Wilfrid

WILFRID, the son of a nobleman, was born in Northumbria around the year 633, and was educated at Lindisfarne. He later went to Canterbury and Rome to study Scripture and canon law. Wilfrid then spent three years at Lyons, France, before he returned to England and assumed the abbotship of Ripon. At the synod of Whitby in 664, he was chosen to be a bishop and he went to France to receive episcopal consecration at Compiègne.

When Wilfred returned several years later, his place as bishop of York had been taken by Chad, and so Wilfrid retired to Ripon. Wilfrid was reinstated as bishop of York three years later in 669. The next twelve years were his most successful, founding monasteries and churches and presiding over a large diocese.

Wilfrid encouraged the queen to separate from her husband, King Egfrid, and to become a nun, which angered the king. When Archbishop Theodore of Canterbury divided Wilfrid's diocese into four without consulting him, Theodore had the king's support. An appeal by Wilfrid to Rome was successful, but the king refused to reinstate him, and Wilfrid went to Sussex to do missionary work. In 686 he was reinstated as bishop of York, but with reduced powers. In 703 he was stripped a second time of his bishopric, but again an appeal to Rome vindicated him. He died two years later and was buried at Ripon.

In art he is shown either as a bishop or as a missionary preaching to the pagans. His feast day is October 12.

Wilfra Apple Cake

PASTRY
3 c. (375 g) flour
¾ c. (200 g) butter
5 Tbsp. cold water
2 Tbsp. sugar
1 tsp. lemon juice
pinch of salt

FILLING
1½ lb. (700 g) cooking apples
¾ c. (120 g) brown sugar
½ c. (60 g) grated mild Cheddar cheese

Put the flour in a bowl, and place the butter, cut into small cubes, in the center, making sure it is at room temperature. Rub the butter into the flour until the mixture resembles bread crumbs. Add the water, sugar and a pinch of salt and work to a smooth dough.

Butter a jelly-roll pan 8 x 12 inch (20 x 30) and line the bottom with half the pastry.

Peel, core and finely slice apples and put on top of pastry. Sprinkle with the sugar and the cheese. Roll out remaining pastry to make a cover over the apples. Brush top with a little milk and sprinkle with sugar. Bake in a preheated oven at 350°F (175°C) for about 40 minutes. When cooled, cut into 24 squares.

Serves 24.

This is an old recipe that is traditionally baked in Ripon, England, on St. Wilfrid's Day.

Ancho chile Mild dried chiles.

Angelica The candied stalks of the angelica plant.

Anise seed The aromatic seeds of a plant used for flavoring cookies and liqueur.

Bain-de-marie A cooking utensil filled with hot water in which containers with pate, sauce or other mixtures can be cooked slowly and gently. A baking tray with a high rim will work quite fine for ramekins.

Balsamic vinegar From the region around Modena in Italy. Local wine is processed specially and aged for years in caskets to give it its distinct flavor. The older the better.

Benedictine A strong brandy-based liqueur flavored with aromatic herbs.

Blanch To immerse something briefly in simmering water to loosen the skin or soften vegetables.

Bouquet garni A bunch of fresh herbs or other flavoring agents in a bundle to season soups or stews. Can be made up with sprigs of parsley, thyme, rosemary, sage, chervil, chives or savory. Often includes bay leaves, leek and celery. Some combinations go better with certain types of meat.

Cantal cheese A type of hard strong French cheese.

Capers The flowerbuds of a southern European shrub, cooked and pickled. Available in jars.

Cassis A brandy-based liqueur made from black currants.

Chipolatas Small sausages about 1 inch long, mildly spiced. Regular breakfast sausage may be substituted.

Chipotle pepper Hot dried smoked jalapeño pepper, available in cans.

Chorizo Highly spiced Spanish or Mexican sausage seasoned with garlic and cayenne pepper. A substitute can be made by mixing 1 pound ground lean pork with 2 tablespoons vinegar, 1 minced garlic clove, 1 teaspoon oregano, 1 teaspoon salt and 2 tablespoons chile powder. Allow to stand 30 minutes at least. Fry until pork is completely done.

Choux pastry A very light pastry enriched with eggs that puffs up when baked.

Cilantro The leafy part of the coriander, also known as Chinese parsley.

Cointreau An orange-flavored liqueur.

Crème fraîche A substitute for French crème fraîche can be made by mixing heavy whipping cream with a little buttermilk. Allow it to thicken slightly and then refrigerate.

Custard A thick sweet vanilla-flavored sauce made with milk and egg yolks. Custard powder is available in cans.

Egg wash A mixture of 1 egg yolk and 1 tablespoon milk used to brush a yeast bread loaf, etc., so it will brown nicely.

Escalope A thin slice of meat without any bone.

Fenugreek A strongly flavored seed used to flavor bread. Also used in curry powder. Use sparingly.

Fettucini A narrow flat noodle about ¼ inch (6 mm) wide.

Glycerin Also known as Glycerol, it is a sweet clear liquid used to soften icing. Available in most drugstores.

Golden syrup A thick sugar-based syrup available in specialty stores. Honey may be substituted.

Grand Marnier A brandy-based orange flavored liqueur.

Gruyère cheese A cheese made in Switzerland. Regular Swiss cheese may be substituted.

Herbs de Provence A mixture of dried herbs popular in French cooking. Use 6 parts each marjoram, thyme and savory, 2 parts each basil and rosemary, one part each sage and fennel seed.

Kirsch A non-sweet, clear, strong liqueur distilled from cherries.

Macaroons Small biscuits made from ground almonds, egg whites and sugar.

Maraschino A strong sweet liqueur made from black cherries.

Mixed peel A mixture of candied peel. The proportions should be approximately 2 parts orange peel, 1 part lemon peel and 1 part citron peel.

Mixed spice A special spice blend. If unavailable use equal parts cinnamon and coriander plus a tiny bit of nutmeg and ground cloves.

Mulato chile Mild dried chiles.

Noissette A small round piece of meat, from the tenderloin of lamb or beef.

Papardelle A thin flat noodle narrower than fettucini.

Phyllo dough Tissue-thin pastry sheets that can be bought frozen in many supermarkets.

Pomegranate An orange-size fruit with a reddish skin and containing many seeds. Available around Christmas time.

Puff pastry Pastry that becomes flaky and light when baked. Puff pastry can be prepared at home, but making it is an involved process, so it is convenient to purchase it in ready-to-bake form from a grocery store.

Ramekin A small dish (½ cup; 125 ml) for baking and serving individual portions of food.

Ratafia biscuit A biscuit flavored with almonds or kernels of peach, apricot or cherry.

288

Ricotta cheese A fresh, unripened, light curd cheese with a full flavor.

Shallot A mild form of onion, highly regarded by French chefs.

Spätzle A thick batter of flour, egg, water and salt that is drizzled into boiling water, cooked for one minute and served as an accompaniment for dishes that have lots of gravy.

Tournedos A small thick cut from a fillet of beef.

Vol-au-vent A small round case of puff pastry normally filled with meat or fish and a sauce.

Bibliography

Benedictine Monks of St. Augustine's Abbey, Ramsgate. *The Book of Saints: A Dictionary of Servants of God Canonised by the Catholic Church; Extracted from the Roman and Other Martyrologies.* 1st ed.: London: A. and C. Black, 1921; 6th ed.: London: Cassell PLC, 1994.

Bentley, J. *A Calendar of Saints.* London: Orbis; Little, Brown and Company, 1986.

Braunfels, W., ed. *Lexikon der Christlichen Ikonographie.* Freiburg im Breisgau: Herder Verlag, 1976.

Coulson, J., ed. *The Saints: A Concise Biographical Dictionary.* New York: Hawthorn Books, 1958. Reprint, New York: Hawthorn Books, 1985.

Cronin, V. *A Calendar of Saints.* Westminster, Md.: Newman Press, 1963.

Delaney, J. J., and J. E. Tobin. *Dictionary of Catholic Biography.* Garden City, N.Y.: Doubleday, 1961.

Delaney, J. J. *Dictionary of Saints.* Garden City, N.Y.: Doubleday, 1980.

De Voragine, J. *The Golden Legend.* Translated by W. G. Ryan. Princeton: Princeton University Press, 1993.

Farmer, D. H. *The Oxford Dictionary of Saints.* Oxford: Clarendon Press, 1978.

Jöckle, C. *Das Grosse Heiligen Lexikon.* Erlangen, Germany: Karl Müller Verlag, 1995.

New Catholic Encyclopedia. New York: McGraw-Hill, 1967.

One Hundred Saints. Boston: Bullfinch Press; Little, Brown and Company, 1993.

Walsh, M. *Butler's Lives of Patron Saints.* London: Burns and Oates, 1987.

Recipe Acknowledgments

Agnesenplätzchen, from *Kochbuch für drei oder mehr Personen*, by H. Lamprecht (K. Dienstlicher Verlag, 1924).

Andreasherzen, from *Regensburger Kochbuch*, by Maria Schandri (Alfons Coppenrath Verlag, 1890).

Apple Marmalade (used in Saint-Andrés recipe), from the Mississippi Cooperative Extension.

Avocado Sainte-Marguerite, from *Elle* cooking magazine. Reproduced with the kind permission of Hachette Fillipachi, New York.

Barbarakuchen, from the back of a Mondamin box. Reproduced with the kind permission of Knorr GMBH, Germany.

Barm Brack, from *Irish Traditional Cooking*, by Darina Allen (London: Kyle Cathie, 1995). Reproduced with kind permission of the publisher.

Bizcocho de San Lorenzo, from *A Continual Feast*, by E. B. Vitz (San Francisco: Ignatius Press, 1991). Reproduced with kind permission of the author.

Brioche Saint-Denis, from *Floyd on France*, by Keith Floyd, reproduced with the permission of BBC Worldwide. © Keith Floyd, 1987.

Brochettes de Coquilles Saint-Jacques, from *Belgian Cookbook*, by Enid Gordon and Shirley Midge (London: MacDonald, 1983). Reproduced with the kind permission of Little, Brown and Co.

Caponata, from <http://www.customcatering.net/>, the website of Custom Catering, Inc. Reproduced with kind permission of Chef Emile L. Stieffel III.

Caprice Saint-Sylvestre, from *Great Dishes of the World*, by Robert Carrier (Sphere Books). Reproduced with kind permission of Little, Brown and Co.

Cassolette de Saint-Jacques à la Normande from *Floyd on France*, by Keith Floyd, reproduced with the permission of BBC Worldwide. © Keith Floyd, 1987.

Catherine Wheel Cookies, from the recipe collection of H. Krebs at <http://www.cuisine.at/>.

Charlotte à la St. José, from *Mrs. Beeton's Cookery*, by I. Beeton (Cassell PLC). Reproduced with kind permission of the publisher.

Chicken St. John, from *Simply Simpatico*, published by the Junior League of Albuquerque. Reproduced with kind permission of the publisher.

Chiles en Nogada, from *The Art of Mexican Cooking*, by Diana Kennedy. © 1989. Reproduced with permission of Bantam Books, a division of Random House.

Chimichangas San Carlos, from *Simply Simpatico*, published by the Junior League of Albuquerque. Reproduced with kind permission of the publisher.

Cochon de Lait Saint-Fortunat, from *Ma Cuisine,* by Auguste Escoffier (London: P. Hamlyn, 1965). Reproduced with kind permission of the publisher.

Coeurs de Sainte-Catherine, from *A Continual Feast,* by E. B. Vitz (San Francisco: Ignatius Press, 1991). Reproduced with kind permission of the author.

Collerette de la Saint-Sylvestre aux Trois Chocolats, from the website <http://home.nordnet.fr/~pestival>, by Patrick Estival. Reproduced with kind permission of the author.

Coniglio Sant'Angelo, from *An Invitation to Italian Cooking*, by Antonio Carluccio (Pavilion Books, 1986). © Antonio Carluccio, 1986. Reproduced with permission of the author c/o Roger, Coleridge and White, 20 Powis Mews, London W11 1JN.

Coniglio San Domenico, from *Italian Feast*, by Antonio Carluccio. Reproduced with the permission of BBC Worldwide. © Antonio Carluccio, 1996.

Coquilles Saint-Jacques Aurore, from *The Best of Gordon Bleu Cookery*, by Rosemary Hume and Muriel Downes (Penguin UK, 1978). © Rosemary Hume and Muriel Downes, 1963. Reproduced with permission of the publisher.

Coquilles Saint-Jacques en Waterzooi, from *Belgian Cookbook*, by Enid Gordon and Shirley Midge (London: MacDonald, 1983). Reproduced with the kind permission of Little, Brown and Co.

Coupe Saint-Jacques, from *The Fannie Farmer Cookbook*, by Marion Cunningham (New York, Alfred Knopf). Reproduced with kind permission of the publisher.

Covezun' di San Giuseppe, from *The All-Italian Cookbook*, by Wilma Reiva LaSasso (New York: Macmillan, 1958). Reproduced with kind permission of the estate of W. R. LaSasso.

Crabmeat St. Martin, from the website <http://www.jfolse.com/>, by Chef John Folse. Reproduced with kind permission of the chef.

Creamed St. George's Day Mushrooms, from *The Festive Food of England,* by Henrietta Green (London: Kyle Cathie). Reproduced with kind permission of the publisher.

Crème Sainte-Anne, from *French Regional Cookery—Brittany*, by Michael Moffat (London: P. Hamlyn). Reproduced with kind permission of the publisher.

Cucia, from *The All-Italian Cookbook*, by Wilma Reiva LaSasso (New York: Macmillan, 1958). Reproduced with kind permission of the estate of W. R. LaSasso.

Daube de la Saint-André, from *The Cooking of South-West France*, by Paula Wolfert (London: Grub Street). Reproduced with kind permission of the publisher.

Eisbecher Santa Lucia, from *Gourmet Menüs für meine Gäste*, by Theodor Böttiger (Gräfe und Unzer). Reproduced with kind permission of the publisher.

Elisabethen Brottorte, from *Regensburger Kochbuch*, by Maria Schandri (Alfons Coppenrath Verlag, 1890).

Elisen Lebkuchen, from *Bayerisches Kochbuch*, by M. Hofmann and H. Lydtin (Birken Verlag). Reproduced with kind permission of the publisher.

Émincé de Veau St. Moritz, from *International Cuisine by the World's Greatest Chefs*, by G. Curran and L. Wholey (Carol Publishing Group). Reproduced by arrangement with the publisher.

Ensalada Festiva de Santa Clara, from *Cocina Monacal de las Hermanas Clarisas* (SPAM Servicios, 1995). Reproduced with permission of the publisher.

Entremets Sainte-Catherine, from the website <http://home.nordnet.fr/~pestival>, by Patrick Estival. Reproduced with kind permission of the author.

Escalope de Veau San Juán, from *Das Weltkochbuch*, by Laura Conti (Künzelsau: Sigloch Ed., 1988). Reproduced with permission of the publisher.

Filets de Sole Saint-Germain, from *Ma Cuisine*, by Auguste Escoffier (London: P. Hamlyn, 1965). Reproduced with kind permission of the publisher.

Filetti di San Pietro in Salsa di Broccoli, from *Entertaining all'Italiana*, by Anna del Conte (Corgi Books, 1984). Reproduced with permission of Sheil Land Associates.

Frischlingskeulen St. Hubertus, from *Gourmet Menüs für meine Gäste*, by Theodor Böttiger (Gräfe und Unzer). Reproduced with kind permission of the publisher.

Gâteau aux Noix le Saint-André from the website <http://www-rodin.inria.fr/~xhumari/gateau.html>, by Florian Xhumari. Reproduced with kind permission of the author.

Gâteau Saint-Florentin, from *Larousse Gastronomique* (London: P. Hamlyn, 1961). Reproduced with kind permission of the publisher.

Gâteau Saint-Michel, from *Larousse Gastronomique* (London: P. Hamlyn, 1961). Reproduced with kind permission of the publisher.

Hildegardplätzchen, from *Schmankerln aus deutschen Landen*, by Helmut Schauer. Reproduced with kind permission of the author.

Jägerbraten Hubertus, from the recipe collection of H. Krebs at <http://www.cuisine.at/>.

Johannisweibl, from *Gebildbrote*, by I. Carius (Langewiesche Buchverlag). Reproduced with kind permission of the author.

Kalbskoteletten à la Saint Cloud, from *Universal Lexikon der Kochkunst* (J. J. Weber, 1909).

Kartoffeltorte St. Valery, from *Gut gekocht für meine Gäste* (Stuttgart, Vienna, Reader's Digest). Reproduced with kind permission of the publisher.

Katharina Lebkuchen, from a handwritten *Kochbuch* of the Bücking family. With kind permission of the family.

Lakror, from *A Continual Feast*, by E. B. Vitz (San Francisco: Ignatius Press, 1991). Reproduced with kind permission of the author.

Lasagna al Forno, from *The All-Italian Cookbook*, by Wilma Reiva LaSasso (New York: Macmillan, 1958). Reproduced with kind permission of the estate of W. R. LaSasso.

Lepre alla Sant'Uberto, from *Valentina Harris' Complete Italian Cookery Course,* by Valentina Harris. Reproduced with permission of BBC Worldwide. © Valentina Harris 1992.

Lienzer Helenenbrot, from *Tiroler Brot,* by Brigitte and Siegfried de Rachewitz (Tyrolia Verlag). Reproduced with permission of the publisher.

Lukasheringe, from *Praktisches Kochbuch,* by Mary Hahn (1924).

Lumache con Salsa, from *The All-Italian Cookbook,* by Wilma Reiva LaSasso (New York: Macmillan, 1958). Reproduced with kind permission of the estate of W. R. LaSasso.

Lussekattor, from the website <http://www.santesson.com/>, by Anne and Johan Santesson. Reproduced with kind permission of Anne and Johan Santesson.

Magdalenenkuchen, from *Regensburger Kochbuch,* by Maria Schandri (Alfons Coppenrath Verlag, 1890).

Magdalenenstriezeln, from *Regensburger Kochbuch,* by Maria Schandri (Alfons Coppenrath Verlag, 1890).

Margaritenlebkuchen, from a cookbook of St. Hildegard of Bingen.

Markusbrot, from *Das Altbayerische Küchenjahr,* by Erna Horn (Prestel Verlag). With kind permission of the publisher.

Martinsente, from *Es weihnachtet sehr,* by Frank Gerhard (Künzelsau: Sigloch Ed., 1998). Reproduced with permission of the publisher.

Martinshörnchen, from *Sachsen: Kulinarische Streifzüge,* by Oda Tietz (Künzelsau: Sigloch Ed., 1993). Reproduced with permission of the publisher.

Meringone di Sant'Ambrogio, from *Good Housekeeping Italian Cookery,* by Anna Conte (Ebury Press). Reproduced with permission of the publisher.

Nikolausstiefel, from *Köstliche Geschenke,* by Sonja Koch (Künzelsau: Sigloch Ed., 1995). Reproduced with permission of the publisher.

Omelette à la Saint-Flour, from *Larousse Gastronomique* (London: P. Hamlyn, 1961). Reproduced with kind permission of the publisher.

Paletta di Mandorla, from *The All-Italian Cookbook,* by Wilma Reiva LaSasso (New York: Macmillan, 1958). Reproduced with kind permission of the estate of W. R. LaSasso.

Pan de Santa Teresa, from *A Continual Feast,* by E. B. Vitz (San Francisco: Ignatius Press, 1991). Reproduced with kind permission of the author.

Pane di San Giuseppe, from *The All-Italian Cookbook,* by Wilma Reiva LaSasso (New York: Macmillan, 1958). Reproduced with kind permission of the estate of W. R. LaSasso.

Pappardelle di San Giuseppe, from *The All-Italian Cookbook,* by Wilma Reiva LaSasso (New York: Macmillan, 1958). Reproduced with kind permission of the estate of W. R. LaSasso.

Pasta Santa Caterina, from *Pasta Fresca,* by Viana Laplace and Evan Kleiman. © 1988 by Viana Laplace and Evan Kleiman. Reprinted by permission of Harper and Collins Publishers, William Morrow.

Pasteis de Santa Clara, from *The Taste of Portugal*, by Edite Vieira (London, Grub Street). Reproduced with permission of the publisher.

Pastelitos Santa Engracia, from *Cocina Monacal de las Hermanas Clarisas* (SPAM Servicios, 1995). Reproduced with permission of the publisher.

Petites Terrines de Lièvre Saint-Hubert, from *La Cuisine Française et Africaine,* by Léon Isnard (1949).

Pizza di San Martino, from *The All-Italian Cookbook,* by Wilma Reiva LaSasso (New York: Macmillan, 1958). Reproduced with kind permission of the estate of W. R. LaSasso.

Pommes de Terre Saint-Flour, from *Larousse Gastronomique* (London: P. Hamlyn, 1961). Reproduced with kind permission of the publisher.

Pommes de Terre Saint-Florentin, from *The Chef's Compendium of Professional Recipes*, by John Fuller and Edward Renold (London, Butterworth-Heinemann). Reproduced with the kind permission of the publisher.

Pork Loin St. Laurent, from the website of Custom Catering Inc. <http://www.customcatering.net/> Reproduced with kind permission of Chef Emile L. Stieffel III.

Porter Cake, from the website <http://www.members.tripod.com/~banaltra/Ireland/BanaltrasIrishRecipes.html>.

Potage Saint-Germain, from *The Flavor of Scotland*, by Brian Hannan (Mainstream Publishing Co.). Reproduced with permission of the publisher.

Potage Saint-Hubert, from *French Country Cooking,* by Elizabeth David (Penguin Books, 1951). Reproduced with permission of the estate of Elizabeth David.

Potage Saint-Jacques, from *The Best of Gordon Bleu Cookery*, by Rosemary Hume and Muriel Downes (Penguin UK, 1978). © Rosemary Hume and Muriel Downes, 1963. Reproduced with permission of the publisher.

Pouding Froid à la Saint-Cloud, from *Mrs. Beeton's Cookery*, by I. Beeton (Cassell PLC). Reproduced with kind permission of the publisher.

Poulet à la Sainte-Ménéhould, from *French Country Cooking*, by Elizabeth David (Penguin Books, 1951). Reproduced with permission of the estate of Elizabeth David.

Poulet Saint-Valentin, from *French Cooking,* by Mabel Bonney (1929).

Puños de San Francisco, from *Cocina Monacal de las Hermanas Clarisas* (SPAM Servicios, 1995). Reproduced with permission of the publisher.

Quenelles of Veal St. Florentine, from *Mrs. Beeton's Cookery*, by I. Beeton (Cassell PLC). Reproduced with kind permission of the publisher.

Ravioli San Giuseppe, from *Keep It Simple*, by Alastair Little (Conran Octopus). Reproduced with the kind permission of the publisher.

Rehkeule St. Hubertus mit Ingwer, from *Berlin, Brandenburg: Kulinarische Streifzüge*, by Frank P. Freudenberg (Künzelsau: Sigloch Ed., 1995). Reproduced with permission of the publisher.

Rindsbraten St. Magdalena mit Kartoffelnudeln, from *Tiroler Kost nach Alten und Neuen Rezepten* (Südtiroler Hotelier and Gastwirtverband). Reproduced with kind permission of the publisher.

Rosquillas de Santa Clara, from *Cocina Monacal de las Hermanas Clarisas* (SPAM Servicios, 1995). Reproduced with permission of the publisher.

San Marco Roast, from Carole Woodard, in *Metropolitan Spirit*, Augusta, Georgia.

St. Clement's Chicken, from *Quick After-Work Entertaining*, by Hilarie Walden (Judy Piatkus). © Hilarie Walden, 1996. Reproduced with kind permission of the publisher.

St. Clement's Mousse with Caramel Oranges, from *The Masterchef Collection* (Random House, UK). Reproduced with permission of the publisher.

St. Clement's Sweet Potatoes, from *The Electric Cookbook*, by Lucille Barber (Conran Octopus, 1984). Reproduced with permission of the publisher.

St. Clement's Tartlets, from the website <http://www.stclement.com/> of the St. Clement Winery in Napa, California. Reproduced with permission of the winery.

St. Cloud Tartlets, from *Mrs. Beeton's Cookery*, by I. Beeton (Cassell PLC). Reproduced with kind permission of the publisher.

St. David's Leek Pie, from *Cooking Month by Month*, by Mary Norvak (Treasure Press). Reproduced with the kind permission of Conran Octopus.

St. Denis Tartlets, from *Mrs. Beeton's Cookery*, by I. Beeton (Cassell PLC). Reproduced with kind permission of the publisher.

Saint-Émilion au Chocolat, from *French Country Cooking*, by Elizabeth David (Penguin Books, 1951). Reproduced with permission of the estate of Elizabeth David.

St. George's Toast, from *Good Savouries*, by Ambrose Heath (Faber and Faber). Reproduced with kind permission of the publisher.

St. Honoré Trifle, from *Mrs. Beeton's Cookery*, by I. Beeton (Cassell PLC). Reproduced with kind permission of the publisher.

St. Lawrence Fried Fish, from *Country Inn Cookbook*, by Anita Stewart (Stoddart Publishing). Reproduced with kind permission of the author.

Saint-Louis Nierchen, from *Rezepte—Ein Leben lang gesammelt*, by Aenne Burda (Verlag A. Burda, 1984). Reproduced with kind permission of the publisher.

St. Nicholas Pudding, from *The Pudding Club Book*, by Keith and Jean Turner. Reproduced with kind permission of the authors.

St. Ninian's Gingery Muffins, from *The Highland Fling Cookbook*, by Sara MacLoud Walker (Atheneum Press, 1971). Reproduced with the permission of Simon & Schuster.

St. Patrick's Bacon, from *Cooking Month by Month*, by Mary Norvak (Treasure Press). Reproduced with the kind permission of Conran Octopus.

St. Patrick's Drunken Fisherman's Pie, from *The Beerfood Cookbook*, by Josh Klein (One Horse Rhino Press). Reproduced with kind permission of the publisher.

St. Peter's Pie, from *The Sunday Telegraph Cookery Book*, by Jean Robertson (The Sunday Telegraph, 1965). © The Sunday Telegraph. Reproduced with permission of the Publisher.

St. Peter's Pudding, from *The New McCall's Cookbook*, by Mary Eckley. © McCall Publishing Company, 1973. Reproduced with permission of Random House.

Saint-Pierre à l'Oseille, from *Floyd on France*, by Keith Floyd. Reproduced with the permission of BBC Worldwide. © Keith Floyd, 1987.

St. Valentine's Day Cake, from *Cooking Month by Month*, by Mary Norvak, (Treasure Press). Reproduced with the kind permission of Conran Octopus.

Salpicon Saint-Hubert, from *The Chef's Compendium of Professional Recipes*, by John Fuller and Edward Renold (London, Butterworth-Heinemann). Reproduced with the kind permission of the publisher.

Santa Lucia Crown, from <http://www.breadworld.com/>, the Fleischmann's Yeast website. Reproduced with the kind permission of Fleischmann's Yeast.

Sfincione di San Vito, from *The All-Italian Cookbook*, by Wilma Reiva LaSasso (New York: Macmillan, 1958). Reproduced with kind permission of the estate of W. R. LaSasso.

Straubinger Josefitorte, from *Das Altbayerische Küchenjahr*, by Erna Horn (Prestel Verlag). With kind permission of the publisher.

Talmouses de Saint-Denis, from *Larousse Gastronomique* (London: P. Hamlyn, 1961). Reproduced with kind permission of the publisher.

Tarte à la Citrouille Sainte-Marthe, from the website of Les Cercles de Fermièrs du Québec. <http://www.servicevie.com/01alimentation/Recette/Recette.html>. Reproduced with their permission.

Timbales de Coquilles Saint-Jacques, from *Floyd on France*, by Keith Floyd. Reproduced with the permission of BBC Worldwide. © Keith Floyd, 1987.

Tintenfisch San Miguel, from *Internationales TV Kochbuch*, by Ekkehard Boesche (VGS Verlagsanstalt). Reproduced with kind permission of the author.

Tire, La, from *Out of Old Nova Scotia Kitchens*, by Marie Nightingale (Nimbus Publications). Reproduced with kind permission of the publisher.

Torcolo di San Costanzo, from *La Cucina Casalinga*, by Susanne Bunzel. © Droemer Knaur Verlag (Munich, 1995). Reproduced with permission of the publisher.

Totano al Forno, from *The All-Italian Cookbook*, by Wilma Reiva LaSasso (New York: Macmillan, 1958). Reproduced with kind permission of the estate of W. R. LaSasso.

Truchas al Horno a la Donostiarra, from *The Home Book of Spanish Cooking*, by Nina Froud and Marina Pereyra del Aznar (Faber and Faber, 1965). Reproduced with the kind permission of the publisher.

Wildschweingulasch Sankt Hubertus, from *Dr. Oetker's Mikrowellen Kochbuch* (Ceres Verlag). Reproduced with kind permission of the publisher.

Wilfra Apple Cake, from *Traditional Cooking*, by Caroline Conran (Conran Octopus).

Xavier Suppe, from *Universal Lexikon der Kochkunst* (J. J. Weber, 1909).

Zeppole di San Giuseppe, from *The All-Italian Cookbook*, by Wilma Reiva LaSasso (New York: Macmillan, 1958). Reproduced with kind permission of the estate of W. R. LaSasso.

Zucchini St. Moritz, from *Simply Simpatico*, published by the Junior League of Albuquerque. Reproduced with kind permission of the publisher

Zuppa di Sant' Antonio, from *The All-Italian Cookbook*, by Wilma Reiva LaSasso (New York: Macmillan, 1958). Reproduced with kind permission of the estate of W. R. LaSasso.

The following are sources for recipes for which every effort has been made to trace the holder of the copyright but with unsuccessful results. Letters were returned or were not answered during a six-month period of continuous effort. In many cases not even the publishers knew the current holder of the copyright of a particular book. Rights holders of any recipes not credited should contact the author via Ignatius Press.

Ambrosius Creme, from *Gut Essen—Bayrische Küche*, by Helga Lederer (Cologne, Pawlak Verlag).

Anna Torte, from *Altdeutsche Backrezepte* (Möwig Verlag).

Bubenschenkel, from *Spezialitäten aus Württemberg und Baden*, by Ursula Grüninger (Munich: W. Heyne, 1969).

Cécilias, from *A Good Housekeeping Cookery Compendium* (London: Waverly Book Company, 1952).

Ciastka Miodowe, from *The Feastday Cookbook*, by Katherine Burton and Helmut Rippenger (New York: David McKay, 1951).

Coquilles Saint-Jacques au Gratin, from the website *<http://dinnercoop.cs.cmu. edu/dinnercoop/recipes/jody/>*, by Jody Prival.

Coquilles Saint-Jacques au Safran, from *Restaurant Dishes of the World*, by Margaret Fulton (Octopus Australia, 1982).

Côtelettes d'Agneau Saint-Michel, from *French Cooking*, by Paul Bocuse (Pantheon Books, 1977).

Côtes de Chevreuil Saint-Hubert, from *The Mushroom Feast*, by Jane Grigson (Lyons Press, 1975).

Coupe Saint-André, from *The Modern Patissier,* by William Barker (Northwood, 1979).

Croustilles Saint-Michel, from *Madame Prunier's Fish Cookbook*, edited by Ambrose Heath (Penguin UK, 1963).

Eggs St. Charles, from the website <http://tilapia.unh.edu/WWWPages/recipe5.html/>; a modification of a recipe originally by Yatcom Communications, Inc.

Hasenrücken St. Hubertus, from *Gut Essen–Bayrische Küche*, by Helga Lederer (Cologne, Pawlak Verlag).

Homard Saint-Honorat, from *Madame Prunier's Fish Cookbook*, edited by Ambrose Heath (Penguin UK, 1963).

Honig-Johannisbrot Laib, from *Das Buch from Honig*, by C. Francis and F. Gontier (H. Hugendubel Verlag, 1980).

Kamhié, from *Visions of Sugar Plums*, by Mimi Sheraton (New York: Random House, 1968).

Lasagna di San Frediano, from *Pasta for Pleasure*, by Moyra Bremner and Liz Filippina (Diamond Books, 1996).

Macarons de Saint-Émilion, from *A Taste of France*, by Robert Freson (Stewart, Tabori and Chang).

Macqueraux Saint-Jacques, from *The Nouvelle Cuisine of Jean and Pierre Troisgras*, by Caroline Conran (London: Macmillan, 1980).

Mole of Santa Clara, from the now-defunct magazine *Chili Pepper*, by Ron West (1998).

Moules Saint-Michel, from *Madame Prunier's Fish Cookbook*, edited by Ambrose Heath (Penguin UK, 1963).

Pasta San Marco, from the website <http://www.floras-hideout.com/recipes>.

Pepernoten, from *Dutch Cooking*, by Helen A. M. Halverhout (Jordan Station, Ontario: Padeira Press).

Peters Fischtopf mit Limettensauce, from *Gut Essen—Friesische Küche* (Cologne: Pawlak Verlag).

Pizzette di San Gennaro, from *La Cocina—The Complete Italian Cookbook*, by Myra Street (London: Orbis Books).

Podkovy, from *The Catholic Cookbook*, by William I. Kaufmann (Lyle and Stuart).

Purée Saint-Germain, from *The Best of Robert Carrier*, by Robert Carrier (London: Bloomsbury).

Râble de Lièvre Saint-Honorat, from *Simply Delicious* (Surrey: Colour Library Books, 1987).

Rissoles de Saint-Flour, from *French Regional Cooking*, by Anne Willan (New York: W. Morrow, 1981).

Roast Michaelmas Goose with Apples and Prunes, from *The Dairy Book of British Food*, by Elizabeth Martyn (Ebury Press, 1988).

Saint-Andrés, from *The Constance Fry Cookery Book,* by Constance Fry (Dutton, 1963).

St. Iago Pork Chops, from *The Complete Book of Caribbean Cooking,* by Elizabeth L. Ortiz (J. B. Lippincott, 1973).

St. Martin's Torte, from *Leckere Spezialitäten* (Cologne: Lingen Verlag, 1973).

St. Moritz, from *A Concise Encyclopedia of Gastronomy,* by Andre L. Simon (London: Collins, 1952).

St. Roch's Fingers, from *The Feastday Cookbook,* by Katherine Burton and Helmut Rippenger (New York: David McKay, 1951).

St. Stephen's Pudding, from *The Windsor Castle Cookery Book.*

Salad St. Regis, from *The Book of Fruit and Fruit Cookery,* by Paul Dinnage (London: Sidgwick and Jackson).

Santa Lucia Leves, from *Az Inyemester Nagy Szak a Csköyve* (New York: K. P. Schick, 1956).

Sardinas Grelhadas, from *The Food of Portugal,* by Jean Anderson (New York, W. Morrow).

Schweinelendchen Barbara, from *Der lachende Feinschmecker,* by Fred Metzler (Falken Verlag, 1979).

Soufflé Saint-Jacques, from *Simply Delicious* (Surrey: Colour Library Books, 1987).

Speculaas, from the website <http://ourworld.compuserve.com/homepages/paulvanv/speculas.htm>

Stephen's Beigli, from *Cakes,* by Barbara Maher (London: Dorling Kindersley).

Struan Micheil, from *The Scots Kitchen,* by Marian MacNeil (Glasgow: Blackie and Sons, 1929).

Tarta de Santiago, from *The Cooking of Spain and Portugal,* by Tony Schmaeling (Chartwell Books, 1983).

Tarte Normande Saint-Nicolas, from *Lenôtres Dessert and Pastries* (Woodbury, N.Y.: Barras).

Thomasstriezeln, from a nineteenth-century cookbook owned by the Firsching family.

Torta Garfagnana, from *The Tuscan Cookbook,* by Wilma Pezzini (Atheneum Publishers).

Vasilopeta, from *The Complete Book of Greek Cooking,* by The Recipe Club of St. Paul's Orthodox Cathedral (Harper and Collins, 1991).

Yemas de Santa Teresa, from *Fare Exchange,* by Dorothy Allen Gray (October House, 1960).

Saint Agnes
Court of the Virgins mosaic, 6th c.
S. Apollinare Nuovo, Ravenna, Italy
Scala / Art Resource, N.Y.

Saint Ambrose
Mosaic, 5th c.
S. Ambrogio, Milan, Italy
Scala / Art Resource, N.Y.

Saint Andrew
El Greco (1541–1614)
Casa y Museo del Greco, Toledo, Spain
Scala / Art Resource, N.Y.

Martyrdom of S. Angelo
Ludovico Carracci (1555–1619)
Pinacoteca Nazionale, Bologna, Italy
Scala / Art Resource, N.Y.

Virgin and Child with Saint Anne
Albrecht Dürer (1471–1528)
Tempera and oil on canvas, 60 x 49.9 cm
The Metropolitan Museum of Art (Bequest of Benjamin Altman, 1913),
    14.50.633
Photograph © 1989 The Metropolitan Museum of Art, New York

The Temptation of Saint Anthony
Hieronymus Bosch (ca. 1450–1516)
Le Prov. Escorial, Museo del Prado, Madrid, Spain
Scala / Art Resource, N.Y.29

Saint Anthony of Padua with the Infant Christ
Giuseppe Bazzani (1690–1769)
Oil on canvas, 85.1 x 69 cm
© National Gallery, London, NG 3663

Saint Augustine Teaching Law, Rhetoric and Philosophy in Rome
Benozzo Gozzoli (1420–1497)
S. Agostino, San Gimignano, Italy
Scala / Art Resource, N.Y.

Saint Barbara
Jan van Eyck (ca. 1390–1441)
Koninklijk Museum voor Schone Kunsten, Antwerp, Belgium
Scala / Art Resource, N.Y.

Saint Basil
Mosaic, 1342–54
S. Marco, Venice, Italy
Scala / Art Resource, N.Y.

Stories of Saint Blaise: *Wolf Giving the Pig Back to the Poor Widow*
Sano di Pietro (1406–1481)
Pinacoteca Nazionale, Siena, Italy
Scala / Art Resource, N.Y.

Saint Bridget (St. Brigid)
Lives of the Saints, manuscript illustration
Bodleian Library, Oxford, MS Tanner 17, fol. 13v
© Bodleian Library, Oxford

Saint Catherine of Alexandria
Artemisia Gentileschi (1597–1651)
Uffizi, Florence, Italy
Scala / Art Resource, N.Y.

Saint Cecilia
Raphael (1483–1520)
Pinacoteca Nazionale, Bologna, Italy
Scala / Art Resource, N.Y.

Saint Charles Borromeo
Orazio Borgianni (1578–1616)
S. Carlo alle Quattro Fontane, Rome
Scala / Art Resource, N.Y.

Saint Clare and Saint Elizabeth of Hungary (detail)
Simone Martini (1284–1344)
Chiesa S. Francesco, Assisi, Italy
Scala / Art Resource, N.Y.

Saint Clement
Icon (with Saint Maoum)
Church of the Virgin Peribleptos, Chrid, Macedonia, Greece
Giraudon / Art Resource, N.Y.

Saint Clou
Engraving, Rd 2, fol. 79A 42319
Bibliothèque Nationale de France, Paris
Photograph © Bibliothèque Nationale de France Service Reproduction

Saint Constance (Constantine)
Pietro Perugino (1448–1523)
From the Polyptich of Saint Augustine
Galleria Nazionale dell'Umbria, Perugia, Italy
Scala / Art Resource, N.Y.

Saint Cunegund
Michael Wolgemuth (1434–1519)
Altar of the Virgin, Langenzenn Parish Church, Bavaria, Germany
Photograph © Dr. Wilfrid Bahnmüller

Saint David, detail, from *Four Saints in the Chapel of the Magdalene*
School of Giotto di Bondone (1266–1336)
Chiesa di S. Francesco, Assisi, Italy
Scala / Art Resource, N.Y.

Saint Denis Hands the French Banner to Jean Clement du Mer around 1230
Stained glass, south transept, Chartres Cathedral, France
Erich Lessing / Art Resource, N.Y.

Madonna and Child with Saints Dominic, Nicholas of Bari, John the Baptist and
   Catherine of Alexandria (detail)
Fra Angelico (1387–1455)
Galleria Nazionale dell'Umbria, Perugia, Italy
Scala / Art Resource, N.Y.

Saint Elisabeth of Thuringia (Hungary)
The Hastings Book of Hours
British Library, MS Add 54782 64v
By permission of the British Library, London

Saint Émilion
Engraving, Rd 2, fol. H17 3793
Bibliothèque Nationale de France
Photograph © Bibliothèque Nationale de France Service Reproduction

The Flagellation of Saint Encratis
Bartolomé Bermejo (ca. 1405–1498)
Oil on wood, 92.5 x 52 cm
Museo de Bellas Artes de Bilbao, Spain
© Archivo fotográfico del Museo de Bellas Artes de Bilbao

Saint Felix and Saint Adauctus (detail)
Early Christian fresco, late 7th c.
Catacomb of Comodilla, Rome
Scala / Art Resource, N.Y.

Saint Florentin of Saumur
Romanesque mural, Hotel Musée Gouin, Tours
Photograph © 2001 Ernst Schuegraf

Saint Flour
Reliquary of Saint-Flour
Cathédrale Saint Pierre, Saint-Flour, France
Photograph © Angela Glover-Chris Beck

Saint Fortunat in the Convent of Saint Radegunde at Ste. Croix
Puvis de Chavanne (1824–1898)
Poitiers Town Hall, France
Photograph © Musées de Poitiers, Ch Vignaud

Saint Francis Preaching to the Birds
Giotto di Bondone (1266–1336)
Chiesa di S. Francesco, Assisi, Italy
Scala / Art Resource, N.Y.

Saint Francis Xavier
Anthony van Dyck (1599–1641)
Pinacoteca, Vatican Museum, Vatican State
Scala / Art Resource, N.Y.

The Madonna and Child Surrounded by Angels with Saint Frediano and Saint Augustine, 1437/1438 (detail)
Fra Filippo Lippi (1406–1469)
Louvre, Paris
Scala / Art Resource, N.Y.

Saint George and the Dragon
Russian icon, School of Novgorod, 14th c.
Tretyakov Gallery, Moscow, Russia
Scala / Art Resource, N.Y.

Saint Geneviève Receiving the Medal from Saint Germain
Antoine Coypel (1661–1722)
Musée des Beaux-Arts, Dijon, France
Erich Lessing / Art Resource, N.Y.

Vitae Beatae Hedwigis, 1353
Court Atelier of Duke Ludwig I of Liegnitz and Prieg
Tempera colors between wood boards covered with red stained pigskin, 34.1
    x 24.8 cm
The J. Paul Getty Museum, MS Ludwig XI 7, fol. l2v
Photograph © The J. Paul Getty Museum, Los Angeles

Proof of the Cross (Saint Helen)
Piero della Francesca (ca. 1415/20–1492)
S. Francesco, Arezzo, Italy
Scala / Art Resource, N.Y.

Saint Hildegard of Bingen: Portrait Inspired by Divine Fire
From "Scivias" Codex Rupertsberg, Lucca, Italy (disappeared during WW II)
Erich Lessing / Art Resource, N.Y.

Saint Honoratus and the Saints of Lerins Island
Icon, 20th century
Abbaye de Lérins, Ile Saint-Honorat
Photograph © Editions Gaud

Saint Honoré of Amiens
Boucicaut Master (active ca. 1400–1415)
Book of Hours, manuscript illustration
Photograph © Institut de France, Musée Jacquemart-André, Paris

The Conversion of Saint Hubert
Master of the Life of the Virgin (active second half of the l5th century)
Oil on wood, 123 x 83.2 cm
© National Gallery, London, NG 252

*Saint Ignatius of Loyola Receives Papal Bull from Pope Paul III Ordaining the Jesuit
    Order* (detail)
Juan de Valdes Leal (1622–1690)
Museo de Bellas Artes, Seville, Spain
Scala / Art Resource, N.Y.

Saint John the Baptist with Saint John the Evangelist and Saint James (detail)
Nardo di Cione (active 1343; d. 1365/1366)
Egg tempera on wood, 159.5 x 147.5 cm
© National Gallery, London, NG 581

The Glory of Saint Gennaro
Giovanni Battistello (1570–1637)
Certosa di S. Martino, Naples, Italy
Scala / Art Resource, N.Y.

Saint John the Baptist
Titian (ca. 1488–1576)
Accademia, Venice, Italy
Cameraphoto / Art Resource, N.Y.

Holy Family with Sparrow (Saint Joseph)
Bartolomeo Esteban Murillo (1617–1682)
Museo del Prado, Madrid, Spain
Scala / Art Resource, N.Y.

Martyrdom of Saint Lawrence
Palma Giovane (Jacopo Palma; 1544–1628)
S. Giacomo dell'Orio, Venice, Italy
Cameraphoto / Art Resource, N.Y.

Saint Louis, King of France, and a Page Boy
El Greco (1541–1614)
Louvre, Paris
Giraudon / Art Resource, N.Y.

Saint Lucy Being Pulled by Bulls
Jacobello del Fiore (14th–15th c.)
Pinacoteca Civica, Fermo, Italy
Scala / Art Resource, N.Y.

Saint Luke Painting the Virgin
Michelino da Besozzo. (d. 1450)
Prayer Book, Milan, Italy, ca. 1420, M. 944, fol. 75v
The Pierpont Morgan Library / Art Resource N.Y.

Saint Margaret of Antioch
The Hastings Book of Hours
British Library, MS Add 54782 62v
By permission of the British Library, London

Saint Mark Seated
Odalricus Peccator Gospel (11th c.)
British Library, MS Harley 2970 2v
By permission of the British Library, London

Christ in the House of Martha and Mary
Jan van Delft (1632–1675)
Oil on canvas, 160 x 142 cm
National Gallery, Edinburgh
© Joachim Blauel / ARTOTHEK

Saint Martin Giving His Cloak to the Beggar
Anthony van Dyck (1599–1641)
Oil on canvas, 32 x 31 cm. Inuhr 2517
© Staatsgallerie, Stuttgart, Germany

Mary Magdalen
Piero della Francesca (ca. 1415/20–1492)
Duomo, Arezzo, Italy
Scala / Art Resource, N.Y.

Saint Erasmus and Saint Mauritius
Matthias Grünewald (ca. 1475–1528)
Oil on wood, 226x 176 cm
Alte Pinakothek, Munich
© Blauel/Gnamm / ARTOTHEK

Saint Ménéhould Receiving the Veil
Stained glass, Église Notre-Dame, Ste-Ménéhould, France
Photograph © 2001 Ernst Schuegraf

Saint Michael
Piero della Francesca (ca. 1415/20–1492)
Oil on wood, 133 x 59.5 cm
© National Gallery, London, NG 769

Saint Nicholas
Byzantine enamel medallion, 10th c.
Museo Lazaro Galdiano, Madrid, Spain
Giraudon / Art Resource, N.Y.

Saint Ninian and the Highlanders, 1854
T. Appolonio
St. Ninian's Cathedral, Antigonish, Nova Scotia
With permission of the Rector, J. W. Crispo
Photograph © 2001 Ernst Schuegraf

Saint Patrick's Window
Magheralin Parish Church, Northern Ireland
Photograph © Northern Ireland Tourist Board

Christ Giving the Keys to Saint Peter, 1820
Ingres, Jean Auguste Dominique (1780–1867)
Oil on canvas, 2.80 x 2.17 m
Musée lngres, Montauban, France
Giraudon / Art Resource, N.Y.

Saint John Francis Regis with Brother Bideau
William H. McNichols, S.J.
Icon, Regis University, Denver, Colorado
Photograph © St. Andrei Rublev Icons, Albuquerque

Saint Roch in the Desert, ca. 1567
Jacopo Tintoretto (1518–1594)
Oil on canvas, 230 x 670 cm
S. Rocco, Venice
Cameraphoto / Art Resource, N.Y.

308

The Martyrdom of Saint Sebastian
Antonio and Piero del Pollaiuolo (ca. 1432–1498; ca. 1441–1496?)
Oil on wood, 281.5 x 202.6 cm
© National Gallery, London, NG 292

The Stoning of Saint Stephen
Adam Elsheimer (1578–1610)
Oil on copper, 34.5 x 28.5 cm
National Gallery, Edinburgh
© Joachim Blauel / ARTOTHEK

Saint Sylvester Raising the Wise Men in the Forum
Maso di Bianco (14th c.)
Bardi di Vemio Chapel, S. Croce, Florence, Italy
Scala / Art Resource, N.Y.

Saint Teresa of Avila, 1827
François Gerard (1770–1837)
Maison Marie-Thérèse, Paris
Erich Lessing / Art Resource, N.Y.

Saint Thomas
Georges de La Tour (1593–1652)
Oil on canvas
Louvre, Paris
Erich Lessing / Art Resource, N.Y.

Saint Valentin Cures the Epileptic and Refuses to Submit to Idolatry
Bartolomeus Zeitblom (1455/60–1518/22)
Oil on wood, 213.8 x 120 cm
Bayer staatsgallerie, Staatsgemäldesammlungen, Augsburg, Germany
© Joachim Blauel / ARTOTHEK

Saint Valery Appearing to Hugo Capet in a Dream
Boucicaut Master (active ca. 1400–1415)
British Library, MS Cotton Nero E II, I, fol. 29
By permission of the British Library, London

Saint Vitus Protector of Livestock
Master Theoderich (1359?–1381)
Tempera on wood, National Gallery, Prague, Czech Republic
Erich Lessing / Art Resource, N.Y.

Saint Wilfred, 1977
Harry Harvey
Stained glass, Ripon Cathedral, Ripon, Yorkshire
With permission of Ripon Cathedral

Index of Recipes by Name

COOKING WITH THE SAINTS

315

COOKING WITH THE SAINTS

Index of Recipes by Type

Index of Recipes by Country

United States